BROWN V. BOARD OF EDUCATION: WITNESS TO A LANDMARK DECISION

ANNIVERSARY EDITION

Brown v. Board of Education, excerpted from
*Crusaders in the Courts, Anniversary Edition:
Legal Battles of the Civil Rights Movement.*

BROWN V. BOARD OF EDUCATION: WITNESS TO A LANDMARK DECISION

ANNIVERSARY EDITION

By

Jack Greenberg

Twelve Tables Press
462 Broome Street, Suite 4W
New York, NY 10013
www.twelvetablespress.com

For My Children and Grandchildren

Josiah, David G., Sarah, Ezra, Suzanne, Bill, Jessica, Sam, Julia, Danny, David C.

CONTENTS

Foreword ix

Preface xi

Part I: Preparing the Ground

1. He Guided Us 3
2. The Ground is Hard 7
3. Law Schools in the Supreme Court 29

Part II: The Battle

4. An End to Segregation—Nothing Else 47
5. Jim Crow and the Voice of God in Kansas 59
6. In the House of the Law 89
7. Back to the Drawing Board 111

Part III: *Brown* Decided: Eyes on the Future

8. A Historic Turn 137
9. The Spirit of Black Revolt Stirs and
   Jim Crow Fights Back 149
10. Lucy and Little Rock: War of All Men Against
    All Men 159
11. Trench Warfare 183

Part IV: The Movement Takes Off

12. Crushing Jim Crow 199

13. Education Following the Defeat of
   "All Deliberate Speed" 227
14. Schools: Final Thoughts and Reflections 249

Appendices 269
A Note on Sources 297
Index 307

FOREWORD

The Dream of Brown v. Board of Education

by *Mrs. Thurgood Marshall*

Over fifty years ago a group of lawyers had a vision of what America should be. In their vision, race and color would no longer be a mark that differentiated some Americans from others in ways that decided who succeeded and who didn't, who enjoyed a good life, whose children would be raised safely, securely, and happily. The lawyers who held this vision aspired to an ambitious ideal, but it could not be realized until America cleansed itself of the heritage of slavery. Imagine! In 1789 our Constitution recognized slavery. A black man until the Civil War had no right that a white man was bound to respect—so said the Supreme Court in the *Dred Scott* case. The Civil War and the Thirteenth, Fourteenth, and Fifteenth Amendments were supposed to wipe that stain on our democracy and consciences from law and life.

But those who enacted the Civil War Amendments could not imagine the depth and persistence of prejudice that the slave system expressed. After the Civil War ended and the nation tried to cleanse itself of all the related injustice, the South and its friends did all they could to return the black person as closely as they could to the status of slave. Before the Southern States could be readmitted to the Union they first had to submit their constitutions for approval. None of those constitutions provided for school segregation. After the seceding states were admitted they then put school segregation into their constitutions and laws. That and many other segregation practices returned black people to second-class citizenship. The fate of African-Americans was sealed when the Supreme Court ratified the defeat of Reconstruction by deciding *Plessy v. Ferguson* in 1896.

Plessy made state-imposed racial segregation constitutional. Until *Plessy* was defeated, the dream of equal, non-racial citizenship would have to remain just that, a dream. The band of lawyers at the NAACP Legal Defense Fund set out, systematically, case by case, to build a body of law that would overrule *Plessy* and make clear, indeed, that all men and women were created equal and had to be treated equally. They succeeded in *Brown v. Board of Education*. *Brown* was argued three times in the Supreme Court to cap a campaign that lasted a generation. The campaign began when Thurgood Marshall and his teacher Charles Houston won the first case ordering a white institution, the University of Maryland, to admit its first black to its law school in 1936. Thurgood, along with colleagues who argued with him, won *Brown*, which required elementary and high schools to admit children without regard to their race. *Brown* amounted to overruling *Plessy* and setting the United States on the path to true equality. It went beyond schools and signaled the end of racial distinctions under law in America.

The partisans of the past mounted their last efforts at physical resistance in Little Rock in 1957 and at the University of Mississippi in 1962 when federal troops had to disperse a ragtag group of bitter-enders from blocking nine children from entering Little Rock high school and James Meredith from enrolling in the University of Mississippi. But while physical obstruction ended, resistance continues.

We certainly are far from equality now, but closer than we were when Thurgood and Charlie Houston started their campaign. We have many more tasks to complete and miles to go until we achieve the goal. We should continue with the resolve that they and their colleagues pursued in 1954 and years before and after that. We surely will overcome!

PREFACE

School Segregation, Gypsies, Roma, Bulgaria?

Roma? Or, as they have been called, Gypsies. Bulgaria? What do they have to do with *Brown v. Board of Education,* decided in 1954? They taught me what *Brown* really meant to the United States, even though I had been a lawyer in *Brown* and for decades worked on cases that followed it. In June 2003 I visited Budapest, Sofia, and two small towns in Bulgaria—Vidin and Montana. I saw the beginnings of school integration of Roma that went so smoothly that it blew me away. How could this be? The ease with which schools desegregated would have been unimaginable in the United States following *Brown.* Riots, troops, political stonewalling were the order of the day in Arkansas, Delaware, Kentucky, Tennessee, where modest integration efforts began early. As late as 1962, eight years after *Brown,* gunfire killed and wounded people on campus when James Meredith, a solitary black man, entered the University of Mississippi under protection of the armed forces. I had always thought of *Brown* as only a school segregation case. But, my visit to Vidin and Montana was a revelation. I saw that *Brown,* fundamentally, broke up a racist political system that had penetrated every aspect of life in the South, and much of the North as well. Until that happened, racial integration could not be achieved, not in schools, jobs, public places or everyday life. Eastern Europe was politically prepared when integration came to Vidin and Montana. There was no way that the American South could have been politically prepared without *Brown. Brown,* before it could integrate schools, had to break up racist control. It set in motion forces that did just that. As I figured it out, there was no other means for clearing that way.

At one Bulgarian school, I attended a meeting of three to four hundred parents, pupils, teachers and administrators—Roma and non-Roma—where for perhaps three hours, one person after another stood up and spoke about the virtues of desegregation. Social workers had visited every Romany family with school-age children. There were tutors, special training for teachers, and food and clothing for families that needed it; Roma and non-Roma children shared outings, social events, and cultural experiences. Politicians and the press supported integration. The President of Bulgaria congratulated the organization that sponsored the desegregation.

In Hungary, in 2004, school desegregation began with integrating Roma and Hungarian students who previously had attended school in the same buildings, but in separate classrooms. The transition has taken place almost without notice.

Political acceptance was in place already in 2000 when the European Union (EU) adopted the Race Equality Directive and desegregation began. Eastern European countries such as Bulgaria, Hungary, Czech Republic, Slovakia and others want to join the European Union. But to be admitted they must first comply with the Race Equality Directive. Bulgaria has enacted a "Framework Program" to implement the Directive. A practical consideration supports Bulgarian integration: Eastern European population is falling because of a low birth rate and emigration. But, Roma population is not. Schools are funded on a per capita basis. Teachers and administrators in the "white" schools, as they are called, welcome the income new Roma students provide.

Not all of Eastern Europe has embraced desegregation positively. There has been inertia and some efforts to evade. There is litigation in local and international courts. There has been anti-Roma violence. In September 2003, a group opposed to desegregation in a town south of Budapest set up what we would call a segregation academy for Hungarian children only. The Hungarian national ombudsman for minority rights announced that such schools would be closed. In the U.S., school boards and public officials coddled segregationist academies for as long as they could get away with it.

Nothing in Eastern Europe resembled reactions during a comparable period in the American South: there was obstruction and troops overcame it. Congressmen and state and federal judges denounced the Supreme Court, and scholars impugned its decisions. States enacted evasive school enrollment laws and laws threatening to close schools; legislatures adopted spurious pre-enrollment administrative remedies, all with the purpose or effect of preventing desegregation. I think of the case of African-American Mack Charles Parker, jailed on a charge of having raped a white woman in Poplarville, Mississippi. In April 1959, a mob broke into the jail and lynched him. The local newspaper linked the lynching to campaigns for civil rights.

The Beginnings of Desegregation in the United States

There was "massive resistance" and much non-productive litigation after 1954. In 1969, after a decade and a half of barely effective lawsuits, I argued *Alexander v. Holmes County Board of Education* in the Supreme Court. The decision made clear that the Court would not stand for further delay. School desegregation in earnest began. In the decade following *Brown* Southern white schools admitted almost no black students; by 1970 the percentage of blacks rose to 33.1; by 1988 it went to 43.5. The effect went beyond schools.

First: *Brown* raised a legal and moral imperative. *Brown* was not merely a pronouncement by the Court. The brief for the United States stated, "The right of children not to be segregated because of race or color is not a technical legal right of little significance or value. It is a fundamental human right, supported by considerations of morality as well as law." The United States argued in another brief: "It is in the context of the present world struggle between freedom and tyranny that the problem of racial discrimination must be viewed. The United States is trying to prove to the people of the world, of every nationality, race, and color, that a free democracy is the most civilized and most secure form of government yet devised by man."

Those who wanted to maintain segregation made no claims about right and wrong. They argued about federalism, local control, the original intent of the Constitution, the sanctity of precedent, the role of the judiciary in a democracy, the difficulty of compliance, the academic inadequacy of blacks. They argued that community attitudes were opposed to integration, that the black population was deficient in "health and morals," that local school boards were "unalterably opposed," and the like. North Carolina argued that integration would create the "likelihood of violence," and that "[p]ublic schools may be abolished." Oklahoma urged that desegregation would create "financial problems." Florida argued that almost 2% of white births in Florida and 24% of Negro births were "illegitimate." Florida reported over 11,000 cases of gonorrhea, of which 10,000 were among the Negro population. There were no claims that segregation was right and moral.

Second: Enforcing *Brown* established national, not regional standards as the measure of equality. Efforts at school desegregation were opposed by a steady drumbeat of physical resistance that was almost always overcome by superior police and military force. There could be no more authoritative endorsement of desegregation than the United States government's determination to suppress force by force. In 1957 in Little Rock, Arkansas, the President summoned the armed forces to assure black children's entry to Little Rock High School. In 1962 another President summoned troops to secure admission of James Meredith to the University of Mississippi and Vivian Malone and James Hood to the University of Alabama. Ultimately, national rule established its superiority by physical force over physical resistance.

Third: A people's movement embraced the principles underlying *Brown* and demonstrated vigorously for their implementation. By 1960 the sit-ins began. The leaders of the first sit-ins had been inspired by *Brown*. Freedom Rides began in 1961, partly in homage to *Brown*, the first ride scheduled to arrive in New Orleans May 17, 1961, its seventh anniversary. Martin Luther King Jr. annually held prayer pilgrimages on May 17. King often preached and spoke about the Supreme Court, referring to its race relations decisions, particularly *Brown*. Rosa Parks, whose act of defiance launched the Montgomery bus boycott, was an NAACP administrator, steeped in *Brown*. The boycott was resolved by *Gayle v. Browder,* in which the Supreme Court, citing *Brown,* held unconstitutional the segregation law that was the subject of the boycott.

Together, the moral imperative of *Brown*, the massive resistance that *Brown* provoked and its defeat—particularly the physical suppression of physical resistance—and the Civil Rights Movement culminated in the Civil Rights Acts of the sixties. Those acts marked the beginning of a political transformation. It has been epitomized in the election of 40 black Congressmen and of black mayors at one time or another in every major city and most smaller ones. Its effects went beyond race relations. On signing the Civil Rights Bills, Lyndon Johnson observed that they meant the end of the Democratic Party in the South and, by implication, southern politics as the country knew it. He was right.

Europe took centuries and many wars to recognize that narrow national and ethnic antagonisms are too destructive to tolerate. The Second World War, the Cold War, and a Roma Holocaust alongside the Jewish Holocaust imparted power to human rights commitments. While brotherly love has not pervaded all Roma and non-Roma relationships, virulence has subsided. We would not expect intergroup warfare to erupt in Western Europe again or, I think, among countries that are, or aspire to be, part of the EU.

Following *Brown,* the United States passed through times that also had profound effect on its human relations. U.S. racial politics had been frozen until 1954. Southern white racist hegemony dominated, keeping blacks in a subordinate position. The school integration decision, if a metaphor may be permitted, acted like a powerful icebreaker.

Supreme Court Justice Robert H. Jackson, chief prosecutor of Nazi war criminals at Nuremberg, used a similar metaphor in describing the path-breaking role of the Nuremberg trials. He told his staff that they had to produce "an ice pick to break up the frozen sea within us." Kafka scholar Stanley Corngold has suggested that Jackson may have found the metaphor in Kafka who wrote that "a book must be the axe for the frozen sea within us."

Like my metaphorical icebreaker or Kafka's metaphorical axe, *Brown* opened channels in a frozen sea through which America arrived at racial change. *Brown* was not merely a school case.

So, when I saw smooth, easy, agreeable, successful school desegregation in Bulgaria, I wondered why *Brown* hadn't gone so smoothly in the U.S. The answer is that *Brown,* while a school case, was doing different work in different circumstances. Schools could not desegregate in the racially hostile atmosphere of the South in the fifties and even later. The laws, state and local legislatures, the Congress, state and federal judges, the society and economy—all would not allow changing arrangements that privileged whites. *Brown* cracked open that frozen sea. It changed minds and rules, challenged hierarchical assumptions, stimulated a social movement that became political, enlisted parts of the country and the world. In its wake, the nation suppressed physical resistance and enacted basic laws that affected power relationships between black and white, North and South. Then South Carolina and Mississippi could respond to our Fourteenth Amendment in the way that half a century later Vidin and Montana, Bulgaria, responded to the European Union Race Equality Directive.

PART I

PREPARING THE GROUND

CHAPTER 1

HE GUIDED US

He guided us through the legal wilderness of second-class citizen-ship. He was truly the Moses of that journey. He lived to see us close to the promised land of full equality under the law, closer than even he dared hope when he set out on that journey and so much closer than would have been possible without his genius and his leadership.

—William H. Hastie, speaking at the funeral of
Charles Hamilton Houston

I met him only once, and my only memory of the man is like a fleeting twenty-frame image of a famous but long-gone relative caught in an old family movie. Thurgood Marshall was walking Charles Hamilton Houston back to his own office, past mine, and he stopped for a moment to introduce me. They went into Thurgood's office and closed the door. That's all.

I recall high cheek bones, receding hairline, wide eyes, a broad, generous face that suggested—maybe reading what I knew of the man into what I was seeing—compassion and pain. I saw in that face everything I'd heard about this special man during the brief time I had been at the NAACP Legal Defense and Educational Fund (LDF). At Houston's funeral in 1950, Thurgood simply repeated what he had been saying to those of us at the Fund all along: "We wouldn't have been any place if Charlie hadn't laid the groundwork for it."

Though I had met him for only that one brief moment, I became immensely curious about the life of this singular man, for while he was only peripherally involved with the work at the Fund during my

3

time there, his shadow was across everything we did. He was taken from us early, at the age of fifty-five, and I have sometimes wondered how differently things might have turned out had he lived longer. His greatest contribution lay in conceiving a grand strategic framework and in educating his students at Howard University Law School to do legal battle for racial equality, and in his continuing guidance of his protégés. And so, at the time of his death, untimely though it was, the struggle was left not leaderless but with an entire generation of talented people who had been well trained to continue the fight.

He conceived of the notion of the litigation campaign. Using it first to launch a broad-based attack on discrimination in the selection of juries, he drafted legal papers that could be used as a model by black lawyers preparing attacks on such discrimination all over the South. He planned and began an effort to equalize the salaries of black teachers. Southern school boards until then unashamedly maintained two salary scales, one for white teachers, another for blacks, thereby mocking their own self-professed belief in the concept of separate-but-equal.

Houston's most important conception may have been the step-by-step assault on segregation in education, which he began in the mid-1930s with a series of cases against all-white professional schools. After a false start with a case against a school of pharmacology in North Carolina, he focused on states that had no law school offering admission to blacks. Judges might be receptive to a young man's desire to avail himself of the good legal education being offered right in his home state, even if the young man's skin was dark. Graduate students would be few and less threatening to the established racist order than large numbers of elementary and high school students. And, because there were few women among law students, the cases wouldn't raise the specter of the ultimate bugbear of white Southerners of the time—black males sitting in classrooms alongside white females.

The struggle in the courts against segregated education indeed was a Houston idea in its inception. Originally it was conceived as an attack on segregated elementary and high schools, but it began at the university level. Moreover, it did not unfold with the precision suggested by the word "campaign." Unanticipated obstacles arose, for example, southern opposition of a fierce intensity that had never been seen before, except perhaps in the resistance to Reconstruction. The analogy is apt, because following *Brown* the South fought against what indeed was a Second Reconstruction. Legal victory translated into unforeseen social movements: when they filed their suits the lawyers, myself included, could not have imagined them leading to sit-ins sweeping the nation, freedom rides that electrified the world, and the triumphs of Martin Luther King Jr. Nor his assassination. Interminable failed efforts to enact civil rights legislation suddenly succeeded and civil rights became enforceable, opening doors to those who had been kept outside, segregation in public accommodations collapsed, the workplace began yielding opportunities to people of color, forty black congressmen took office. Yet, resistance and backlash rolled back many gains. School integration peaked and declined. Affirmative action erupted into a national controversy. The law of unforeseen consequences worked its powers with vigor. If campaign is the apt word, then it alludes to armies that in unanticipated ways advance, retreat, stall, see-saw, meander, yet continue to move towards victory.

In 1936, Houston was working in New York as staff counsel to the NAACP and brought one of his star pupils at Howard, Thurgood Marshall, North to work with him. In 1938, he left Thurgood in charge and returned to Washington to go back into private practice with his father. When Houston left he told Thurgood, "Shock troops don't occupy towns." By 1950, under Thurgood's leadership, and by winning some of the first cases on which I worked after coming to the Fund, LDF had succeeded in the graduate and professional school campaign that Houston had begun fifteen years earlier. Tragically, in April 1950, before Houston could rejoice in these hard-won victories, he died of a heart attack. He had been working at the time on the precursor to the District of Columbia case that became one of five cases later known as the School Segregation Cases, or *Brown v. Board of Education,* decided by the Supreme Court in 1954,[1] although strictly

---

[1] Brown v. Board of Education, 347 U.S. 483 (1954); Bolling v. Sharpe, 347 U.S. 497 (1954) (the District of Columbia case).

speaking the District of Columbia case, *Bolling v. Sharpe,* was decided under a different name, with a separate opinion, and on a different theory.

At most difficult moments those carrying the struggle did not have the world at their shoulder telling them that the way they were going about it was right. At the outset of the attack on school segregation in the mid-1930s some black leaders, including W. E. B. Du Bois, counseled against it. On the eve of *Brown,* Marjorie McKenzie, a prominent black journalist, opposed our efforts. White liberals, like Harry Ashmore, editor of the *Arkansas Gazette,* argued that there was so much opposition to desegregating schools that the Supreme Court would rule against us. Senator William Fulbright, whose fellowships added luster to his name and made him a darling of the academy, filed a brief against us in the Supreme Court when we opposed Arkansas Governor Orville Faubus's attempt to suspend integration in Little Rock in 1958. President Dwight Eisenhower's decision to nationalize the Arkansas Guard, and then to post troops to Little Rock to enforce the court order, was criticized by some of the national press as too provocative, too draconian, taken too early in the negotiations—a general's solution, some said, to a political problem. It is not surprising, then, that when we tried to bring about the court-ordered admission of James Meredith to the University of Mississippi in 1962, John F. Kennedy waffled, attempting to negotiate with the racists who had promised to block Meredith's way. Finally, unable to bribe, placate, or win over the state's governor, Ross Barnett, Kennedy belatedly directed federal marshals to enforce the court order we had won, by force if necessary, and Meredith entered the university through tear gas and gunfire that cost several lives.

Although the struggle in *Brown v. Board of Education* and in some of the cases that *Brown* precipitated are today well-known, they would have been for naught without the careful preparation and strategic acumen of Thurgood and the LDF's staff.

CHAPTER 2

THE GROUND IS HARD

Freedom House, 1949

In September 1949, when I came to work at the NAACP Legal Defense and Educational Fund, its offices were on the fourth floor of Freedom House at 20 West Fortieth Street, just west of Fifth Avenue, in New York City. Earlier in the century, the seven-storied red brick and granite structure had been a German-American clubhouse. It was later subdivided into offices, its sculpted interior decorations painted over many times, its lovely fireplaces sealed, the original flooring covered with linoleum tiles. The basement, once a beer cellar, was our conference room. A little of the building's history lingered. Once I reached under a radiator to retrieve a coin I'd dropped and found a dust-encrusted microphone. Thurgood called the police, thinking that we were being bugged, but the police had trouble identifying the microphone, a really old piece of business, as any model then in use. Eventually it was decided that it must have been under that radiator for decades. In *The Zimmerman Telegram*, Barbara Tuchman writes of the bugging of another German-American club in New York during the First World War, and upon reading her book, I later thought that our ancient microphone might have been part of a similar attempt by American intelligence to eavesdrop on our German-American club.

Three of us—Constance Baker Motley, Franklin H. Williams, and I—all assistant counsel, worked in a large high-ceilinged office with big windows facing north, overlooking Fortieth Street, the monumental New York Public Library, and the green lawn and shrubbery of Bryant Park. To our left, also facing Fortieth Street and separated

7

from us by a small office for two secretaries, Thurgood Marshall occupied another office; his desk was at the far end of the room from us. Annette Peyser, a sociologist, sat at a table on the opposite wall, her back to him when she faced her work. At right angles to their room, Robert L. Carter, Thurgood's first assistant counsel, had his own small office. That was the entire staff in those days of the NAACP Legal Defense and Educational Fund, Inc., the organization directing a legal revolution for American blacks, which, by 1949, was already well advanced.

Thurgood Marshall was not only the boss, he was the commanding presence. I first met him in 1947, while working as a law student on a project for LDF. In 1949 he interviewed me for a job with LDF. The interview was brief. After all, Walter Gellhorn, his good friend and sometime collaborator, had been my teacher for four semesters, and probably told him more about me than he could have learned in a dozen long interviews.

Thurgood was well over six feet tall. While he was of muscular build, I'm pretty sure that he never engaged in any athletic activity. Someone not long ago told me that he had heard Thurgood used to play squash with Telford Taylor, a Columbia professor and former Nuremburg prosecutor. I flatly declared that was impossible, as indeed it was, a false report. He has been described, more or less accurately, as resembling a Sikh warrior. His nose curved downward as is often seen in that part of the world. He kept fit by maintaining a frantic travel and litigation schedule. As a judge, living a sedentary life, he developed the ample shape that appears in pictures of his later years.

My First Days

I went to work my first day at LDF not knowing what I would be asked to do, only vaguely aware of the cases in the office, hardly knowing the people. That first morning Thurgood called me in and asked me to do research for a friend-of-the-court brief in a case that was not an LDF case at all. His friend Loren Miller, a civil rights pioneer in California, who was involved in a range of dissident causes, represented members of the Progressive party who had been beaten up by a group of men wearing the caps of American Legionnaires. They sued, claiming that their assailants had deprived them of their constitutional rights. I was asked to make an argument in their support. I holed up in the bar association library for a week and produced a memorandum that, although it greatly pleased Loren, didn't help: he lost the case.[1] Then Thurgood asked me to prepare a presentation to a conference dealing with why the New York State Commission Against Discrimination was ineffective. I asked around and studied and researched and concluded, like others before me, that it was lack of political will and lack of real power. Very nervous, I delivered my conclusions to a group at a nearby hotel. Though I told them nothing new the exercise was part of an ongoing struggle to pressure the commission to act more effectively.

My work became a little more exciting. In January 1950, Thurgood assigned me to represent John McCray, the publisher of the Columbia South Carolina *Lighthouse and Informer,* the only black newspaper in the state. A black defendant was awaiting execution for a rape of a white girl, the daughter of the county solicitor, and in October 1949, McCray printed the man's story, including his contention that the girl and her boyfriend had asked him to find some whiskey for them and then invited him to have intercourse with her in their car. Harold Boulware, the first black lawyer ever to appear in that county, had represented the defendant, who refused to testify about the consensual sex, possibly because he thought he would be treated leniently if he kept quiet about what had actually happened. He was convicted, refused to appeal, and was electrocuted. For publishing his story with the allegation that a white female had had consensual sex with a black male, McCray was charged with criminal libel. Today, none of this could have occurred. The death penalty for a rape is prohibited as cruel and unusual punishment, and a conviction for criminal libel for printing the defendant's claim of innocence would be inconceivable because the First Amendment protects against such prosecutions.

---

[1] Collins v. Hardyman, 341 U.S. 651 (1951).

I traveled back and forth to Columbia and came up with a few defenses, but never was able to put them to the test because in June McCray pleaded guilty to avoid jail and paid a fine. If the case had come to trial, this being the early 1950s, I almost surely would not have succeeded. In fact, the atmosphere was so hostile that a white lawyer in Columbia, who covertly helped us, asked us to enter his house at night through the back door. He would have been ruined if his involvement became known.

The court sentenced McCray to three years' probation, during which he was not permitted to leave the state, although his parole officer explained that he might take short trips for business purposes. But, in August 1951, the court revoked his probation, because he had gone briefly out of state on two occasions, and sentenced him to two months on the chain gang. The real reason for the court's anger with him was likely his newspaper's support for the School Segregation Cases, then being argued in South Carolina. McCray suspected that such an order must have come directly from South Carolina Governor James Byrnes, for many years a power in the Democratic party, a former associate justice of the Supreme Court, war effort organizer under Franklin Roosevelt, and secretary of state under Truman. Because McCray had already pleaded guilty, the only legal issue became whether the parole had been properly revoked, and on that there was no second-guessing the state courts.

I soon got an assignment working on cases involving the integration of the University of Texas Law School and the University of Oklahoma Graduate School of Education, both about to be argued in the Supreme Court. Though the cases involved heady constitutional issues, my role was not at the level of great intellectual challenge. It was becoming apparent that being a good civil rights lawyer meant first being a good lawyer, which required doing many things that were not terribly exciting or important. But I knew also that there *were* great issues being debated, if not in the work I was doing, certainly in the work of the other lawyers, whose work was supported by my own.

I slowly became immersed in the core of LDF work as I attended staff meetings, the frequent conferences that Thurgood called with law professors and "visiting firemen" to deal with higher education cases, and after-hours bull sessions in the office, in the 440 Club down the street, and in colleagues' homes. I also knew there was a master plan guiding what seemed to be an endless stream of diverse cases.

Thurgood often referred to something he called the "Margold Report," so I got it out of the file, a blue-backed lawyer's document, and read it during my first few weeks at the Fund. The report was the product of a small committee, directed by Nathan Margold, a protégé of Felix Frankfurter, set up for the NAACP in 1930 to outline the direction it should take in the courts. The report was made possible by $20,000 provided by the American Fund for Public Service, a foundation set up by a young man, Charles Garland, who had inherited funds he declined to spend on himself. The committee's recommendations were remarkably bold and prescient, setting the direction we traveled, although with frequent deviation.

In 1930, when Margold was drawing up his plan, there were basically only a few important Supreme Court cases dealing directly, or even by implication, with discrimination based on race. One might have thought that the Fourteenth Amendment's equal protection clause, adopted after the Civil War, would have given blacks first-class citizenship. And, indeed, not long after the amendment was adopted the Court seemed to be following that course. *Strauder v. West Virginia,* decided in 1880, held that excluding blacks from juries was "practically a brand upon them, affixed by the law: an assertion of their inferiority, and a stimulant to that race prejudice . . . an impediment to . . . equal justice."[2] But around that time the Court began to waver. In 1883, *The Civil Rights Cases*[3] held that in enforcing the Fourteenth Amendment, which provided that no "state shall deny to any person . . . the equal protection of the laws," the federal government had no power to pass laws prohibiting *individuals* from discriminating. Individuals were not the "state." They could keep blacks out of privately owned restaurants, opera houses, ferryboats, and other places, immune from the federal civil rights statutes that

[2] Strauder v. West Virginia, 100 U.S. 303, 308 (1880).
[3] Civil Rights Cases, 109 U.S. 3 (1883).

were enacted to prevent such discrimination. This decision gave rise to what became known as the "state action" doctrine and later stimulated debates over what is the state and what is state action, warming the hearts of political scientists, but contributing little to racial justice. This issue was reprised in the sit-in cases of the 1960s, when demonstrators sat in at private establishments to force change in racist policies followed universally within certain states, and rigorously enforced by police and judges. Were the policies examples of private or state-imposed discrimination?

Civil rights did not always lose in the late 1800s. *Yick Wo v. Hopkins,*[4] decided in 1886, held unconstitutional a San Francisco ordinance that had a discriminatory impact on Chinese by banning laundries in wooden buildings, which is where the Chinese typically located their businesses. The Court said that the law was employed with "an evil eye and an unequal hand" and denied the Chinese their constitutional rights. Perhaps it is important in understanding this decision to recall that *Yick Wo* involved San Francisco and not the American South and did not involve blacks, the racial group singled out for disparate treatment more often than any other.

In 1896 the Supreme Court, in what became the dominant decision governing the lives of blacks for almost sixty years, repudiated the principal purpose of the Fourteenth Amendment in the infamous case of *Plessy v. Ferguson,*[5] which ruled that states had the power to *require* segregation. *Plessy,* in upholding a Louisiana law that segregated railroad cars, said that "in the nature of things": the Fourteenth Amendment could not have been intended "to abolish distinctions based upon color, or to enforce social, as distinguished from political, equality, or a coming together of the two races upon terms unsatisfactory to either." It opined that if segregation made blacks feel inferior it was because they chose "to put that construction on it"; if the roles were reversed whites would never feel that way. Law could not change "racial instincts." The decision created

---

[4] Yick Wo v. Hopkins, 118 U.S. 356, 373–74 (1886).

[5] Plessy v. Ferguson, 163 U.S. 537, 544, 551, 559 (1896).

the legal doctrine of "separate-but-equal," under which excluding blacks from opportunities and conveniences enjoyed by whites was okay as long as blacks were offered equal accommodations. Though it would seem to any fair-minded person that separate-but-equal could never obtain in the real world, the decision set a new obstacle in the way of civil rights lawyers, an obligation to prove to the satisfaction of a court that the separate accommodations were not in fact equal.

The Supreme Court had no evidence before it upon which to base its assertions about inferiority and instincts. These supposedly were statements about facts, but told more about the Court's values. Years later, in *Brown v. Board of Education*, the Court would confront issues about a sense of inferiority once more, this time after plaintiffs had indeed presented evidence on the subject. Based upon this evidence, or perhaps expressing contemporary values, it came to a contrary conclusion, which provoked a firestorm of criticism directed at what was called "inadequate evidence."

Plessy had one saving grace. Justice John Marshal Harlan dissented, writing that "our constitution is color-blind, and neither knows nor tolerates classes among its citizens. In respect of civil rights, all citizens are equal before the law."

Following *Plessy,* not only were individuals allowed to discriminate against fellow citizens, free of federal prohibition, but the states could now require and enforce such discrimination. Predictably, with the power of the state now behind it, rigid Jim Crow segregation soon defined all aspects of Southern society.

Why the switch from a pro- to an anti-egalitarian interpretation of the Constitution? C. Vann Woodward has written that the 1877 presidential election between Republican Rutherford B. Hayes and Democrat Samuel J. Tilden was so close that a few electors could have decided it. Hayes offered a deal to Southern Democrats: withdrawal of Northern troops from the South, abandonment of blacks, and federal support of economic development in return for the votes of the white South needed to assure victory. They accepted; the bargain became known as the Compromise of 1877. It gave a free hand to Southerners to return blacks to a condition as close to slavery as could be achieved. The law can be a great teacher. It is also sometimes an obedient pupil, and in the years after 1877, the law began to reflect the new social and political reality.

Plessy metastasized, infecting more than half a century of constitutional law. As late as 1927, a unanimous court, on which Holmes, Brandeis, and Stone sat, applied *Plessy* to schools, in a case that permitted Mississippi to require a Chinese girl to attend black schools, *Gong Lum v. Rice.*[6] But Harlan's *Plessy* dissent continued to loom, as Charles Evans Hughes once described some dissents, like "an appeal to the brooding spirit of the law, to the intelligence of a future day."

There were some cracks in the united front. *Strauder,* the case proscribing discrimination in the selection of juries, never was overruled, merely distinguished as being applicable solely to the deprivation of "political" rights, a term never defined precisely. Therefore, its doctrine of prohibiting the state from imposing a stigma on blacks remained latent, available for use in later years. Twenty years after *Plessy, Buchanan v. Warley,*[7] a 1917 NAACP case, held unconstitutional a Louisville law barring blacks from living in certain parts of town, a residential apartheid resembling that which until recently existed in South Africa. The case pointed out that *Plessy* dealt only with rail travel, and rejected the argument that the state's action in establishing residential segregation was necessary to prevent violence and intermarriage. *Yick Wo,* the Chinese laundry case, remained available to challenge rules that were written to appear evenhanded but that were clearly intended to discriminate.

A Strategy Emerges

Faced with this state of the law, Margold first considered whether the NAACP should acquiesce in the *Plessy* framework and bring suits to force school districts to maintain completely equal, though separate, schools. There had been an earlier proposal to file such cases in South Carolina, Georgia, Mississippi, Louisiana, Florida,

---

[6] Gong Lum v. Rice, 275 U.S. 78 (1927).

[7] Buchanan v. Warley, 245 U.S. 60, 81 (1917).

Alabama, and Arkansas in order to make separate schools so expensive that segregation would have to be abolished, a theme to be heard almost until the *Brown* decision. But, Margold argued, few districts would be equalized, soon they would slip back into inequality, and the struggle would have to start all over again. He concluded that:

> It would be a great mistake to fritter away our limited funds on sporadic attempts to force making of equal divisions of school funds in the few instances where such attempts might be expected to succeed. Such an effort would eliminate only a minor part of discrimination and only temporarily. It would not establish new principles or have any general effect. . . . *We should be leaving wholly untouched the very essence of the existing evils.* If we boldly challenge the constitutional validity of segregation if and when accompanied irremediably by discrimination, we can strike directly at the most prolific sources of discrimination.

He proposed exploiting the concept of *Yick Wo,* which condemned discrimination administered "with an evil eye and an unequal hand," as central to his legal theory. The idea was that if wherever there was segregation there also was inequality, which was invariably the case, segregation, therefore, was unconstitutional.

An equally prescient aspect of Margold's report was that the litigation effort would "stir . . . the spirit of revolt among blacks" and cause whites to view them with more respect. Indeed, that turned out to be the case.

At the conclusion of his report, Margold wrote, curiously, that we "are not trying to deprive southern states of their acknowledged privilege of providing separate accommodations for the two races. We are trying only to force them to comply with their equally acknowledged duty to provide 'equal if separate' accommodations in white and colored schools." He urged publicity to avert the danger of alienating "enlightened public opinion," perhaps a sop to those who feared stirring adverse public reaction. Maybe the passage was put in by a conservative member of the committee.

During the same period black leaders conducted a similar debate over equalization versus integration. W. E. B. Du Bois, a towering black scholar, a founder of the NAACP, and the editor of *The*

Crisis until 1934, was forced to resign for having written an editorial that stated that "thinking colored people of the United States must stop being stampeded by the word segregation. . . . It is the race conscious black man co-operating together in his own institutions and movements who will eventually emancipate the colored race." Bill Hastie, ordinarily a man of measured tones, attacked Du Bois in language uncharacteristically harsh: "For fifty years prejudiced white men and abject boot-licking, gut-lacking, knee-bending, favor-seeking Negroes have been insulting our intelligence with a tale that goes like this: Segregation is not an evil. Negroes are better off by themselves . . . in theory there can be segregation without unequal . . . treatment." Hastie unequivocally rejected that view.

In a major debate in 1935, Du Bois argued that there was nothing wrong with integration in theory, but he opposed sending black children to white schools where they would be received with hostility and lack of understanding. Charles Thompson, dean of the Howard University Graduate School of Education, replied that black children could be treated equally only in an integrated system. Black schools did not always educate black children more sympathetically. Members of both races could learn mutual respect only if educated together. The NAACP, and LDF when it came into being, held the Thompson view. The Du Bois view remains very much alive today, although among nearly all of those within the civil rights leadership, Martin Luther King, Jr.'s dream of a fully integrated society remains the driving force.

As NAACP lawyers faced a thoroughly segregated South on the eve of the Second World War, they could find possibly effective legal tools in the constitutional melange of the previous half-century or so, and could turn them in a direction proposed by the Margold plan. In this, they were fortified by the values articulated by black integrationist civil rights lawyers and educators, like Bill Hastie and Charles Thompson.

Around the same time the law began taking a more favorable turn and fresh legal doctrines became available. In 1938, in one of the most influential passages in American constitutional history, Justice Harlan F. Stone, in a footnote, expressed a philosophy that gave primacy to constitutional rights protecting participation in the political process. One part of that footnote asserted:

> It is unnecessary to consider now whether legislation which restricts those political processes which can ordinarily be expected to bring about repeal of undesirable legislation, is to be subjected to more exacting judicial scrutiny under the general prohibitions of the Fourteenth Amendment than are most other types of legislation . . . [and] whether prejudice against discrete and insular minorities may be a special condition, which tends seriously to curtail the operation of those political processes ordinarily to be relied upon to protect minorities, and which may call for a correspondingly more searching judicial inquiry.[8]

As America entered the Second World War, Supreme Court doctrine took a further egalitarian turn, although the practical outcome of the cases sometimes was otherwise. In 1943, in a case involving wartime curfews of Japanese-Americans, the Court upheld the restrictions on the basis of wartime necessity, but asserted that "distinctions between citizens solely because of their ancestry are by their very nature odious to a free people whose institutions are founded upon the doctrine of equality."[9] A 1944 case involving Japanese removal from the West Coast during the war decided that "all legal restrictions which curtail the civil rights of a single racial group are immediately suspect. That is not to say that all such restrictions are unconstitutional. It is to say that courts must subject them to the most rigid scrutiny."[10]

The Court also began making inroads into the state action doctrine, or how much private individuals might act free of constitutional restraint. In 1946 it reversed trespass convictions of Jehovah's Witnesses for proselytizing in a company town, holding that "the more an owner, for his advantage, opens up his property for use by

---

[8] United States v. Carolene Products, 304 U.S. 144, 153 (1938).

[9] Hirabayashi v. United States, 320 U.S. 81, 100 (1943).

[10] Korematsu v. United States, 323 U.S. 214, 216 (1944).

the public in general, the more do his rights become circumscribed by the statutory and constitutional rights of those who use it."[11]

Our job was to exploit the favorable decisions and use them to overwhelm the unfavorable ones.

National and International Attitudes Evolve

As LDF probed how far and fast it might go, a national political consensus began to emerge. In September 1946, Walter White, as head of a National Emergency Committee Against Mob Violence, visited the White House to ask that President Truman call a special session of Congress and undertake a study of American race relations. In response, the president, in December 1946, appointed the President's Committee on Civil Rights. Its mandate was broad: "To inquire into and to determine whether and in what respect current law-enforcement measures and the authority and means possessed by Federal, State, and local governments may be strengthened and improved to safeguard the civil rights of the people." The committee included Morris Ernst, of the LDF National Legal Committee, and Channing Tobias, chairman of the NAACP board. Thurgood testified before the committee urging a wide range of legislation and LDF filed a brief arguing the legal basis for federal protection of civil rights.

Like all presidents, Truman appointed a committee to propose what he wanted to do; he was not disappointed. Its historic 1947 report, *To Secure These Rights,* called for reforms that, within twenty-one years, were adopted in toto by the Congress and the Supreme Court. The report was a catalyst, regularly cited in briefs and before congressional committees. The President's Committee on Civil Rights recommended:

The elimination of segregation, based on race, color, creed, or national origin.

---

[11] Marsh v. Alabama, 326 U.S. 501, 506 (1946).

The conditioning by Congress of all . . . federal assistance to public or private agencies for any purpose on the absence of discrimination and segregation.

The enactment by Congress of a law stating that discrimination and segregation, based on race, color, creed, or national origin, in the rendering of all public services by the national government is contrary to public policy.

The enactment by Congress of a law prohibiting discrimination or segregation . . . in interstate transportation. . . .

Prohibition of discrimination and segregation . . . in all public or publicly supported hospitals, parks, recreational facilities, housing projects, welfare agencies, penal institutions, and concessions on public property.

The establishment of a fair educational practice program . . . in the admission of students to private educational institutions.

The establishment of a fair health practice program forbidding discrimination and segregation by public or private agencies. . . .

The outlawing of restrictive covenants.

Granting equal access to places of public accommodation.

On October 30, 1947, the day following issuance of the report of the President's committee, Truman's Solicitor General, Philip Perlman, filed a friend-of-the-court brief in the Restrictive Covenant Cases supporting the LDF position that court enforcement of restrictive covenants was unconstitutional. Earlier, Truman addressed the NAACP annual convention and called for progress in civil rights.

Moving Ahead in Higher Education: Maryland, Missouri, Oklahoma

The nation and the Court clearly seemed primed to move ahead on civil rights, but the question was *how* primed. NAACP and LDF lawyers proceeded principally with a campaign against segregation in higher education, not exactly following Margold, who had aimed at elementary and high schools, or his primary legal theory, which rested on *Yick Wo*. They also found it impossible to confine their efforts to schools only, tackling teachers' salaries, voting, housing, transportation, criminal cases, and other subjects. But the Margold Report had established the importance of a long-range goal and a plan for reaching it, lessons the LDF followed even as it adjusted the plan and occasionally substituted short-range goals.

In 1936, Thurgood and Charles Houston won *Pearson v. Murray*[12] in the Maryland courts, requiring the state to admit Donald Murray, a black applicant who didn't want to go out of state, to Maryland's white law school because it didn't have a black one. The state didn't appeal to the United States Supreme Court and so no nationally binding precedent was established. Murray entered the University of Maryland Law School, graduated, and went into practice. (I knew him as a quiet, cheerful legal aid lawyer when I traveled to Baltimore. He showed up at NAACP events, but never participated in civil rights cases.)

Then in 1938, Houston, with Thurgood, Leon Ransom, and Sidney Redmond, early associates whose participation waned in later years, won a case against the University of Missouri[13] on the same grounds as in the Maryland case, this time in the United States Supreme Court. That should have made clear that, at least when there was no comparable black institution, blacks had to be admitted to the white school. The Missouri plaintiff, Lloyd Gaines, disappeared, however, and, unlike Donald Murray, never did enjoy the fruits of his victory. Rumors flew about foul play, that he couldn't take the pressure and had run off to Mexico, and so forth. But no one ever discovered anything. Missouri opened a black law school, so that if the issue were to arise again, it wouldn't have to admit blacks to its white universities. So far as the South was concerned, the Maryland and Missouri cases had never been decided. No other Southern state

---

[12] Pearson v. Murray, 169 Md. 478, 182 A. 590 (1936).

[13] Missouri ex rel. Gaines v. Canada, 305 U.S. 337 (1938).

admitted black students because of their precedent. Then there were no further Supreme Court decisions in higher education until the mid-1940s, probably because the war made it difficult to find plaintiffs. The Association's efforts during the war and early postwar years focused on the White Primary Cases.

In a cautious approach, the NAACP, as late as 1945, though committed to ending segregation, nevertheless resolved to implement the earlier victories by stressing inequality rather than attacking segregation itself. A 1945 legal department report stated:

> The NAACP still believes that segregation in public education is unconstitutional. However, in view of the present decisions of the United States Supreme Court, it is believed that an affirmative campaign to compel the southern states to give absolute equality in its segregated schools will not only give Negro children equal educational facilities but the tremendous cost of maintaining an equal dual school system will eventually destroy segregation.

Higher education remained the model case of inequality: whites had graduate and professional schools and blacks had virtually nothing. Admission to the white institution would be the appropriate relief. In 1946, Ada Lois Sipuel's LDF lawyers—Thurgood and Amos Hall (a Tulsa private practitioner who worked with us in some cases)—sought a court order requiring Oklahoma to admit her to its all-white law school. Oklahoma, too, had no law school for blacks, but defended on the ground that there weren't enough black applicants to make opening one worthwhile. Hall had invited Thurgood to enter the case because his office was the fount of expertise on segregation issues. I knew Hall principally as a Prince Hall Mason, the black Masonic group to which Thurgood also belonged, and they bonded together closely in that relationship and its rituals.

Around the same time another law school applicant appeared in Texas. Heman Marion Sweatt's LDF lawyers—Thurgood, W. J. Durham, and James M. Nabrit, Jr. (both in private practice, sometimes working with us)—applied for a court order admitting him to the University of Texas Law School. (Nabrit later taught the first civil rights course in the United States. His son, James M. Nabrit, III was to become my closest colleague). Texas didn't have a black law school either. Here we were all over again—virtually a decade later—still fighting over the same issues.

The Oklahoma Supreme Court ruled against Sipuel saying that she should have asked for a separate black law school and that she could have had a scholarship to attend school out of state. The Texas courts took a different tack, giving the university six months to offer legal instruction "substantially equivalent" to that at the University of Texas. Texas then announced it would establish a law school for blacks that would be equal to the University of Texas Law School. It would be in the basement of a petroleum company building in downtown Austin, and consist of three medium-sized rooms, one smaller room, and a toilet, which had been leased for $125 per month. There would be no library, but students might use the library in the state capitol; the faculty would be three University of Texas professors who would teach part-time. There were no other students, moot court, legal aid clinic, law review, honorary societies, or scholarship fund. Charles T. McCormick, dean of the University of Texas, was made dean also of the new black school. He was a celebrated legal scholar, author of leading texts on evidence and damages. Demonstrating that status as a scholar was no guarantee that one would speak intelligently, McCormick testified that the two law schools were equal. If testifying honestly had crossed his mind, he would have considered that the state legislature could retaliate with devastating disapproval.

Then in May 1947, Thurgood, Durham, and Nabrit conducted a full-scale trial to prove the obvious—the two Texas schools weren't equal and never could be. They built on an approach developed by Bob Carter in a 1946 friend-of-the-court brief that attacked segregation of Mexican Americans in California by documenting the psychological consequences of segregation.[14] Social science materials had been used before, but not a great deal. Louis D. Brandeis had in 1908 written a pioneering brief that marshaled social scientific data

---

[14] Brief for NAACP, amicus curiae, Westminster School District v. Mendez, 161 F.2d 774 (9th Cir. 1947) (No. 11,310).

in support of a law that limited the number of hours women might work. He showed that the law had a reasonable basis and argued that it was, therefore, constitutional.[15] But, in the higher education cases, LDF lawyers went beyond published materials. They commissioned research and called sociologists, psychologists, psychiatrists, educators, and others as expert witnesses. Unlike Brandeis, who argued in support of a law, they used social scientific evidence to strike one down.

The evidence concerning library, faculty, classrooms, and other facilities was what one might have expected. But more important was social scientific testimony about intangible aspects of education presented by Robert Redfield, chairman of the department of anthropology at the University of Chicago, who also was a lawyer, and Earl Harrison, dean of the University of Pennsylvania Law School. They testified that race is not relevant to ability to learn and that segregation interferes with law school education. Charles Thompson, dean of Howard University's Graduate School of Education, testified that wherever segregation existed, black schools were vastly inferior to white ones in measurable respects. As was probably expected, it all went for naught in the Texas courts, which ruled that the schools were equal. To play it safe, Texas moved to upgrade the black law school. Thurgood and Durham headed for the Supreme Court.

As *Sweatt* was pending, Thurgood took *Sipuel* to the Supreme Court also, arguing it one week before his argument in the Restrictive Covenant Cases, which sought to invalidate a commonly used artifice to segregate housing: judicially enforced agreements among white neighbors that they would not sell their homes to blacks. Along with the education cases, the covenant cases comprised much of the LDF's early litigation campaign. Two such important arguments in a week is pretty much like the iron-man feat of pitching a double-header. After *Gaines, Sipuel* should have been a piece of cake, and it

---

[15] Brief for Defendant, Muller v. Oregon, 208 U.S. 412 (1908) (No. 107). Linda Kerber has brought to my attention the fact that the material Brandeis used was assembled and drafted by Josephine Goldmark of the Consumers League.

was. The Court held that "the State must provide [legal education] to her in conformity with the equal protection clause of the Fourteenth Amendment and provide it *as soon as* it does for applicants of any other group."[16] Arguments concluded on January 8, 1948. The Court announced its decision in record time on January 12.[17] It meant *"as soon as"* quite emphatically.

Though the *"as soon as"* language seemed to rule out any attempts to circumvent the decision by promising Miss Sipuel her own law school, Oklahoma did not accept Miss Sipuel graciously. The local court ordered that "unless and until the separate school of law for Negroes . . . is established and ready to function," authorities were required to enroll her in the University of Oklahoma *or* "not enroll any applicant of any group in said class until said separate school is established and ready to function." Oklahoma then set up a separate law school for Miss Sipuel by roping off a portion of the state capitol and calling it a law school for colored students.

Thurgood went back to the Supreme Court and asked for an order requiring Oklahoma to admit her. Now he unequivocally asked for an end to segregation per se. He argued that a legal education, like any good education, is *collegial,* in that students often learn as much from frank discussion with each other as they learn from their professors, and that, moreover, segregation brands blacks with a "badge of inferiority." But, rather than react with indignation at Oklahoma's response to its earlier ruling, the Supreme Court backed off. Maybe the justices had hoped that their first decision would cause segregation to crumble, and, that not having been the case, found themselves unwilling to provoke a direct challenge to the authority of the Court by the politically formidable South. In February 1948, over a vigorous dissent by Justice Rutledge and a milder one by Justice Murphy, the Court said that it never had ordered Oklahoma to admit Miss Sipuel, only to not treat her unequally.

---

[16] Sipuel v. Board of Regents of the University of Oklahoma, 332 U.S. 631, 633 (1948) (emphasis supplied).

[17] It took the Court longer—from January 16 until May 3—to invalidate racially restrictive covenants and bring that line of LDF litigation to its denouement. Shelley v. Kraemer, 334 U.S. 1 (1948).

Further hearings in lower courts would be needed to determine whether the new school was unequal and whether requiring Miss Sipuel to go to a segregated school was unconstitutional. The experience taught that going for an end to segregation, and that alone, presented a big risk. After the second *Sipuel* argument, all of our school litigation rested on two legs, a demand for an end to segregation as such and a claim that it should be abolished because black and white offerings were unequal, in a physical sense obviously, but also unequal because of the educational and psychological effects of segregation itself.

Thurgood and his colleagues returned to the trial court and presented virtually the same evidence on the effects of segregation that they had offered in May 1947 in the Texas case, with a few more witnesses, including Erwin Griswold, dean of Harvard Law School, and Walter Gellhorn. They lost again in the Oklahoma courts in August 1948.

That month LDF lawyers commenced another higher education case, *McLaurin v. Oklahoma,*[18] using a procedure they had never tried before—filing in a three-judge United States District Court. McLaurin, then in his sixties, had applied in early 1948 to the University of Oklahoma's Graduate School in Education. (His wife had applied and been rejected on racial grounds in 1923!) But more than litigation was going on. The state also was under pressure from its own citizens. In January 1948, one thousand of the university's twelve thousand students protested segregation by cremating a copy of the Fourteenth Amendment and sending the ashes to President Truman.

In October 1948, the three-judge court held that Oklahoma was violating the Constitution by excluding McLaurin because it had no graduate instruction for him at a black school—the word was getting around, at last. But the court refrained from issuing an order because the governor, in a letter to the court, promised to propose legislation to permit blacks to attend white universities. The rights of blacks could wait—a common official reaction, which persisted through the *Brown* case. Before the new law was passed, however,

---

[18] McLaurin v. Oklahoma, 339 U.S. 637 (1950).

the university admitted McLaurin, and introduced a new twist, which might seem cruelly comic today, but which could only frustrate and humiliate him. They would teach him a lesson! He would not be permitted to sit in the classroom with white students; instead, he was assigned to an anteroom from which he looked into the classroom occupied by whites. As the desegregation controversy swirled, the Oklahoma legislature in June 1949 amended its laws to permit blacks to attend white graduate and professional programs, where such programs were not given in black schools, *but on a segregated basis only.* Around the same time the university admitted Ada Lois Sipuel under the new law, but didn't segregate her, and her case dissolved. Maybe a black female was seen as less threatening than a black male, even one in his sixties.

McLaurin's segregated status, however, continued to present a real issue, and Thurgood wanted to pursue his case. But he reported to the LDF board that there was a problem with Amos Hall, which he didn't describe, who like some other black lawyers at that time was not eager to attack segregation. My guess is that Hall and others like him were afraid to rock the boat, believing that pushing too hard, too fast would be counterproductive. McLaurin, however, wanted to push on, which was the decisive factor and determined that LDF lawyers would appeal. After all, McLaurin's wife had been waiting since 1923 for things to change. Thurgood and Hall went back to the district court seeking an order prohibiting segregation. McLaurin testified about sitting in the antechamber, saying it was "quite strange and humiliating to be placed out in that position, and it handicaps me in doing effective work."

But the district court again said no. LDF lawyers appealed and, when *McLaurin* reached the Supreme Court, confining McLaurin to the anteroom seemed so ludicrous that he was admitted into the classroom—but once inside, he was limited to a seat for blacks only. In the cafeteria and library, too, he was confined to blacks-only chairs and tables. The case had begun with exclusion, moved to the anteroom, then to Jim Crow seats in the classroom, library, and cafeteria. So in the Supreme Court the case increasingly looked like one of segregation per se.

During this period LDF pursued a raft of cases involving higher education, teachers' salaries, voting, and other matters.[19]

The World Around Them

In this environment, international and political developments inspired hope. The more than 900,000 black soldiers who risked their lives for the four freedoms laid a powerful claim to the right to enjoy them. Also, service in the armed forces developed in many Americans a more spacious and less xenophobic view of the world: different peoples, cultures, colors became more familiar, less strange. Whites could not ignore that blacks' blood had been shed in defense of their country. Everyone felt more sensitively the opprobrium with which other countries viewed American apartheid. Hitler had given scientific racism a bad name and the country's "National Origins" immigration policy increasingly became an embarrassment. Articles about Africans clad in tribal robes, served in Southern restaurants or seated in white Pullman cars, while American blacks were Jim Crowed, became almost commonplace. Sometimes American blacks faked being African diplomats and were served in places where they would have been excluded in mufti. When they revealed who they were there would be a lot of publicity ridiculing racism. White journalists, disguised as blacks, traveled in the South and wrote about the experience. The Soviet Union missed few opportunities to denounce the United States for its racial practices. And while we decried European colonialism, it was difficult to demand that Europeans cease ruling countries inhabited by darker races while we persisted in similar practices. In a South Carolina voting case, Judge J. Waties

---

[19] Wilson v. Board of Supervisors of Louisiana State University, 340 U.S. 909 (1951); Wrighten v. Board of Trustees University of South Carolina, 72 F. Supp. 948 (E.D.S.C. 1947); Davis v. Cook, 178 F.2d 595 (5th Cir. 1949), *cert. denied,* 340 U.S. 811 (1950); Bates v. Batte, 187 F.2d 142 (5th Cir.), *cert. denied,* 342 U.S. 815 (1951).

Waring wrote, "When this country is taking the lead in maintaining the democratic process and attempting to show to the world that the American government and the American way of life is the fairest and best that has yet been suggested, it is time for us to take stock of our internal affairs."[20]

---

[20] Elmore v. Rice, 72 F. Supp. 516, 527 (E.D.S.C. 1947).

CHAPTER 3

LAW SCHOOLS IN THE SUPREME COURT

Sweatt and *McLaurin*

My role in both *Sweatt* and *McLaurin* was slight. In *Sweatt* I did such low-level things as spending day and night in the library researching cases, constitutional history, and social science literature, and reading proof at the printer. Having taken *McLaurin* to the Supreme Court, Thurgood then questioned whether we'd followed the proper procedure for three-judge courts—a little late, but everything was not programmed neatly. Three-judge courts were established in 1910 to hear cases in which a plaintiff wanted to enjoin operation of a state statute. The idea was that so serious a decision should not be left to a single, perhaps idiosyncratic judge. Three-judge courts had some advantages, a great one being that the case was heard promptly and appeals went immediately to the Supreme Court, swiftly bypassing the court of appeals. Besides, as the three-judge law was written, the Supreme Court was obliged to hear a case, which went up under a mandatory jurisdiction called *appeal,* and could not slough it off as it usually did under its discretionary jurisdiction, called *certiorari.* Of course, if the Court wanted to avoid deciding a case, it often found a way. The three-judge court jurisdiction was fairly untried and I was supposed to become expert in it to anticipate any tricky questions that might arise during argument. I researched the law to a fare-thee-well and finally concluded that I was wrestling with a phantom question; by the time I was through everyone was satisfied that the three-judge court presented no difficulty, and it didn't.

The *Sweatt* brief, filed in February 1950, flatly attacked the constitutionality of segregation. Yet, it made arguments that could bring victory while allowing decision on grounds short of overruling *Plessy.* First, it asserted, *Plessy* was a railroad car case and inapplicable to schools. It also urged that equal protection prohibits segregation in education because it cannot be justified on any ground, including keeping the peace or alleged intellectual differences between the races; and it said that segregation invidiously penalizes blacks, demoralizes whites, and disrupts democratic institutions. Here the brief elaborated on psychological, sociological, and anthropological material offered by witnesses at the *Sweatt* and *Sipuel* trials. Second, it argued that earlier cases assumed the validity of segregation in education, but didn't decide it.

Finally, however, if *Plessy* applied to education, it should be overruled, the *Sweatt* brief claimed, because the framers of the Fourteenth Amendment rejected separate-but-equal and because segregation inevitably resulted in inequality. The brief showed the tangible ways in which blacks' higher education in Texas was inferior to whites'. White plant was valued at more than $72,000,000, black at $4,000,000; per capita black investment was one-quarter of that for whites. Whites had 106 fields of specialization, blacks only 49, including mattress making, auto mechanics, carpeting, laundering, and dry cleaning. Whites could get graduate degrees in 40 fields, blacks in 13. Texas gave whites 212 doctorates between 1940 and 1945; no black institution qualified to grant a doctorate. The University of Texas library had more than 750,000 volumes; the black school about 82,000.

The brief then turned to the law schools. The University of Texas library had 65,000 volumes, the black school none of its own. The university had sixteen full-time faculty, the black school none, other than three of the white school's faculty who were supposed to teach at the black school. The university had 850 students; if Sweatt had gone to the black school he would have been alone. The university had a moot court, legal aid clinic, law review, honor society, and scholarship fund. The black school had none of these. This litany supported two arguments: Sweatt should be admitted because of the tangible inequalities. The brief also pushed hard the social and psychological consequences of segregation, from which it argued that segregation per se was unconstitutional.

The *Sweatt* approach, arguing from inequality and segregation per se, wasn't viable in *McLaurin* where everything tangible was equal: McLaurin was in the same classroom, had the same teachers at the same time, used the same library and cafeteria. *McLaurin* was an attractive case because, on the one hand, it offered the Court no escape (we thought) from deciding the issue of segregation; it was dangerous because it allowed no victory on grounds short of overruling *Plessy*, which the Court might be reluctant to do. The *McLaurin* brief argued that "to admit appellant and then single him out solely because of his race and to require him to sit outside the regular classroom could be for no purpose other than to humiliate and degrade him—to place a badge of inferiority upon him." There was a secondary argument to the effect that *Plessy*, which dealt with travel, shouldn't govern education.

LDF lawyers urged other interest groups to file briefs to inform the Court of the broader implications of LDF cases. Thurgood lobbied the solicitor general (who represents the government in the Supreme Court), the attorney general, and even the President to get the government on our side in cases. We polished, edited, and reedited everything. The briefs and legal papers looked good because we proofread everything carefully, reading aloud to one another. There were no erasures, no strike-overs, no smudges, no wrinkles. When Thurgood was in law school he once carried some legal papers to court for a black practitioner. They were messy. The clerk looked them over and commented, "A nigger brief." Thurgood vowed we never would file "nigger briefs."

Despite the hedging arguments aimed at winning on grounds short of overthrowing segregation, Thurgood focused on the end of Jim Crow. In 1950, in acerbic correspondence with Carter Wesley, a Texas lawyer-publisher, Thurgood wrote: "A segregated school can never be the equal of any school which has all other racial and ethnic groups in it . . . even if the two schools were practically identical as to plant, library, curriculum, and faculty."

Standing Up Before the Court

Sweatt and *McLaurin* introduced me to how to prepare a Supreme Court argument, a skill at which Thurgood excelled. He dictated an argument not to read in court, but as a base from which to speak extemporaneously and to which he might return if distracted by questions. Standing before the Court he might, however, sometimes read the portions of the written argument that dealt with particularly sensitive issues. He would also craft in writing answers to questions that a justice might ask and turn to that text if necessary. One explosive issue was interracial sex: would overruling *Plessy* mean invalidating interracial sex laws, sometimes referred to as miscegenation and cohabitation statutes? The white South was insane on the issue—Northern attitudes weren't very rational either—contributing to the large number of capital sentences imposed on black men convicted of raping white women. White mobs lynched blacks who dated or had personal relationships with white women. The attorneys general of eleven Southern states filed a brief in *Sweatt* that raised high the sex issue: "Negro men do not want their daughters, wives, and sweethearts dancing, dating, and playing with white men any more than white men want their women folk in intimate social contact with Negro men. 'White trash' is the hated name which Southern Negroes apply to white men who keep the company of their women folk. Worse names are applied to Negro men who 'cross the line.'"

To assert that laws prohibiting miscegenation or interracial sex were unconstitutional would bring down a firestorm of criticism and possibly intimidate the Court or some of its justices. But to deny that those laws were unconstitutional would be wrong and lack credibility. Moreover, some blacks would view such a position as craven. The thing to do would be to duck, artfully, if possible. Answers were prepared in the nature of "that's not this case," "the considerations which govern the two situations are very different," and so forth. In *Sweatt* and *McLaurin* the justices, as it turned out, were not interested in exacerbating the issue, so the prepared formulations never had to be used.

Thurgood would also prepare a notebook of summaries of all the pertinent cases for quick reference; the summaries were later replaced by edited photocopies. He thoroughly indexed the record with tabs—and kept the case summaries and index at his side during argument for quick reference.

There was also the "dry run." We were perhaps the first to have dry runs before Supreme Court arguments—at least on a regular basis. LDF never had a Supreme Court argument in those days that was not first argued at Howard Law School before a panel of lawyers and professors who asked every imaginable question they thought might come from the Court. Most focused on what Justice Frankfurter might ask—he was the most prolific questioner on the bench. I did a count of his questioning during the School Segregation Cases: he asked more questions—punctuated by rocking and swiveling back and forth and all around in his chair—than all the other justices combined, and that was typical of him. Neither I nor any LDF lawyer was ever asked a question in actual argument that had not first been asked at the dry run—until Warren Burger became chief justice. Some of his questions were so idiosyncratic that no one could predict them. Whereas a Supreme Court argument used to take an hour, dry runs kept you on your feet for two or three hours; I sometimes quit with a sore back.

And, finally, like a boxer going into training, for the period of preparation—about a week before argument—Thurgood would limit himself to one glass of wine at dinnertime, usually sherry, and no other alcohol.

The Court heard *Sweatt* and *McLaurin* with a third case, *Henderson v. United States,* which arose out of a Southern railway practice of refusing to serve black passengers in dining cars, except during a brief period when blacks might be served behind a curtain. (*Henderson* was the only important civil rights case that was not an LDF case until at least a decade after I got to the Fund.) The railroad installed curtains to separate the two tables nearest the kitchen from adjoining tables, drawing them into position before mealtime and placing "reserved" cards on them. Should all other seats be taken before any black passenger entered the diner, the curtain would be pushed back, the cards removed, and white passengers would be served at those tables. Should a colored passenger appear he would be served behind drawn curtains as soon as the end tables were vacated. Elmer

Henderson, a black field representative of the President's Committee on Fair Employment Practices, filed a complaint against this practice in 1942 and, as in *McLaurin,* the railway squirmed to substitute something it thought more acceptable, but made things worse, if that was possible. It put up a permanent partition in one diner behind which was a table always set aside for blacks and had begun reconstructing all its dining cars by the time *Henderson* got to the Supreme Court.

Perhaps most important about Henderson's case was that the United States government intervened on his side—peculiar, in that it was attacking the Interstate Commerce Commission, part of the government. In any event, the government argued not merely that the regulation was illegal, but that if it were justified by *Plessy v. Ferguson, Plessy* should be overruled. The brief alluded to Communist efforts to infiltrate black groups; quoted Dean Acheson, then secretary of state, as testifying "that the existence of discriminations against minority groups in the United States is a handicap in our relations with other countries"; cited the United Nations Charter and its human rights provisions; and quoted Soviet attacks on American racial practices. It concluded, "It is neither reasonable nor right that colored citizens of the United States should be subjected to the humiliation of being segregated by law, on the pretense that they are being treated as equals."

In *Sweatt* and *McLaurin* the government filed another, more concise amicus brief, concluding that "the 'separate-but-equal' theory of *Plessy v. Ferguson* is wrong as a matter of law, history, and policy." Most persuasive was that the United States came out four-square against segregation. That political act reflected the inexorable movement toward racial equality manifested in the 1947 report of the President's Committee on Civil Rights and the influence of black voters in the 1948 election.

Well aware that in the Supreme Court law intersects with politics, Southern segregationists enlisted Sam Hobbs, a member of the House Judiciary Committee (which could propose laws determining the Court's jurisdiction and set its budget), to argue as a friend of the court for segregation aboard railways.

On April 3 and 4, 1950, Thurgood argued *Sweatt* and Bob argued *McLaurin* along with Belford Lawson and Jawn Sandifer, private lawyers who argued *Henderson*. The marble four-storied Supreme Court building, which resembles a Greek temple, occupies a square block and is set back from the street, its second-floor entrance atop a lengthy staircase, nearly a hundred feet wide. On its pediment is inscribed "Equal Justice Under Law," a maxim later adopted by LDF as the name of its newsletter and, often, as the title of its annual convocations, which review recent civil rights events. Inside, the courtroom is forty feet high, and about eighty feet wide by ninety feet long. Some have ridiculed as overdone and un-American its classic grandeur, massive columns inside and out, coffered and rosetted ceiling, rich dark woods and deep red velvet fabrics, and sculpture of scenes and personalities representing themes of law and justice. But from the beginning I was awed, as I still am when the marshal, who sits to the right of the bench, calls court to order with "Oyez, oyez, oyez," which is Old French for "hear, hear, hear," ending with "God save the United States and this honorable Court" and a rap of the gavel. Upon first entering the building I felt a nakedness on my head, as if I were in a synagogue and not wearing a skullcap.

Goose quill pens, which now sell in the Court's gift shop for seventy-five dollars, with which no one possibly could write, were placed in front of counsel. Lawyers brought them home as souvenirs. A lectern, which lawyers could raise and lower, separated the two sets of opponents. There were two lights on the lectern, a red and a white one. The white light was to warn that the allotted time for argument would soon expire. Before argument the advocate was supposed to tell the marshal how many minutes should be saved for rebuttal and how far in advance the white light should be turned on. The illuminated red light meant time was up. At that point, it was said, you were supposed to stop in the middle of the word "if." Thurgood loved telling of Francis Biddle, who once, in arguing a case, was being particularly hard-pressed. As the red light lit up, instead of answering, he placed one foot on the other and exclaimed, "Red light!" as if saying "Safe!"

Reporters would write notes, place them in cylinders, and drop them into pneumatic tubes that sucked them to the press room. Behind the rail were seats for perhaps three hundred members of the general public, some reserved for guests of lawyers who were arguing cases. Throughout the courthouse and courtroom were marshals in blue serge suits who quietly and efficiently kept order, directing people to where they ought to go and keeping them out of where they shouldn't be.

The raised bench at which the justices sat, and on which they placed their papers, overlooked all this. The bench was a long mahogany desk that ran the length of nine high-backed leather swivel chairs, each individually crafted for a particular justice. Behind the chairs were the red velvet drapes from which the justices emerged when the marshal rapped his gavel and called the Court to order. Today it is all virtually the same, although Chief Justice Burger introduced innovations. The justices' bench is in three sections, with a right and left wing jutting into the courtroom, connected at shallow angles to the center section, three justices sitting at each section. Burger also gave each justice a silver cup in place of their ordinary drinking glasses. Some skeptics made the irreverent suggestion that it was to conceal what they were drinking. Burger didn't like the activity of note taking, and preferred to isolate it; he wouldn't allow lawyers to take notes if they weren't seated at counsel table. Jack McKenzie of the *New York Times,* who was a Supreme Court reporter at the time of the change, did not get along well with Burger and often criticized him. McKenzie tells that Burger explained to the press that he was moving them to the new area and that perhaps it would be enclosed in glass. McKenzie asked, "Will there be oxygen?" eliciting a look of strong disapproval. Burger always was rearranging and refurbishing the courthouse. One day, while Thurgood was a justice, he ambled down a corridor, his law clerks trailing behind him, muttering, "Warren Burger sure knows how to pick good carpets." Chief Justice Rehnquist's innovation was robes for himself as Chief festooned with gold braid, a design of his creation.

At the argument there were no surprises and no fireworks. Attorney General J. Howard McGrath argued that segregation was unconstitutional, calling it "ceremonial," an imposition of legally enforced caste status; few things could be more humiliating than to be publicly labeled as inferior; unless segregation were ended the United States would suffer seriously in world affairs. Solicitor General Philip Perlman mainly fenced with Justice Frankfurter over whether the Court had to decide the constitutional question in *Henderson* if it could dispose of the case by the Interstate Commerce Act's requirement that passengers should be treated without prejudice.

Bob Carter, in *McLaurin,* argued that *Plessy* was inapplicable—it dealt only with travel—and had been wrongly decided. Thurgood, in *Sweatt,* also attacked segregation: "They can build an exact duplicate but if it is segregated, it is unequal." His rhetoric was concrete and tinged with irony: Texas had argued, he said, that the black law school in a basement in Austin was better than the University of Texas, but then it built a new black school in Houston. Now, didn't the white students have cause for complaint? But, carefully, one step at a time, he said that this case would not decide the fate of elementary and high schools or swimming pools, only law schools. And he was not looking for a remedy against personal prejudice: "We want to remove governmental restriction—if they want to, they can keep their prejudices."

In 1950 opponents lunched together. Checking into the clerk's office in the morning, the lawyers who were scheduled to argue and a few close associates would indicate their orders on a menu. At lunch break a marshal would usher them down a restricted back staircase to a private dining room on the ground floor where lunch would be delivered on a wheeled cart and served by Court attendants, who were always black. There wasn't an express rule that we had to eat together, but if it weren't required, hard-bitten segregationists never would have dined with us, as they regularly did until much later when Burger introduced new lunching arrangements—now a marshal takes lawyers to the head of the cafeteria line. Blacks and whites dining together was high on the list of racist taboos; we took special delight at being seated at the same table as Southern attorneys general who before and after lunch would rail at the social disruption we were trying to create. But at the table they were never unpleasant; occasionally they were affable, although mostly each side talked only among themselves. If there is an index of social discomfort generated by being forced to dine with unwilling partners, it peaked when Jim Nabrit, III and I invited Dick Gregory to join us at lunch in the Supreme Court in the early 1960s. We had run into him in the elevator of the Statler-Hilton the night before I had an argument and suggested that he come to the Court and listen. At the lunch break, he approached us and I impulsively took him along to lunch. As he dined with us and our uncomfortable opponents he said loudly, "Them cats in the white robes are trying to take it away from us, Jack, but the guys in the black robes are going to give it back."

On June 5, 1950, the Court decided *Sweatt, McLaurin,* and *Henderson.* In *Sweatt,* after reciting that the black law school was inferior in building, library, and faculty, the Court turned to "qualities that are incapable of objective measurement" in which the black school also was inferior. These included "reputation of the faculty, experience of the administration, position and influence of the alumni, standing in the community, traditions and prestige." The Court went on to state that

> the law school in which Texas is willing to admit petitioner excludes from its student body members of the racial groups which number 85% of the population of the State and include most of the lawyers, witnesses, jurors, judges and other officials with whom petitioner will inevitably be dealing when he becomes a member of the Texas Bar. With such a substantial and significant segment of society excluded, we cannot conclude that the education offered petitioner is substantially equal.[1]

In the *McLaurin* decision the Court held that confining McLaurin to certain seats in the classroom, library, and cafeteria "handicapped [him] in his pursuit of effective graduate instruction. Such restrictions impair and inhibit his ability to study, to engage in discussions and exchange views with other students, and, in general, to learn his profession."

The most intriguing aspect of *McLaurin* was the observation that treating black teachers in an inferior manner would hurt black pupils: "[As our] society grows increasingly complex . . . our need

---

[1] Sweatt v. Painter, 339 U.S. 629, 634 (1950).

for trained leaders increases correspondingly. . . . Those who will come under his guidance and influence must be directly affected by the education he receives. Their own education and development will necessarily suffer to the extent that his training is unequal."[2]

Henderson was decided simply on the grounds that the railroad had violated the Interstate Commerce Act: "The curtains, partitions and signs emphasize the artificiality of a difference in treatment which serves only to call attention to a racial classification of passengers holding identical tickets and using the same public dining facility."[3]

A clean sweep! But while *Sweatt* had appeared to offer a way of winning without ruling on the constitutionality of segregation, *McLaurin* had seemed to present the issue of segregation and nothing else. Nevertheless, saying that McLaurin was being treated unequally was not the same as deciding the issue of segregation. Of course, that might mean that all segregation amounted to inequality, which the Court carefully avoided saying. That afternoon I attended the victory party in the office at 20 West Fortieth Street. There was lots of Scotch and bourbon, clouds of cigarette smoke, lots of laughter and noise and bragging, jokes about race and racial banter, and the almost obligatory poker game. Bobbie Branch, the office manager, an ample woman who resembled Bloody Mary in *South Pacific,* swaggered around, swearing like a marine with great glee. Everyone stayed late, visitors came by, the press was on the phone. The euphoria went on and on. I was elated and swept up in the partying, a new experience. After the party was all over, it seemed that the victory had been so easy, although it really hadn't been. We had researched the law, written briefs, put our coin into the machine, and the right answer came out. And we had a great time doing it. Everyone was psyched up for the next great adventure, the assault on elementary and high schools that *Sweatt* and *McLaurin* invited. We knew also that the work at higher levels of education was far from done.

---

[2] McLaurin v. Oklahoma, 339 U.S. 637, 641 (1950).

[3] Henderson v. United States, 339 U.S. 816, 825 (1950).

The Court's reasoning suggested how next to attack segregated education at elementary, high school, and undergraduate levels—go after the intangibles.

Following *Sweatt,* the University of Texas Law School admitted blacks, but not many. Texas developed the law school it had created for Sweatt in ironic and unanticipated ways as part of Texas Southern University for black students, changing its name to Thurgood Marshall Law School. The enrollment has evolved so that in 2000–2001, the United States Civil Rights Commission reported it as 57% black, with whites and Hispanics about 17% and Asians 4%. The numbers have fluctuated in recent years during which blacks have been around half the student body. Recent black enrollment at the University of Texas has responded up and down to changes in affirmative action policies.

The World the Decisions Confronted

Higher education for blacks continued to be difficult to achieve. Even after the higher education victories, 80 percent of black Americans lived in the South, which continued to take the position that separate-but-equal was still the law of the land. White colleges and universities continued to deny admission to blacks, and we had to continue to litigate in every single state. The deficit that black Americans faced in higher education was so enormous that it would not yield readily—indeed it has not yet been entirely overcome. Of the 1,685 institutions of higher education in the United States in 1945, only 106 were black. In 1947, only about 74,173 of 2,330,000 persons enrolled in colleges and universities were blacks who attended those black institutions. Fewer than fifty blacks, from only three Southern states and the District of Columbia, attended white institutions. Ninety to ninety-five percent of blacks who graduated from college and professional school had gone to black colleges and universities. The disparities were compounded by a gap in curricula and degrees. In the South whites had fifteen medical schools, sixteen law schools, and seventeen schools of engineering; blacks had two medical schools, one accredited law school in Washington, D.C., and no engineering schools. No Southern state, except Maryland (which had been forced by court action), admitted blacks to its white law school. In the arts and sciences, education, commerce, agriculture, home economics, engineering, architecture, and the trades, offerings in white schools far outdistanced those for blacks. Not a single black institution provided work leading to the Ph.D. In engineering and architecture, blacks could not even earn a master's degree. In sum, though blacks were 10 percent of the population, they received only slightly more than 1 percent of the advanced degrees earned in the United States during 1947, none above the master's level except for eight of 3,375 doctoral degrees awarded by nonsegregated institutions.

Some states claimed that they compensated by scholarships to study out of state. In 1954, about 125 black students left Alabama to attend Columbia, Cornell, Harvard, Michigan, Penn, and other elite Northern schools to study medicine, dentistry, law, pharmacology, and to pursue graduate work across the arts and sciences; others scattered to less well-known schools. The overwhelming number went to black institutions like Atlanta University, Howard, and Meharry. Among that year's holders of Alabama out-of-state scholarships was Coretta Scott King, who went to the New England Conservatory of Music. Out-of-state scholarship programs were no more adequately funded than those of in-state black colleges and universities. A black Texan attending Teachers College of Columbia University in New York would have to spend $508 more than he or she would to attend college in Texas. The Texas grant allowed only $235 for tuition and travel.

Lest one think this is ancient history, it is worth remembering that today's blacks who are in mid-career are the near descendants of a generation that was, for all practical purposes, shut out of higher education.

The Black Bar at Mid-Century

Whatever obstacles they faced in obtaining their education, we five—Thurgood, Bob, Frank, Connie, and I—could have done nothing without the lawyers on the frontlines in the South. Long ago in

England, knowledge of the law consisted largely in knowing which form of writ to use for which kind of action. There developed an old English lawyers' saying, "No writ, no right"—without a procedure to pursue a legal claim, it might as well not exist. Similarly, "No lawyer, no law."

Because the prospects for a black lawyer trying to earn a living practicing in the South were so dim, there was little incentive and less reason to spend money traveling North for a legal education. As a consequence, many of the black lawyers in the South had managed to get their legal education in poor schools with part-time faculties, such as Howard Law School had been before Charles Houston turned it into a competitive, fully reputable, and accredited law school. Some took correspondence courses. Others apprenticed themselves to lawyers to learn law. Still, black lawyers operating at the local level were essential to civil rights claimants. Only a couple of Southern white lawyers handled integration cases before the mid-1960s. The Department of Justice had no effective civil rights jurisdiction and was politically shackled.

When black people asked each other how many lawyers (or doctors or undertakers) could be found in such and such a town or county, they were asking in effect how many *black* lawyers (or doctors or undertakers) could be found there. Usually in the South, often in the North, the answer would be one or two, or none. Even in New York City there were only a handful in active civil rights practice. Black lawyers in the South especially had a tough existence in those days. Instead of practicing law a few went into business, several started insurance companies, and some of those who continued to practice did so part-time. A few worked in the post office or as teachers or Pullman porters or wherever they could get a job to feed their families while they struggled to build a practice in a society where the only people who would hire them could not pay a great deal. The few blacks who could afford to hire lawyers often wouldn't hire black lawyers because they anticipated that the courts wouldn't treat them fairly; some may have come to accept white stereotypes of black incompetence. I knew and worked with every black civil rights practitioner in the South after I came to LDF.

Into the 1950s

The NAACP Legal Department's 1951 annual report (which was still reporting on LDF activities as its own) reported that staff lawyers that year had traveled 72,000 miles. It described 77 court cases and more than 700 other matters, many of which were courts-martial or applications for change of military discharge, referrals to the Department of Justice, administrative proceedings, and informal advice in response to letters or walk-ins. We referred most walk-ins to the New York branch of the NAACP. Every now and then an escaped prisoner from a Southern chain gang came in. Thurgood required us to tell them we could not even talk to them, because that might constitute the crime of harboring an escaped felon, but that if they ever were arrested, or turned themselves in to the authorities, they might contact us for help. Some were arrested and we fought their extradition, in a few instances to the Supreme Court, without success. In some cases, we persuaded governors not to sign extradition papers, having argued that the convict was innocent or that the chain gang was cruel and unusual punishment.

By year's end, 1951, we had twenty elementary and high school cases, a dozen higher education cases, five in housing—against segregated public housing projects in Detroit and Schenectady; against Birmingham, Alabama's racial zoning ordinance; one against Levittown, on Long Island, New York, which openly refused to sell to blacks (we lost *Levittown,* because there was no state action in a constitutional sense, although in fact there was)—five against railway and bus companies; a half-dozen in recreation (several involved golf courses on which black doctors and dentists wanted to play); one voting case; a couple of teachers' salary cases; a great many courts-martial; and a variety of miscellaneous matters. Among eleven major criminal cases those with a sex factor loomed large, partly because of the death penalty for rape. Southern irrationality about interracial sex made all such charges suspect.

Now it was onward—toward an end to all segregation—and downward—to colleges, high schools, and grade schools.

PART II

THE BATTLE

CHAPTER 4

AN END TO SEGREGATION—
NOTHING ELSE

The New Strategy

The Association and its lawyers, who at that time for all practical purposes constituted LDF, edged toward a decision to file only cases that asked for an end to segregation. The turning point was 1950. That year, following *Sweatt* and *McLaurin*, they convinced the Association's national convention, held in Boston, to adopt such a resolution. That year, too, I headed irrevocably down the path of a lifetime civil rights career, which I had started upon a year earlier.

In a memorandum to the convention, Thurgood and the legal staff, citing the two recent victories (*Henderson*, as will be recalled, was another victory won by lawyers not affiliated with us and, at any rate, was decided on the very narrow basis that the railroad had violated the Interstate Commerce Act), assigned priorities for the assault on Jim Crow in the following order: public education; transportation with emphasis on local street cars and buses; health, housing, and recreational facilities; public gatherings; places of public accommodation. A tall order for the South, which was totally segregated in all these aspects.

What this decision to attack Jim Crow head-on meant in practical terms, however, was not entirely clear. We were, in our aggressive program to end segregation, out in front of many members of the black community. Among the reasons was that school integration would create problems for black teachers, who reasonably anticipated that whites would fight against their teaching white children;

we didn't fully appreciate how serious this problem would become. In response, rather than allowing the teachers to be kept hostage by segregationists, we vowed to research how to deal with that problem, though we didn't really know what could be done about it that would be effective. Even so, Thurgood knew that the black population might not be ready. He told a board meeting that "some of the lawyers are ready to fight through the college level but are not ready through the high school and elementary level. They will accept a good Jim Crow school. Many desire to leave it up to the local community and to go as far as they want to go." The board response was recorded as "we can't back out at this time but must try and educate the people."

In January 1951, the board refused to assist the Athens, Georgia, NAACP branch in bringing a school case based on the separate-but-equal theory: "We cannot waive our rule in this case." But they decided to ask Walter White, head of NAACP, then scheduled to be in Atlanta, to meet with the branch to try to convince it of the "desirability and necessity of filing an anti-segregation suit."

In Memphis, in 1950, the NAACP branch complained about having access to the zoo on Thursdays only, the rest of the week being reserved for whites. They didn't object to segregation, but protested that on the Thursday that was Thanksgiving the zoo had been turned over to whites. They asked not for an end to the segregation, but for days "proportionate to population and citizenship." This was an occasion on which, as Thurgood sometimes would say, "the easy part of the job is fighting the white folks."

At the same time, even among ourselves, the decision to seek an end to segregation in all cases left open the question of whether we would attack only *Plessy* or also point out the inequality of buildings, books, and expenditures as reasons why a court should end segregation, either as a remedy for particular situations or as recognition that *Plessy* never had and never could secure even tangible equality. Implicit in the latter strategy was that the inequality might be remedied and Jim Crow retained. To ask for integration because a school was physically inferior *and* segregation was unconstitutional was viewed by some as cowardly and unprincipled. Jim Nabrit, Jr., for example, rejected this approach and attacked only segregation per se in the District of Columbia school case. He would have nothing to do with anything that even faintly suggested that if schools were equalized segregation might be acceptable.

But Thurgood was a conservative on this question. Up to the very end of the struggle, he wanted to give judges an opportunity to rule with us on the basis of physical inequalities, whether or not they shared our moral outrage. In the meantime we continued work as we had before, case by case, one day at a time.

As for me, in 1950, I not only got my first real cases but I was asked to participate in matters that were critical to the main work of the Fund.

Though *Sweatt* and *McLaurin* dealt only with graduate and professional education, they clearly implied that all higher education had to desegregate, down to the undergraduate level. But no white Southern public undergraduate college made a move to admit blacks. Not even the not very Southern, former slaveholding state of Delaware was ready to comply. I was delighted when Thurgood called me in one day and said that Louis Redding, the sole black lawyer in Delaware, needed our help to attack segregation at the undergraduate college of the University of Delaware—the first case challenging segregated college education. Delaware had black and white schools of higher education—the University of Delaware (white) and unaccredited Delaware State College (black). He picked me because my in-laws lived in Delaware, not a bad reason and an expression of the personal, free-form way Thurgood ran the office. The case was mine.

My First Big Case: The First to Integrate a College

In 1929, Redding had become the only black lawyer in Delaware, a solitary role that he filled for almost three decades. He had gone to Brown and Harvard Law School and returned home at the urging of his father, a Howard graduate who was a letter carrier and wanted Louis to become the first black lawyer in the state. Lou's brother, Jay Saunders Redding, became a professor of English at Cornell and wrote books on black history and culture. Lou spoke in cultured tones, slowly, considering every word. He was of medium height, with close-cropped hair and a trim mustache, and was always impeccably dressed. He wore Brooks Brothers and J. Press suits, button-down shirts, silk rep or paisley neckties, and usually carried or dangled from his lips an unlit cigarette, filter end outward. Lou did not suffer fools lightly. Some called him an arrogant snob. His first wife, Ruth, told of the time at a wedding when a man from the congregation offered a long prayer that she said had affected her emotionally. Lou responded, "The grammar was terrible." A so-called white liberal said, "If that man was white I could learn to hate him." But I loved Lou for many reasons, in part, perhaps, because I saw in his manner, which was admittedly more reserved than mine, something resembling my own taciturnity and intolerance of nonsense.

Lou's office was one flight up in a walk-up building in downtown Wilmington, where he shared the second floor with a photographer. He knew the landlord, who rented to him though he was the only black in the neighborhood. He practiced alone, with a secretary, and handled a wide variety of matters throughout Delaware, like title closings, mortgages, divorces, wills, major and minor criminal cases. On the long automobile trip from Wilmington to the state capital in Dover, where his practice regularly took him, there was only one place where blacks could stop for a cup of coffee. In Wilmington, the only places he and I could lunch together were at the railroad station and the Negro Y. Early in his career court officials tried to segregate him in the courtroom, but he wouldn't submit. He fought the policy of segregating black plaintiffs, defendants, witnesses, and spectators. He wouldn't live in Delaware, but resided at first in New Jersey and later in Pennsylvania in a wonderful eighteenth-century farmhouse, and commuted to Wilmington to minimize his contact with segregation. He regularly did his research on weekends in New York at the County Lawyers Association or the Association of the Bar of the City of New York. In 1992, when Lou was ninety, the city of Wilmington named the city-county building after him and dedicated a bronze statue of him. It took them a long time to recognize the greatness of one who, while insulted by the dominant powers in his home state, had returned to be close to his family and origins, and to make it better for everyone.

We prepared the college case by digging through records and visiting faculty of the black school at night in their homes. They feared reprisals and knew that if we succeeded their school might be closed and they might lose their jobs, but they spoke to us anyway. I tracked down educational experts to testify on the differences between the schools and the inequality created by segregation per se. We visited the president of the University of Delaware, who was the defendant. Segregation was so pervasive that we had no way of knowing his attitude until we actually interviewed him. To our surprise he cooperated and wished us well. He was embarrassed that he had to segregate. I did a lot of legal research to demonstrate the obvious, that the university was a state institution—it was founded and funded by the state—which its lawyers denied. The university's lawyers denied the obvious up and down the line. How embarrassed *they* were, if at all, at having to utter such nonsense, I never learned.

The state court judge, Collins J. Seitz, who had the ancient English title of vice-chancellor, had been elected by the state legislature and would have to think twice about whether he would be reelected, promoted, or forced to return to private practice before ruling in our favor. During the trial he decided to see for himself and drove to both schools at breakneck speed, our car in pursuit, to inspect them. Among my witnesses was Charles Thompson, who helped launch the campaign against segregated education and had clashed with W. E. B. Du Bois in the celebrated 1935 *Journal of Negro Education* issue that reported the debate of black leadership over whether to go down the road of equalization or integration. Thompson demonstrated that the college was inferior to the university. He offered the opinion that separate-but-equal education is impractical, uneconomical, and theoretically impossible. He cited the dire effects of segregation on the personalities of black boys and girls and on whites as well. He referred also to the U.S. struggle with the Soviet Union for the allegiance of the colored peoples of the world. One might wonder at the legal relevance, but he wanted to say it anyway. Admitted into evidence or not, factors like those influenced legal development.

Besides the argument that the University of Delaware was not a state institution, lawyers for the university claimed that it provided no better an education than that offered at the unaccredited black school. They apparently had no shame, for this was another blatantly ridiculous argument. In curricula, faculty, buildings and grounds, library, money, and every other imaginable respect the university, situated on a beautiful campus, was vastly better than the shabby, decrepit college.

Of course, we most wanted a decision that segregation was unconstitutional. But Vice-Chancellor Seitz, despite his political vulnerability, exercised courage not often seen even in federal judges with lifetime appointments. He ruled that, while he had no authority to hold segregation unconstitutional, bound as he was by Supreme Court precedent, the schools, if separate, were required to be equal, and they were grossly unequal. He ordered the university to admit blacks. No order to go and equalize. Delaware had had its chance. To our delight Lou and I won the first case requiring an undergraduate school to admit blacks—heady stuff for a twenty-five-year-old lawyer.[1]

But it is often easier to win a lawsuit than it is to change hearts and minds. In April 2003, Delaware State College invited me to speak on the occasion of the impending 50th anniversary of *Brown* and, of course, to say something about the University of Delaware case. To prepare I looked up both schools on the internet. The University of Delaware's black enrollment was four percent. Delaware State College was at least three-quarters black. The Supreme Court has ruled that historic black colleges and universities (HBCUs) are obliged to eliminate all vestiges of segregation. To that end, considerable federal funds were appropriated for the HBCUs. Delaware used much of its money to enhance the campus: wide boulevards, impressive plantings, modern buildings and renovated classic ones, not at all the ramshackle, crumbling structures that existed in 1950. The evening of my talk I had dinner with college faculty, almost all of whom were black, and inquired why there had been virtually no

---

[1] Parker v. University of Delaware, 31 Del. Ch. 381 (Del. Ch. 1950).

integration at the University and so little at the college. Everyone agreed that black high school guidance counselors steered black high school students who could have been admitted to the university to the college. They explained that the counselors felt a commitment to preserve the college and what they perceived as its role in the black society and economy. My dinner companions deplored this, but had no suggestion about what might be done to change it.

Taking the Fight to the South

LDF was waging the battle on a broad front. In Tennessee, the state adopted a grade-a-year plan for higher education, the case went to the Supreme Court on procedural nonsense, and we finally won on the merits in the court of appeals, with one judge dissenting.[2] But Tennessee for a time required one case per university. Texas required more cases for schools other than the University of Texas—they wouldn't follow *Sweatt* without court orders directed precisely at each.[3]

We fought Virgil Hawkins's case to enter the University of Florida Law School until he gave up in 1959 and went to Boston University to get a degree in public relations. Then, from 1961 to 1965, Hawkins went to New England School of Law, from which he graduated at the age of fifty-eight. But because the school was not accredited, he could not be admitted to the Florida bar. In 1976, when Hawkins was seventy, the Florida Supreme Court admitted him to practice, waiving the requirement that he take the bar examination, relying on a precedent in which the state attorney general's brother had been admitted even though he had flunked the bar exam four times. In 1983, when Hawkins was seventy-seven, the Florida bar disciplined him for alleged unprofessional conduct and that year the state

---

[2] Gray v. Board of Trustees of University of Tennessee, 100 F. Supp. 113 (E.D. Tenn. 1951).

[3] Battle v. Wichita Falls Jr. College District, 101 F. Supp. 82 (N.D. Tex 1951).

legislature established ten law fellowships at the University of Florida and Florida State University in his name.[4]

When *Sweatt* came down, we had a case in Maryland to admit Esther McCready to the School of Nursing. Because Southern states couldn't afford to duplicate white facilities, they created a regional compact with the Board of Control for Southern Regional Education to maintain cooperatively a few schools for blacks from all over the South, pressing Congress to ratify the compact, thinking it might thereby become immune to litigation. Thurgood testified against the proposal and Congress refused the board's request. Nevertheless, Maryland directed McCready to Meharry School of Nursing in Nashville, which had places for three Maryland students. The trial court approved, but the state court of appeals reversed. Maryland went to the Supreme Court and lost.[5]

In Louisiana, Thurgood and A. P. Tureaud sued the state university to admit Roy Wilson to law school. After winning in the Supreme Court in 1951,[6] Wilson withdrew because someone discovered that he had received a less than honorable discharge from the armed forces. But Robert Collins and Ernest Morial did enroll that year and graduated in 1954. (In 1978, Collins became the first black federal judge in Louisiana and Morial the first black mayor of New Orleans.)

---

[4] State ex rel. Hawkins v. Board of Control, 47 So.2d 608 (1950), *motion denied,* 53 So.2d 116, *cert. denied sub. nom.* Florida ex rel Hawkins v. Board of Control, 342 U.S. 877 (1951), and *motion denied,* 60 So.2d 162 (1952), *vacated,* 347 U.S. 971 (1954), *recalled, vacated,* 350 U.S. 413 (1956), *reh'g denied,* 351 U.S. 915 (1956), and *on remand* 83 So.2d 20 (1955), *motion denied,* 93 So.2d 354 (1957), *cert. denied,* 355 U.S. 839 (1957), Hawkins v. Board of Control, 253 F.2d 752 (5th Cir. 1958), *on remand,* 162 F. Supp. 851 (1958).

[5] McCready v. Byrd, 195 Md. 131, *cert. denied,* 340 U.S. 827 (1950).

[6] Wilson v. Board of Supervisors of Louisiana State University, 92 F. Supp. 986 (E.D. La. 1950), *aff'd,* 340 U.S. 909 (1951). *See also* Constantine v. Southwestern Louisiana Institute, 120 F. Supp. 417 (W.D. La. 1954); Board of Supervisors of Louisiana State University and Agricultural & Mechanical College v. Tureaud, 351 U.S. 924 (1956); Ludley v. Louisiana State Board of Education, 150 F. Supp. 900 (E.D. La. 1957), and Louisiana State Board of Education v. Lark, 358 U.S. 820 (1958).

Bob Carter sued the University of North Carolina in late 1950 for excluding Floyd McKissick, later to become president of CORE, from law school. The trial court held that the black law school at North Carolina College for Negroes was equal to the white state school. The court of appeals reversed; the university petitioned the Supreme Court, which in 1951 refused to hear the case. McKissick later transferred to the state's black law school.[7]

Georgia fought back doggedly, successfully keeping out Horace Ward, who decided to go to Northwestern rather than waste time in a lengthy lawsuit. (He later became Georgia's first black federal district judge.) Like Louisiana, Georgia required a certificate signed by two alumni for admittance to a state institution of higher learning.[8] The University of Virginia Law School folded after a brief hearing.[9] Only Arkansas, among Southern states, integrated higher education without an LDF lawsuit, though they were threatened by one.

As early as 1952 a score of private Southern universities, including Johns Hopkins and St. Johns in Maryland, Washington University in St. Louis, and American University in Washington, D.C., taking their cue from the courts, began admitting blacks for the first time.

The atmosphere was inhospitable at the white schools, while black schools were receptive and had experience in educating under-prepared students. Black elementary and high school education remained essentially segregated until 1970, and its quality was terrible, equipping few black youngsters to enter white institutions on an equal footing with whites. Also, the white colleges and graduate schools were more expensive than the black schools. Finally, somewhat out of shame,

---

[7] Epps v. Carmichael, 93 F. Supp. 327 (M.D. N.C. 1950), *rev'd sub. nom.,* McKissick v. Carmichael, 187 F.2d 949 (4th Cir.), *cert. denied,* 341 U.S. 951 (1951). In 1951, North Carolina admitted Lolita Harrison to its graduate school, then discovered she was black and tried to keep her out of the dorms. We sued; they admitted her to the dorm. But in 1956, well after *Brown,* North Carolina continued to keep blacks out of the undergraduate schools. That year we won a decision against the university in the Supreme Court.

[8] Ward v. Regents of the University System of Georgia, dropped without a reported decision; and Holmes v. Danner, 191 F. Supp. 385 (M.D. Ga. 1960).

[9] Swanson v. University of Virginia, No. 30 (W.D. Va. September, 1950).

but also as a last-ditch attempt to stave off desegregation, the states began to build up black colleges and universities. Where white schools had programs like nursing or accounting that black ones lacked, states set up duplicates in black schools to entice black students. Some black educators began developing vested interests in keeping the all-black schools as institutions of choice for black students.

I Commit Myself to Stay at LDF

Not long after the Delaware decision, Milton Handler, the country's leading authority on antitrust law, who was one of my law school teachers, and for whom I had been a student research assistant, invited me to join his law firm, now known as Kaye, Scholer. The firm then had a handful of lawyers, although now it has more than four hundred. The offer was attractive. I liked Milton. I was interested in antitrust law, though my sympathies usually were not with the defendants, whom he usually represented. I was not so sure about the rest of my career. Was there a future for me in civil rights? Could I earn a decent living? Although it hadn't so far, would being white handicap me in an organization run by blacks? I said to the partner who extended the offer that I had just won the first case ordering blacks admitted to a white college. It would probably be appealed to the Delaware Supreme Court later in the year and I would argue the appeal with Louis Redding. Would it be possible for me to come to work for the firm after the appeal? He replied that I would be no more valuable to the firm for having argued that appeal. I went home and mulled it over. I had just won the first case to gain admission for blacks to a white college. And he didn't think I would be any more valuable for having argued the appeal! I might have asked Milton for the extra time, but I turned down the offer. Maybe I wouldn't be more valuable, but I didn't want to work at a place like that. In fact, the state later decided not to appeal.

This decision was key for the rest of my career. The fact is that I might not have been very successful at the firm. I have to care about what I do. It's hard to tell how that would have played out. I wouldn't have cared too much about most of the kinds of clients I would get, although I might have identified with some of them. There was also the professionalism and craftsmanship of legal practice that I might bring to bear on cases of those with whom I might have no particular personal sympathy.

I toyed with the idea of leaving LDF only one time, not long after this, when Rutgers Law School offered me a teaching job. But by then I had the action and thrill of actual combat in a cause I cared about and wasn't ready to turn to the more tranquil, reflective life of the academy. Oliver Wendell Holmes, Jr., once wrote, "It is required of a man that he should share the passion and action of his time at peril of being judged not to have lived." LDF was my best opportunity to do just that.

CHAPTER 5

JIM CROW AND THE VOICE OF GOD IN KANSAS

A Black Summit Assesses the Options

At the same time that it was pursuing desegregation in higher education, the LDF was engaging in litigation around the country to end segregation in primary and secondary schools. This was a considerably more controversial move. In April 1952, under the sponsorship of the *Journal of Negro Education,* Charles Thompson assembled at Howard University a group of scholars, lawyers, journalists, organizational leaders, and others, black and white, from North and South, advocates of extreme gradualism and those who demanded an immediate end to segregation. Charlie was not staging an academic exercise. He was aggressively gathering support for our campaign, while trying to defuse the opposition—not that of segregationists, most of whom were hopelessly intransigent, but of some blacks and white liberals who held their own strong views about what ought to be done next. At one extreme, Harry Ashmore, editor of the *Arkansas Gazette,* was opposed to segregation in principle, but hardly in favor of attacking it.

Marjorie McKenzie, a black lawyer and columnist for the *Pittsburgh Courier,* had written columns criticizing an all-out attack on segregation because she too thought we would lose. She argued that we should present the cases the same way we argued *Sweatt* and *McLaurin.* Of course, we felt that this was precisely what we were doing. She charged that the lawyers had allowed "too much distance to come between them and their plans, and the people to be affected,"

and advocated putting pressure "on the Executive and on the Legislative branches as well." Her advice about legislative and executive
action didn't address the question of how we were to get past the
Southern stranglehold on Congress and the presidency.

In between, Thurgood and others offered a tempered view of
what the courts were likely to do and how the country might react.
Thurgood observed:

> If anybody thinks you are going to get the Supreme Court, in any
> decision in the foreseeable future, to say that all segregation under
> any circumstances on any ground is unconstitutional, [that person
> is] crazy. The most that anyone asks the Supreme Court to rule is in
> so far as segregation is applied to this phase of what we are talking
> about, that it is unconstitutional. . . . If the Supreme Court says
> everything we ask them to say, it will only be that the segregation
> statutes as applied to elementary and high schools are unconstitu-
> tional. It will not touch transportation; it will not touch assembly;
> it will not touch barber shops; it will not touch bulldogs . . . ("bull-
> dog" was the metaphor Thurgood used when others might have
> said "whatever"). I believe quite firmly that we will have to go
> from county to county and from state to state even after we get it,
> whichever kind of decision we get. Bear in mind in Georgia you
> have two hundred and some counties. So I still say there is no short-
> cut to it.

Spotts Robinson added that lawyers' ability to influence events
was constrained:

> [It is] an improper assumption . . . that we, the lawyers, had a full
> freedom of choice . . . For a period of more than two and a half
> years we even tried to substantially solve the problem without
> making a head-on, direct attack on segregation.
>
> We had four cases. . . . In each of the four cases . . . we had to go
> back to court because the injunctions—equalization injunctions,
> mind you—were not abided by. . . . Contempt was not the answer. . . .
> To get the problem solved we must go back and this time seek fur-
> ther relief which involves a direct attack on segregation itself.
>
> Our situation [in Virginia] . . . was a consequence of a decision
> which was forced upon us, not by people in New England or New

York; not by people outside the State of Virginia, but indeed by
Virginians themselves. . . . Negroes would never in Virginia have
waited the length of time it would have taken for us to see tangible
progress in the public schools so long as we had confined ourselves
within the boundaries of the separate-but-equal doctrine.

At the other end of the spectrum, Jim Nabrit, Jr., advocated an
all-out attack on segregation per se. Jim was medium height, slim,
with a reddish, freckled complexion and slightly reddish curly hair
(some called him "Red"). He almost always carried immense, excellent cigars, which he chain-smoked. He spoke with a deep accent
exuding his Georgia roots overlaid with seven years of Texas, where
he lived before coming to Washington. He spoke as if lots of excla-
mation marks were sprinkled throughout and at the end of sentences:

I believe that the Constitution gives the Negro the fundamental
right to enjoy *now* all benefits offered by the state, without any
limitations based on race. Since that is our right, why disguise our
fight for it? Why try to sneak up on it? Why not make a bold assault for it? The attack should be waged with the most devastating
forces at hand.

Mordecai Johnson, president of Howard University, summed up:

Now is the time to attack. Now is the time to proceed. Now is the
time to precipitate the decisive combat. And let us be aware that if
we are to prevail, we must pray that the God who enabled us to
overcome the slave system will give our members of the Supreme
Court and our national leadership the wisdom to see that the decision on segregation *must* come now—or else, the Communists may
not need to *take* the world, we may have folded it in a nice piece of
paper, wrapped it up, put an Easter ribbon around it, and handed it
to them.

Out of all this deeply held, but often conflicting advice came the
style of attack as the school cases moved from trial courts to the
Supreme Court: a clear eye on the goal, cautious probing, with a
simultaneous willingness to retreat a bit or accept only modest gains

rather than risk a total setback. The legal leadership of the LDF, while always idealists, were never ideologues.

Brown and the Other School Segregation Cases

Statistics alone can't depict the stigma so often imposed by black children's tarpaper shack schools, outhouses, and hand-me-down books. But some numbers offer a shorthand summary. In 1940, the average South-wide annual educational expenditure on black children was less than half that on whites, $21.54 per black school child compared to $50.14 per white child. By 1952, the average Southern state was spending $115.08 per black child and $164.83 per white child, still almost 50 percent more for whites. In 1940, capital outlays for black schools were 23 percent of those for white schools. While by 1952, the black share had risen, it was still only 82 percent of the per capita expenditure for white schools. The number of books in school libraries was another damning indicator. Five states kept such statistics: Georgia, Louisiana, North Carolina, South Carolina, and Texas. In 1940, the average white child in those states had 3.3 library books, the average black, 0.8 books; by 1952 whites had 4.7 books per child and blacks 1.8.

The School Segregation Cases became known as *Brown* only by accident. Brown was the surname of one plaintiff, Oliver Brown (the father of Linda Brown), who had been listed near the end of a score of plaintiffs in one of the cases, the one coming out of Topeka, Kansas, before the list was alphabetized. Actually, another plaintiff family, that of Darlene Brown, should have appeared before Oliver Brown. But, in what today would be seen as an irony, Oliver was listed first because he was a man. Originally, among five cases from four states and the District of Columbia, that we (and in the District, James M. Nabrit, Jr.) had in trial courts around the same time and that the Supreme Court combined for argument and decision, Topeka was listed second, because it was the second to be appealed. Had nothing changed, the School Segregation Cases might have been known as *Briggs v. Elliott* (from South Carolina), the name of the first case to be appealed. But the Supreme Court sent *Briggs* back to the trial court for further hearings, and *Brown* moved up to number one. Among ourselves we called them the "school cases," rather than by one name. A TV film on the cases shows Earl Warren deciding to name them *Brown*, suggesting that he did so to indicate that they dealt with the rights of brown-skinned people. But the Court had it listed as the lead case in 1953 even before Earl Warren's appointment as chief justice.

The cases, as they finally were decided under that single name, were:

No. 1: Oliver Brown, et al. v. Board of Education of Topeka, Shawnee County, Kansas, et al.

No. 2: Harry Briggs, Jr., et al. v. R. W. Elliot, et al. (South Carolina case).

No. 4: Dorothy E. Davis, et al. v. County School Board of Prince Edward County, Virginia, et al.

No. 8: Spottswood Thomas Bolling, et al. v. C. Melvin Sharpe, et al. (District of Columbia case).

No. 10: Francis B. Gebhart, et al. v. Ethel Louise Belton, et al. (Delaware case).

Bolling was not an LDF case. A District of Columbia parents' group, at first represented by Charlie Houston, sponsored it. He had been preparing a school equalization suit for them when he was stricken with a heart attack and sent the group's leader, Gardner Bishop, to Jim Nabrit, Jr., to ask him to take over. "Big Jim" (whose son James M. Nabrit, III became my dear friend and indispensable colleague) refused to argue for equalization but assented to represent the group if it would attack segregation. He was teaching full-time at Howard and not in practice and, therefore, brought in George E. C. Hayes, also a Howard law professor and one of Washington's leading black practitioners. *Bolling* differed from the LDF cases in one other way: the Fourteenth Amendment said "no state" might discriminate. The District of Columbia is not a state and the Washington lawyers had to look to other arguments.

For the four cases the LDF brought, when we counseled desegregation, plaintiffs and their lawyers, if not already convinced, went along. Bob Carter has written of the period: "I believe that the majority sentiment in the black community was a desire to secure for blacks all of the educational nurturing available to whites. If ending school segregation was the way to that objective, fine; if on the other hand, securing equal facilities was the way, that too was fine."

At an executive committee meeting in 1951, Thurgood reported that "we need non-lawyers on the staff to educate the public concerning the importance of our school cases." He referred to a program of North Carolina branches to bring a number of separate-but-equal cases and said, "They must be educated to our way and start to listen to us." He hired two staff members "to work with our branches in an attempt to educate the public about the evils of segregation and to insure community support for our cases."

Several years earlier the Clarendon County, South Carolina plaintiffs who spearheaded *Briggs,* the first LDF case to be filed, hadn't been asking for desegregation. They had begun by trying only to obtain busing; white children were bused, blacks walked. Harold Boulware represented them with remote backup from our office, but they lost their case on a technicality—the only plaintiff lived just over the district line. How could Boulware make such a mistake? He practiced alone, had limited experience in complex cases, and mostly handled marginal matters. Once I accompanied him to a judge's chambers in a divorce case. I was shocked when he took out a bottle of whiskey he had brought along and offered it to the judge as a token of good will. I was slightly startled, but the judge took it without a word and put it in a bottom drawer of his desk. I later observed the same gesture in an Indian village court in Chiapas, Mexico, a ragged peasant propitiating the judge who was considering his case.

Black schools remained so intolerable that the parents in the dismissed case regrouped and once more asked for help. In March 1949, Thurgood went to South Carolina and advised a black community meeting that they should attack inequality in all its aspects. But, by November 1950, when the complaint was filed in *Briggs v. Elliot,* the new standard applied—we would ask only for desegregation.

Soon many of Clarendon County's black leaders, their families, and other blacks were fired from jobs, denied credit, forced to pay up on long-standing debts, refused renewal of leases on farmland, had trouble getting their cotton ginned, were sued for slander, and threatened by the Klan. One black person was beaten to death. They stuck it out.

In the second LDF case to be filed, in March 1951, *Brown v. Board of Education of Topeka,* the plaintiffs and the black community had for several years been trying to get their schools desegregated. Teachers' salaries, teacher training, teacher load for black and white schools were about the same. The precipitating factor in filing the suit was that some black children were bused to remote schools, while their white neighbors walked to nearby schools. Much later, when school busing to end segregation became a national debate, many blacks wondered why opponents of busing hadn't objected when it had been so widely used to *ensure* segregation. But the goal of the Kansas NAACP at the time was not merely a black school in every black neighborhood. Indeed, the pro-separate-but-equal president of the Coffeyville, Kansas, NAACP branch was overwhelmingly voted down when he objected to integration because he expected, accurately, that it would cause black teachers to lose their jobs.

The third of the School Segregation Cases that LDF filed, in May 1951, was *Davis v. County School Board.* It came out of Prince Edward County, Virginia, where, as in South Carolina, intolerable conditions precipitated the suit. The white community didn't want to spend the money it would require to upgrade black schools, so the situation dragged on until it erupted into a two-week student strike.

The students at first wanted a new high school and wrote for help to Spottswood Robinson and Oliver Hill in Richmond. But Spotts and Oliver, although dubious about a desegregation suit in rural, heavily black Prince Edward County, explained that in keeping with NAACP policy it would have to be that or nothing. The students and parents agreed.

In Delaware, suburban Claymont had no black high school. Blacks had to commute to Howard High School in Wilmington, eighteen miles away. The plaintiff, who had no interest in having a black school built, wanted integration—to go to Claymont High School. On the other hand, the Hockessin elementary school case began with a mother's effort just to get equal bus transportation because it was inconvenient to drive her child to school. Louis Redding told her that we would file only a desegregation case. She readily agreed; he filed the fourth and final LDF case, *Gebhart v. Belton,* in July 1951.

We began with all the available theories:

1. That separate schools never were equal anywhere in America, that the systems in our cases weren't equal either;
2. That the inequalities stigmatized black children;
3. Moreover, severe and persistent inequalities amounted to law administered with an evil eye and an unequal hand— Margold's original theory based on the *Yick Wo* Chinese laundry case;
4. Segregation was unconstitutional because, as in cases involving Japanese Americans subjected to curfews and sent to relocation camps, "distinctions between citizens solely because of their ancestry are by their very nature odious to a free people whose institutions are founded upon the doctrine of equality" and "all legal restrictions which curtail the civil rights of a single racial group are immediately suspect . . . [and] courts must subject them to the most rigid scrutiny."[1]
5. Standard equal protection doctrine, developed in economic regulation cases, held that a classification violates equal protection if based upon differences not reasonably related to a proper legislative objective.

We also would follow *Sweatt* and *McLaurin:* certain aspects of education can never be equal under segregation, for example, the ability to exchange ideas with white fellow students. Related argu-

---

[1] Hirabayashi v. United States, 320 U.S. 81 (1943); Korematsu v. United States, 323 U.S. 214 (1944).

ments drew upon studies that showed that segregation does psychological harm to children.

Much of this could be characterized as common sense, based on perceptions so widely held that it was not necessary to prove them. Indeed, in *Plessy v. Ferguson* there had been no evidence for the Court's conclusion that segregation does *no* harm. No one had proved in *Strauder* that excluding blacks from juries inflicts a stigma. These were views of the world, not derived from evidence, such as when a court concludes that an automobile did pass a red light. But we felt that, as in *Sweatt* and *McLaurin,* where we had presented evidence or materials in briefs on the effects of segregation, we should give the Court all the information about educated attitudes on the subject we could get. The Supreme Court heard this evidence and took judicial notice of it, leading to charges after our victory that the school cases rested on social science, not law.

Briggs v. Elliott

Bob Carter enlisted a group of social scientists to testify in *Briggs v. Elliott,* the Clarendon County, South Carolina, case. The federal district court judge, J. Waties Waring, had shown that he would hear claims of racial discrimination sympathetically. In the early 1940s, he had ruled with black plaintiffs in a teachers' salary case as well as in a pre-*Sweatt* law school case that concluded with setting up separate-but-(allegedly) equal legal education—an advanced view for that period.[2] In 1947, he held the South Carolina white primary unconstitutional. He had prohibited the use of race in jury selection and segregated seating of spectators in his court, and appointed the only black bailiff in any Southern federal court.

Briggs, the case that Thurgood and Harold Boulware filed in his court, could have been framed two ways: It could have asked for an injunction to prohibit enforcement of the South Carolina school segregation *statutes* as unconstitutional or merely could have claimed

---

[2] Rice v. Elmore, 165 F.2d 387 (4th Cir. 1947), *cert. denied,* 333 U.S. 875 (1948).

that segregation and inequality were unconstitutional—with no mention of the statutes. If the former, the case would be heard by three judges—as *McLaurin* was. The other two judges probably would be John J. Parker, chief judge of the Court of Appeals for the Fourth Circuit, who would be unsympathetic to ending segregation, and George Bell Timmerman, an outspoken racist. If the case did not seek to enjoin enforcement of the statute, it would be heard by Waring alone.

A lawyer attacking segregation would presumably prefer to be before Waring alone. But there was a problem. Any attack on segregation would run into a defense that it was required by the statute, and so, whether you liked it or not, the statute would be put in issue and three judges might be summoned. Even if Waring agreed to try the case alone, an appellate court might overrule him and order a three-judge hearing. On the other hand, the three-judge statute had been construed very technically, and by a close reading of its *language* might not cover a case where the plaintiff did not literally ask to enjoin enforcing a statute—so it was worth a shot. The complaint, therefore, claimed that the plaintiffs were denied equal protection by the "policy, custom, usage, and practice of the defendants in maintaining public schools for Negro children because of their race and color which are in every respect inferior to those maintained for white children." Thurgood and Bob planned then to introduce the social science evidence and make legal arguments, as in the past, that segregation was per se unconstitutional.

But Waring had another agenda. He had grown increasingly estranged from the Charleston white community, ideologically and personally. Whites there criticized his race decisions and also his recent divorce and remarriage to a Northerner, a woman from Detroit. He was the object of personal abuse, including physical harassment. He was in contact with Hubert Delany and John Hammond, NAACP board members, who thought Thurgood was not militant enough and told Waring so. (Delany was an influential black lawyer and political figure whose membership in the left-wing National Lawyers Guild set him apart from Thurgood politically. Hammond, a talent scout and record producer, has been described as "the most influential non-performing" individual in the field of jazz.)

Waring scheduled a pretrial hearing for November 17, 1950. At that time, because the three-judge court statute very well may have prohibited him from hearing the case alone, but more because he wanted to confront segregation head-on, he refused to hear the case alone. He suggested that Thurgood withdraw the complaint and file a new one attacking South Carolina's school segregation laws. Thurgood, having no choice, filed a new case, asking for an injunction against South Carolina's segregation statutes; it came to trial May 28, 1951. But Waring's efforts to push Thurgood to measures he didn't want to take, his backdoor dealings with Walter White and NAACP board members (he urged Walter to enlist other organizations to file amicus briefs in the school cases), and efforts to instruct Thurgood about strategy and argument irritated Thurgood and made him a bit uncomfortable about the propriety of being in that court. If Waring's extrajudicial communications became public, it could cause trouble nobody needed. Thurgood dealt with Waring circumspectly then and later, after Waring retired and moved to New York. Indeed, Waring complained that when Thurgood called him about a dinner planned in Waring's honor in April 1952, it was the first communication from him in nine months.

The May 28 trial commenced before Waring, Parker, and Timmerman and produced several memorable exchanges. Herbert Hoover had nominated Parker to the Supreme Court, but the Senate rejected him, responding to opposition from the NAACP and organized labor. Thurgood, while believing that Parker would decide for the state, thought that he would act decently, follow the law—which, of course, was against us—but employ fair procedure and find facts accurately. Indeed, he had thought so well of Parker that, when a possibility arose again that he might be nominated to the Court, Thurgood promised that if the NAACP were to oppose him once more, Thurgood would support him. But Harold Burton got the appointment and the matter never arose. Counsel for the defendants, Robert McC. Figg, Jr., put up no defense for the disgraceful condition of the black schools and commenced with the best tactic when confronted with an overwhelming argument: give away what your opponent can take away. He conceded that the black schools were inferior, justifying the inferiority on the ground that education in rural districts had not kept pace with urban ones and that the inequality wasn't intentional. Moreover, the state had just passed a 3 percent sales tax, to take effect in July, to raise $75,000,000 for education and to equalize the schools. He did not oppose an order requiring equalization and asked for "a reasonable time to formulate a plan for ending such inequalities and for bringing about equality of educational opportunity."

Thurgood insisted on presenting details of the inequalities and put on witnesses who described them in detail. Beyond that, one of our expert witnesses, Horace McNally, professor of education at Teachers College of Columbia University, testified in support of our main theme in the school cases: "There is basically implied in the separation . . . that there is some difference in the two groups which does not make it feasible for them to be educated together, which I would hold to be untrue. Furthermore, by separating the two groups, there is implied a stigma on at least one of them." Ellis Knox, a professor of education at Howard, testified similarly: "When children are segregated . . . segregation cannot exist without discrimination, disadvantages to the minority group, and that the children in the Negro schools very definitely are not prepared for the same type of American citizenship as the children in the white schools."

Our main witness was Kenneth B. Clark, then a young assistant professor of psychology at City College of New York, who would become one of America's foremost social scientists. Bob Carter recruited him through Otto Klineberg, a professor of social psychology at Columbia, indeed a creator of modern social psychology, who had been Kenneth's professor and had supervised his Ph.D. dissertation. He and his wife, Mamie Phipps Clark, who also had a Ph.D. in psychology, had done path-breaking work to ascertain the psychological effects of segregation on the self-image and self-esteem of black children. We brought him to Clarendon County to repeat this research on black children there.

In what are called projective tests, the Clarks placed in front of children dolls that were identical except for skin color, one white, the other brown, and asked questions such as, "Show me the doll that you like best or that you'd like to play with," "Show me the doll that is the 'nice' doll," "Show me the doll that looks 'bad,'" and "Give me the doll that looks like you." Kenneth gave these tests to sixteen black elementary school children in Clarendon County between the ages of six and nine. As he later described it, some of the children responded with statements like "I'm a nigger, that's a nigger." He viewed the tests not as making a precise statement on *school* segregation, but rather as describing the effect of societal discrimination, of which school segregation was a part.

The Clarendon County results were consistent with tests Kenneth previously had given to more than three hundred children. In Clarendon County ten of the sixteen black children liked the white doll better and thought it was nice. Eleven picked the brown doll as looking "bad," while more than half identified themselves with the "bad" doll. Seven of the black children, when asked to pick the doll that looked most like themselves, picked the white doll, all of which he interpreted to mean that the "Negro child accepts as early as six, seven or eight the negative stereotypes about his own group," and that a "fundamental effect of segregation is basic confusion in the individuals and their concept about themselves conflicting in their self images." He concluded that "children in Clarendon County, like other human beings who are subjected to an obviously inferior status in the society in which they live, have been definitely harmed in the development of their personalities." It was the kind of injury that would endure or last as long as the situation endured, changing only in its form and in the way it manifested itself.

He described also "confusion in the child's concept of his own self esteem—basic feelings of inferiority, conflict, confusion in his self image, resentment, hostility towards himself, hostility toward whites, intensification of sometimes a desire to resolve his basic conflict by sometimes escaping or withdrawing." Later the doll tests were attacked as having been based on faulty research. Not all of us were in favor of using Kenneth's testimony. Bob Ming and Bill Coleman opposed the doll test evidence because they didn't believe in it. But Thurgood wanted to use everything he could. I was a bit skeptical myself, but certainly believed that Dr. Clark's conclusions were right. We didn't have the luxury of time to do further testing and answer every doubt the evidence might raise, as if we were writing a Ph.D. thesis. If the decision had been mine alone I would have used the evidence.

With one witness Bob stepped over the sometimes not terribly clear line between social science and policy. He asked Louis Kesselman, associate professor of political science at the University of Louisville, whether a segregated public school system "would have adverse effects in operation among the individuals."

Figg objected: "I don't think that this witness has been qualified. . . ." Bob replied: "He is a person who has studied the science of government." Parker turned to Thurgood, in whom he apparently had as much confidence as Thurgood had in him:

PARKER: Do you seriously contend he is qualified to testify as an educational expert? What do you say about that, Mr. Marshall?

THURGOOD (evasively): We had been trying to . . . present as many experts in the field with as many different reasons why we consider that segregation in and of itself is injurious. . . .

PARKER: Are you going to offer any more witnesses along this line?

THURGOOD: No, sir. The other witnesses are REAL scientists. (Here the court reporter used capital letters, seeking to indicate Thurgood's emphasis.)

Kesselman then testified: "Segregation . . . prevents them from gaining an understanding of the needs and interests of both groups . . . breeds suspicion and distrust . . . and . . . enforced by law, it may even breed distrust to the point of conflict."

Thurgood cross-examined one witness in surgical strokes that bared South Carolina's adamant opposition to integration. E. R. Crow, director of the State Educational Finance Commission, testified that recent legislation would soon provide much more money to Clarendon County schools. (Outside of court, his name, although not "*Jim* Crow," was occasion for joking; during the Supreme Court argument Thurgood poked fun at it.) Crow testified that to abolish segregation "would eliminate public schools in most, if not all of the communities in the State." He was "sure" that there would be "a probability of violent emotional reaction." Thurgood questioned him:

Q: About what is the percentage of Negro population to white population in South Carolina?

A: . . . About forty percent, or forty-five.

Q: . . . Are there any Negroes on your Commission?

A: No.

Q: Would the fact that Negroes have been admitted to public schools in Indiana for the first time within the last year, change your opinion [that if schools were mixed the public schools of the state would be abandoned]?

A: No. . . . We have in South Carolina a different ratio of the two races. . . .

Q: Mr. Crow, assuming that in Clarendon County, specially in School District No. 22, the population was 95% white and 5% Negro, would that change your opinion?

A: No.

Thurgood read into the record the testimony in *Sweatt* of Robert Redfield, the University of Chicago law teacher, that "differences in intellectual capacity or inability to learn have not been shown to exist as between negroes and whites."

And that was the end of the first trial. Less than a month later, on June 23, 1951, the Court ruled against us. Parker (Timmerman joined him) held that the district had to equalize the schools and report in six months what it had done. He refused to hold segregation unconstitutional. In summary, his opinion said: States had power to legislate about safety, morals, health, and general welfare; *Plessy* held that they have authority to segregate schools; *Sweatt* and *McLaurin* expressly refused to overrule *Plessy*; *McLaurin* "involved humiliating and embarrassing treatment of a Negro law student (actually a graduate student) to which no one should have been required to submit"; "if public education is to have the support of the people through their legislatures, it must not go contrary to what they deem [to be in] the best interests of their children." How about the testimony of the social scientists? They had presented issues to be resolved by the legislatures. Seventeen states and Congress (for the District of Columbia) for three-quarters of a century had required segregated schools.

Judge Waring, in a long and passionate opinion, concluded that "all of the legal guideposts, expert testimony, common sense and reason point unerringly to the conclusion that the system of segregation in education adopted and practiced in the State of South Carolina must go and must go now. *Segregation is per se inequality.*" He couldn't resist taking a swipe at the "witness, significantly named Crow."

Brown v. Board of Education

Two days later, on June 25, Bob Carter and I, along with the brothers John and Charles Scott, our lawyers in Topeka, began the Topeka trial, *Brown v. Board of Education.* As early as September 1948, Isabel Lurie, a Topeka NAACP branch member, had visited our office, asking for help in filing a lawsuit attacking school segregation. Under the state's segregation law only the lower grades were segregated, with children transferring to integrated schools in seventh grade. In 1948, however, neither *Sweatt* nor *McLaurin* had been decided and LDF bided its time. The local branch got nowhere in continuous negotiations with the school board. In September 1950, McKinley Burnett, the branch president, wrote to Walter White that the school board had referred the branch to the state legislature to seek repeal of the school segregation law. "Words will not express the humiliation and disrespect in this matter," he added. Shortly afterward, Connie Motley sent Burnett a model complaint used in Virginia equalization cases, adding (in view of the June 1950 mandate that all school cases should ask for an end to segregation), "It will be necessary . . . to add in the prayer for relief a specific *prayer for the admission of Negro children to the white schools.*" Between October and December 1950, Bob Carter and Charles Bledsoe of Topeka corresponded, Bob urging him to sign up a large number of plaintiffs and discussing whether the case should be in a one- or three-judge court.

In November, the Topeka lawyers had sent us a list of twenty children as plaintiffs; the twentieth entry on the list was "Linda Carol Brown, Father: Oliver Brown." But when they drafted the complaint, because Brown was first in alphabetical order, they captioned the case *"Oliver Brown, et al. v. Board of Education of Topeka, Shawnee County, Kansas,"* bestowing immortality on a family that was neither more nor less involved than any of the other nineteen. I redrafted the complaint to request a three-judge court and an injunction against the school segregation law as unconstitutional. *Brown v. Board of Education* was ready to go. Bledsoe filed it on February 28, 1951.

In March, at the suggestion of the Kansas City director of the Community Relations Bureau of the American Jewish Committee, who had been enlisted by its New York headquarters, I recruited Hugh Speer, head of the Department of Education of the University of Kansas City, to survey the Topeka schools. On May 29, he sent me a telegram: "PRELIMINARY EVIDENCE REVEALS NO SIGNIFICANT DISCRIMINATION ON TEACHER PREPARATION SALARY OR CROWDED CONDITIONS PROBABLY SOME INFERIORITY IN BUILDINGS TRANSPORTATION SPECIAL TEACHERS AND CURRICULUM SUGGEST EMPHASIS ON SOCIAL AND PSYCHOLOGICAL HANDICAPS OF SEGREGATION PER SE."

By the end of May, I was looking for social scientists for the Kansas case, scheduled for trial at the end of June, and the Delaware cases, which would be filed in August. I telephoned and wrote to the sociologist Robert S. Lynd at Columbia, author of the great Middletown study, because I knew him slightly. Once, while on leave in the navy, I had visited him, seeking suggestions about what to read. Among his recommendations was his own book *Knowledge for What,* a powerful argument that scholars should devote their energies to addressing social problems about which they might make a difference. But Lynd said he couldn't help us. Karl Menninger (a member of the original Committee of 100, the fund raising group of notable names assembled by our fundraiser Harold Oram), of the famed psychiatric clinic located in Topeka bearing his name, was opposed to segregation; Hugh Speer solicited his testimony but received no reply. Some speculated that he preferred not to have a collision with authorities in Topeka, but, later, Menninger said he had not been asked. After the lower court decision, however, he helped raise funds to pay for the case. I was particularly interested in recruiting social scientists from the Midwest, to keep travel expenses down, so I wrote to a long list, including another eminent scholar, Arnold Rose, a professor at the University of Minnesota and a collaborator with Gunnar Myrdal on the *American Dilemma*. Rose at first agreed but then couldn't appear, although he offered to write an affidavit. He suggested various names, including Louisa Holt of the University of Kansas, who happened to live in Topeka. With the trial scheduled for June 25, I worked out the appearance of eight experts from Midwestern universities, making arrangements with some less than a week before trial.

On June 13, Bob sent Thurgood a memorandum stressing that the case might be important because we might win: "Our possibilities for winning here seem much better than they are in South Carolina, particularly in view of the fact that the statutes involved in this case are permissive and give cities of certain size in Kansas the right to enforce segregation, if they so desire. Thus, the pressure for the maintenance of the segregated system is not as great as it would be in southern communities." He pointed out that the Topeka case would go to the Supreme Court with South Carolina.

Topeka was a Jim Crow city, but some public accommodations took in blacks who came properly recommended. A local lawyer offered to arrange for Bob and me to stay at the Jayhawk, the best hotel in town and ordinarily for whites only, but we wouldn't become exceptions to the general rule. Another suggestion was that I stay in a white hotel and Bob stay in a black one. I declined. So, I flew out four days before trial, on a particularly bumpy Lockheed Constellation, to join Bob and went to a black hotel. Shortly after checking in, I went to the bathroom, a sort of enclosure down the hall, lath showing through the crumbling plaster of its walls, which did not quite reach the ceiling, and pulled the light cord, which brought down a large chunk of ceiling. That was enough. We moved to a private home where we stayed for the duration of the case. The night before the trial we all went to Louisa Holt's house and discussed each witness's testimony.

Walter A. Huxman of the Court of Appeals for the Tenth Circuit and two district judges, Arthur J. Mellott and Delmas C. Hill, presided at the trial. Bob and I were joined by our local counsel, John and Charles Scott, of the firm of Scott, Scott and Scott. The third Scott was their father, Elisha, a legendary black lawyer, who began practicing at a time when black lawyers were even scarcer than in the early 1950s. He was said to be so good that white racketeers sought him out as counsel.

The trial first developed that black and white schools were un-equal and that black children who lived near white schools had to travel considerable distances to black ones, often waiting for buses in the rain and cold, unable to come home for lunch as the white children did. One of the black parents whom John Scott examined on such matters gave us a fright. Silas Fleming testified that his chil-dren took the city bus past white schools, at some expense, because the school bus stopped more than six blocks from his home.

Then suddenly he said: "I would ask this [*sic*] for a few minutes to explain why I got into the suit whole soul and body."

After some initial confusion, Judge Huxman asked, "Didn't you consent to be a plaintiff in this case?"

Fleming responded, "That's right."

Now, it would have been more than an embarrassment if Fleming testified that he had not voluntarily brought the suit, or that he had been pressured into suing; it could have caused real trouble. It was then a crime and grounds for disbarment to engage in "champerty," "maintenance," "running and capping," and colloquially, "ambu-lance chasing." Even after solicitation came to be held legal in civil rights cases, there was no right to file suit for someone who hadn't given permission. The colloquy between witness and judge was for a while confused:

JUDGE HUXMAN: You did not?
JUDGE MELLOTT: He said he did, but he wants to tell the reason why.
THE WITNESS: I want to tell the cause.
JUDGE HUXMAN: You want to tell the Court why you joined this lawsuit?
THE WITNESS: That's right.

JUDGE HUXMAN: All right, go ahead and tell it.

THE WITNESS: Well, it wasn't for the sake of hot dogs. It wasn't to cast any insinuations that our teachers are not capable of teaching our children because they are supreme, extremely intelligent and are capable of teaching my kids or white or black kids. But my point was that not only I and my children are craving light, the entire colored race is craving light, and the only way to reach the light is to start our children together in their infancy and they come up together.

JUDGE HUXMAN: All right, now you have answered and given us your reason.

We breathed sighs of relief. But more than that, Fleming inspired us and, maybe, the judges.

I examined Hugh Speer, who described respects in which the black schools were inferior to the white ones, like buildings, sites, books, staffs, and so forth. The differences weren't enormous but they certainly existed. Then, suddenly, during defense counsel Lester Goodell's cross-examination of Speer, Elisha Scott, the senior Scott, who until then had nothing to do with the case, appeared.

MR. SCOTT: I object to that.

JUDGE HUXMAN: Mr. Scott, are you entered here as an attorney of record?

MR. SCOTT: I am supposed to be.

JUDGE HUXMAN: Go Ahead.

MR. SCOTT: I object to that because he is invading the rights, and he is answering a question not based upon the evidence adduced or could be adduced.

MR. GOODELL: You just got here; you wouldn't know.

MR. SCOTT: Yes, I do know.

JUDGE HUXMAN: Objection will be overruled.

Elisha Scott, unhappily, was drunk. But the judges knew him well and didn't react unkindly. The court declared a brief recess, he was hustled out of the courtroom, and the trial resumed.

We had a half-dozen social scientific witnesses, three white women, the others men, and had decided that Bob Carter should take the testimony of the white women, while I would examine the men, simply because we thought that would irritate the other side. If any single social scientist had more impact than the others in the Topeka case, it was Louisa Holt. After describing her credentials (bachelor's, master's and Ph.D. degrees in the Department of Social Relations at Radcliffe) and teaching and research positions, including her current teaching post at the University of Kansas, she answered Bob's questions:

Q: Mrs. Holt, are you at all familiar with the school system in Topeka?

A: Yes; I have one child who entered that system this last year and another who enters next September.

Q: Based upon your experience and your knowledge, taking the segregated factor alone in the school system in Topeka, in your opinion does enforced legal separation have any adverse effect upon the personality development of the Negro child?

A: The fact that it is enforced, that it is legal I think, has more importance than the mere fact of segregation by itself does because this gives legal and official sanction to a policy which inevitably is interpreted both by white people and by Negroes as denoting the inferiority of the Negro group. Were it not for the sense that one group is inferior to the other, there would be no basis, and I am not granting that this is a rational basis, for such segregation.

A sense of inferiority must always affect one's motivation for learning since it affects the feeling one has of one's self as a person, as a personality or a self or an ego identity, as Erik Erickson has recently expressed it. That sense of ego identity is built up on the basis of attitudes that are expressed toward a person by others who are important. First the parents and then the teachers, other people in the community, whether they are older or one's own peers. It is other people's reactions to one's self which most basically affects the conception of one's self that one has. If these attitudes that are reflected back and then internalized or projected, are unfavorable ones, then one develops a sense of one's self as an inferior being. That may not be deleterious necessarily from the standpoint of educational motivation. I believe in some cases it can lead to stronger motivation to achieve well in academic pursuits, to strive to disprove to the world that one is inferior since the world feels that one is inferior. In other cases, of course, the reaction may be the opposite and apathetic acceptance, fatalistic submission to the feeling others have expressed that one is inferior and therefore any efforts to prove otherwise would be doomed to failure.

On August 3, 1951, the court handed down its decision.[3] We lost, but in that loss were the seeds of ultimate victory. The court held that it was bound by *Plessy*. Judge Huxman's opinion recognized that *Sweatt* and *McLaurin* had made inroads into that doctrine. In fact, unlike Judge Parker, who wrote that there were meaningful differences between higher and lower schools that justified a difference in outcome between the Clarendon County case and the graduate and professional school cases, Huxman wrote that

> if segregation within a school as in the *McLaurin* case is a denial of due process [actually it was equal protection], it is difficult to see why segregation in separate schools would not result in the same denial. Or if the denial of the right to commingle with the majority group in higher institutions of learning as in the *Sweatt* case and gain the educational advantages resulting therefrom, is lack of due process, it is difficult to see why such denial would not result in the same lack of due process if practiced in the lower grades.

Nevertheless, he made two important findings, first, that schools for blacks and whites in Topeka were equal (although in fact they weren't—there were real, though slight, differences), possibly to highlight the second key finding: no matter how equal the facilities, segregation injures the black child. Adopting almost verbatim Louisa Holt's testimony, he concluded:

---

[3] Brown v. Board of Education of Topeka, 98 F. Supp. 797, 800 (D. Kan. 1951).

Segregation of white and colored children in public schools has a detrimental effect upon the colored children. The impact is greater when it has the sanction of the law; for the policy of separating the races is usually interpreted as denoting the inferiority of the negro group. A sense of inferiority affects the motivation of a child to learn. Segregation with the sanction of law, therefore, has a tendency to retard the educational and mental development of negro children and to deprive them of some of the benefits they would receive in a racially integrated school system.

Louisa's words, which found their way into Huxman's findings, later were adopted by the Supreme Court in critical passages of *Brown v. Board of Education*. Huxman, in finding the schools equal in all respects, except for the fact of segregation, was trying to box in the Supreme Court. In 1967, he told Hugh Speer, one of our experts, "I tried to wrap it up in such a way that they could not duck it. They had whittled away at it long enough."

After the trial, the school placed Louisa's daughter in the slowest first-grade reading group, which she felt was a retaliation for her testimony. In Berkeley, California, where they moved shortly afterwards, her daughter placed in the highest group.

I sent thank you letters to all the witnesses. In looking over the correspondence as I prepared to write these pages, I blanched as I read my letter to Louisa Holt. After expressing appreciation, I added: "It is rare that an expert witness combines the qualities of scholarship, residence in the community about which she is testifying, two children in the school system and the irrefutable authority of being exceedingly attractive." Those last words today would be viewed as not politically correct. At that time, however, nothing of the sort would have occurred to me. Later I spoke with Louisa (whose name had become Louisa Howe) about her recollections. She reminded me that she had not expected to testify until several days later and was unprepared when we called her as a witness. While she was not religious, she felt that a God-given eloquence had descended upon her. I asked about the letter. She laughed, "I guess I was reasonably O.K. looking those days."

Appeal from a three-judge court went directly to the Supreme Court of the United States.

Davis v. County School Board

The trial of *Davis v. County School Board of Prince Edward County, Virginia*[4] ran from February 25 to 29, 1952. It went pretty much like the other cases: Witnesses described the material differences between black and white schools. Our social scientists, including Kenneth Clark, testified. Virginia differed from the others in two respects; defense counsel was openly racist and for the first time the state called its own expert witnesses. The chief defense counsel, Justin Moore, acting like the Nazi heavy in an old war movie, behaved like the racist he was, asking our social science witness Isadore Chein, "What kind of name is that? What sort of racial background does that indicate?" "Are you one hundred percent Jewish?" "Were your parents native born in the United States?" He asked Kenneth Clark where he was born (Panama), and then, "What percentage, as near as you can tell us, are you white and what percentage some other?"

For the first time, defendants called their own social scientists and educators as witnesses. But one, William H. Kelly, a child psychiatrist, conceded that racial segregation "is adverse to the personality." In response to Bob Carter's question on cross-examination, "Do you feel that racial segregation has an adverse effect on a healthy personality development?" the psychologist John Nelson Buck admitted that, "As an abstract statement—as a generality, let us put it that way—I should say, yes." Henry Garrett, the state's star social scientist, who had been Kenneth Clark's teacher at Columbia, attacked Kenneth's testimony and that of the plaintiffs' other social scientists. But he, too, had to admit on cross-examination that, "Wherever a person is cut off from the main body of society or a group, if he is put in a position that stigmatizes him and makes him feel inferior, I would say yes, it is detrimental and deleterious to him."

On March 7, 1952, the court entered a decree declaring that there was inequality in buildings, facilities, curricula, and "conveyances." It ordered the school board to immediately equalize curricula

---

[4] Davis v. County School Board of Prince Edward County, 103 F. Supp. 337, 340 (E.D. Va. 1952).

and transportation, and to pursue with "diligence and dispatch their present program, now afoot and progressing," to equalize buildings and equipment. But it refused to hold segregation unconstitutional: "So ingrained and wrought in the texture of their life is the principle of separate schools, that the president of the University of Virginia expressed to the Court his judgment that its involuntary elimination would severely lessen the interest of the people of the State in the public schools, lessen the financial support, and so injure both races."

The Delaware Cases

The University of Delaware case Lou Redding and I had won had been heard by Vice-Chancellor Collins J. Seitz, so it would have made good sense to file the elementary and high school cases in his court, but Seitz was up for promotion to chancellor. Segregationists in Delaware, of whom there were plenty, hated Seitz, and downstate legislators were already lining up in opposition. We hardly wanted to reward his courage by costing him the votes he needed for promotion. So we filed two cases, *Wilson v. Beebe* and *Johnson v. Beebe,* in federal court on June 2, 1951.

The state, however, moved that the federal court do nothing until the state court had first had an opportunity to construe the segregation statute. There is a doctrine called abstention, which allows state courts first to interpret their statutes to have a meaning that would be constitutional, obviating the possibility that federal courts will declare them unconstitutional. The argument was ridiculous in this case, because it could hardly be contended that state law permitted integration. In the meantime, however, the legislature confirmed Seitz as chancellor. Now without any reason to fight the abstention motion, in July and August we filed *Belton v. Gebhart* and *Bulah v. Gebhart* in state court, and these ultimately became the Delaware school segregation cases in the United States Supreme Court. When Lou told the federal court that we would proceed in state court, the judges seemed so clearly sympathetic that we wondered whether we shouldn't have tried to stay there.

Early in August, I began assembling a group of expert witnesses. As in Topeka and South Carolina, we needed someone to survey the schools, and once more there were the social scientists. I put together a great crew, including some distinguished scholars who had never testified before. Kenneth Clark agreed to test some of the Wilmington children. Among the new witnesses were Jerome Bruner, who has since become one of the world's foremost social scientists; Otto Klineberg, one of the founders of social psychology, who later became a good friend; and Fredric Wertham, a famous psychiatrist who ran a mental health clinic for black youngsters in Harlem and who cared deeply about discrimination.

Wertham and I agreed that it would be best if he were to spend time speaking with some of the children from Delaware. I arranged to bring batches of kids to New York to be interviewed at the Lafargue Clinic, Wertham's facility at St. Philip's Episcopal Church in Harlem. The clinic had a staff of thirty professionals and was open two nights a week. A member of the Wilmington NAACP accompanied a small group of black and white children to New York City (a two-hour train trip) on three or four occasions. I met them at Pennsylvania Station, took them to the clinic, and, after their interviews, back to the station for the trip home.

The first time they came up I thought I would treat them to dinner in a Chinese restaurant, a new experience for all of them. That turned out to be a big mistake; as they went about sampling all the strange and exotic dishes they had never seen before, I began to wonder whether or not I'd have enough money to pay the bill.

Wertham was of an imperious nature and quite temperamental, and everything had to be precisely as he wanted it. He insisted on testifying first, ahead of the other experts, offering the reason that by the time the trial began he would have examined the children and his testimony would be the most detailed, and he didn't want to face the burden of defending the testimony of preceding witnesses. He had an injured knee and until almost the last minute I couldn't be sure that he would show up. One point of tension was Wertham's view that comic books, particularly those that depicted sadism, violence, and racism, had a very harmful influence on children. As we discussed his testimony Wertham kept veering off into denouncing the malignant influence of comic books, and I kept trying to steer him back to the case at hand, thinking the comic book issue irrelevant and distracting.

The trial began on October 22, 1951. It went much like the Clarendon County and Topeka cases. Stephen Wright, dean of Hampton Institute, and Ellis Knox and Paul Lawrence, professors of education at Howard, testified about material aspects of the schools. In a delicious twist, Louis Redding called as a witness Maurice Thomasson, acting president of Delaware State College, to which black students had been restricted until our case of the previous year integrating the University of Delaware. In light of how some whites, as well as some blacks, might react, it took courage for Thomasson to testify. He offered the opinion that the white schools were materially better than the black ones and that segregation per se indicated a belief that "the persons designated for [the separate] school[s] are not quite fit to go to the regular schools."

Kenneth Clark's social scientific testimony was about the same as at the Clarendon County trials: segregation impaired the self-esteem of black children and confused their sense of identity. Otto Klineberg testified that there are no racial differences in intelligence.

Only Wertham's testimony was different than expected—he captivated the courtroom. The Viennese accent helped, but the impact came from what he had to say. He responded to my questions:

> It is my opinion that the State . . . injures the child's health. . . . I hold the scientific opinion that if a rosebush should produce twelve roses and if only one rose grows, it is not a healthy rosebush. . . .
>
> Now, the fact of segregation in public and high school creates in the mind of the child an unsolvable conflict. . . .
>
> One way to overcome such a conflict is to have a realistic understanding of why it is that one group of children to which one belongs is excluded and another group of children to which one does not belong is included. . . . I have found that the children cannot find such a realistic rationalization for the simple reason that the adults don't give it to them and . . . the State . . . cannot give an understandable explanation. . . .
>
> If the State of Delaware would employ Professor Einstein to teach Physics in marble halls to these children, I would still say

everything I have said goes: It is the fact of segregation in general and the problems that come out of it that to my mind is anti-educational, by which I mean that education in the larger sense is interfered with.

Now, of course these facts that I have mentioned are not caused only by the school segregation, but the school segregation is important, of paramount importance. . . .

In the first place, it is absolutely clear cut.

Secondly, the State does it.

Thirdly, it is not just the discrimination—it is discrimination of very long duration. . . .

Fourth, it is bound up with the whole educational process.

He was very powerful, and, up to this point, he hadn't got into the comic books. I was hoping he wouldn't get the chance. But then he told of a child he had interviewed who had with him a copy of Jumbo Comics. I stood powerless as Wertham turned to the chancellor:

THE WITNESS [WERTHAM]: I would like to show a picture which shows a cage up in a tree, and there are colored people in there, clearly understood by these children as being Negroes, and it says, quote: Helpless natives left to starve or to be prey to any prowling beast.

There is a white girl underneath looking upward (indicating). Can I show this to you?

THE COURT: You will have to introduce it through your counsel.

I tried to be casual:

MR. GREENBERG: May I introduce this in evidence? It is a photostat of a comic book from one of the children whom Dr. Wertham examined.

THE WITNESS: And this one is a close-up (indicating). And in this one there are Negroes tied to a tree and being beaten.

The attorney general started asking questions about the original documents. I had no way out and introduced the photocopies of the comic book into evidence, as well as the comic book itself, as if I had planned to do so all along. I tried to link the comic books to school segregation with a few questions and Wertham helped a bit:

> The children read that, and they are there indoctrinated with the fact that you can do all kinds of things to colored races. Now, the school problem partly, as you say, reinforces that, but it is very much more, because after all these commercial people who sell these things to children do so to make money. The State does it as acting morally. . . . So that the State really stabs very much deeper than these things do.

Wertham's summary was the best part of his testimony:

> Segregation in schools legally decreed by statute, as in the State of Delaware, interferes with the healthy development of children. It doesn't necessarily cause an emotional disorder in every child. I compare that with the disease of tuberculosis. In New York thousands of people have the tubercle bacilli in their lungs—hundreds of thousands—and they don't get tuberculosis. But they do have the germ of illness in them at one time or another, and the fact that hundreds of them don't develop tuberculosis doesn't make me say, "never mind the tubercle bacillus; it doesn't harm people, so let it go."

Lou and I wrote briefs and waited for the decision. Then, on April 1, 1952, Lou Redding and I won the first case ever to order black children admitted to white schools.[5] The chancellor held that the black and white schools were unequal in material respects and that black children should be admitted to the white schools. "Such a plaintiff is entitled to relief immediately, in the only way it is available, namely, by admission to the school with the superior facilities. To postpone such relief is to deny relief." But he went a step further than simply ruling that the only way to bring about equality in a timely way was to end segregation. He expressed approval of our testimony on the psychological effects of segregation irrespective of

---

[5] Belton v. Gebhart, 32 Del. Ch. 343, 87 A.2d 862, 864, 870 (Del. Ch. 1952).

whether or not the segregated facilities were equal. Referring to Wertham as "one of America's foremost psychiatrists," he accepted his testimony that "State enforced segregation is important, because it is 'clear cut' and gives legal sanction to the differences, and is of continuous duration."

The judge concluded, "From the testimony . . . in our Delaware society, State-imposed segregation in education itself results in the Negro children, as a class, receiving educational opportunities which are substantially inferior." He refused to hold segregation unconstitutional, however, because it had been upheld by the Supreme Court. Now we had to hope that the state would appeal, because Delaware would be a great case to take to the Supreme Court.

Thurgood had called the Delaware school case "our best case." True, it was a border state, and thus more moderate on racial issues, but a court had ordered what, until then, would have been unthinkable to many. It was an entering wedge that might persuade the Supreme Court that it could do likewise. It's always easier to undertake a difficult task when you see that someone else has done it successfully.

CHAPTER 6

IN THE HOUSE OF THE LAW

First Pass at the Supreme Court

In July 1951, Spotts Robinson, Bob Carter, and Thurgood appealed the South Carolina case *Briggs v. Elliott*. On October 1, Bob, Thurgood, and I, along with the Kansas lawyers, appealed *Brown v. Board of Education,* the Kansas decision. In December, Clarendon County filed a report that told of progress in equalizing facilities, which the district court forwarded to the Supreme Court. The Supreme Court, in turn, sent the report back to the district court for appropriate action. Physical improvements had nothing to do with segregation, and Justices Black and Douglas dissented[1] on the grounds that any additional facts were "wholly irrelevant to the constitutional questions."

Back in the district court in March 1952, Thurgood once more pushed for a decision on the unconstitutionality of segregation. J. Waties Waring had retired and, although Judge Parker invited him to take part, he declined to do so. Thurgood conceded, "They are proceeding to lay the plans for the buildings which will eventually furnish equal facilities." The colloquy turned testy:

JUDGE PARKER: Well, none of us can build a building overnight. . . .
MR. MARSHALL: I might say, sir, that every day they are not equal, these plaintiffs are losing rights, for which they cannot be adequately compensated.

---

[1] Briggs v. Elliot, 342 U.S. 350, 352 (1952).

JUDGE DOBIE [who had replaced Waring]: Well, what can we do about that? . . . They can't do any more at this stage, can they?

MR. MARSHALL: No, sir, they cannot physically do more. It is impossible for them to build those schools overnight.

JUDGE TIMMERMAN: Well, do you want us to put them in jail for not doing something that you know they can't do?

MR. MARSHALL: It is something they can do, sir. They could break down the segregation.

JUDGE DOBIE: Let that alone.

Thurgood hadn't been overly ambitious in the district court. He said he was "not saying to strike it down on the basis of segregation per se, but on the basis that the facilities that are being offered the Negroes are not equal as of today"—the basis of the decision soon to be handed down in the Delaware cases. But, of course, the South Carolina trial court would have none of it, approved what the school district was doing, and on March 13, 1952, denied further relief. Observing Thurgood, Bob, and Spotts's chortling, thigh-slapping, and mimicking when they recounted what had occurred after the hearing, one might not have guessed that we had lost. They took particular delight in imitating Dobie's "let that alone."

On May 10, 1952, Thurgood and his co-counsel appealed to the Supreme Court in *Briggs v. Elliot* for the second time. In June the Court agreed to hear *Briggs* and *Brown*, scheduling argument for October 13. That left three cases in lower courts: Delaware, Washington, D.C. (Jim Nabrit, Jr.'s case), and Virginia. A few days earlier, on March 7, the Virginia court had ruled against us, in *Davis,* and on July 12, Thurgood and associates appealed and suggested that it be heard with South Carolina and Kansas.

On April 1, 1952, we won the Delaware cases. The state attorney general appealed immediately. Lou Redding and I argued the appeal in the tiny colonial Delaware Supreme Court courthouse in Dover, downstate Delaware, before the three-judge supreme court. At the end of August, we won again—the Delaware Supreme Court affirmed the chancellor's order that required admitting the black plaintiffs because the schools were unequal. Now we had to hope that Delaware would appeal. The Supreme Court finds it easier to affirm lower court decisions than to overturn them and to follow a precedent rather than break new ground. One winning case before the Court would improve the chances of all the cases. Ego was involved, too: we wanted *our* case up there.

Just before the arguments in South Carolina and Kansas were due to begin on October 13, the Court postponed them until December and agreed to hear *Davis* from Virginia at the same time. The Court clerk also called Jim Nabrit, at the direction of Chief Justice Vinson, and requested that he file a petition in the D.C. case, even though it had not yet been decided in the court of appeals. It was like the Navy, where a request from an officer is the equivalent of a command. The Court also entered an order stating that the "Court will entertain a petition for certiorari in the case of *Bolling v. Sharpe,* which if presented and granted will"[2] be heard with the other cases. Jim did as he was told, and then the Court, in a rarely employed procedure, granted the petition for a writ of certiorari before judgment was rendered in the court of appeals.

We were startled in the Kansas case, where the district court had held the schools to be equal and segregation constitutional, when a newly elected school board majority decided it would no longer defend the case. The state attorney general took the position that it was a local question, and that if the local board was willing to go along with whatever the Supreme Court might decide, he was not going to Washington to argue the case. The Supreme Court, however, as demonstrated in *Bolling,* wanted a comprehensive picture of school segregation throughout the country. At the end of November, it requested, which again amounted to requiring, the Kansas attorney general to appear on behalf of the state, and he complied.

Toward the end of November, as the ninety-day filing period was running out, the Delaware attorney general broke the suspense and filed a petition for writ of certiorari; apparently, if he couldn't have the Deep South cases decided first he wasn't going to forfeit his right to Supreme Court review. Lou and I immediately filed a re-

---

[2] *Brown v. Board of Education of Topeka,* 344 U.S. 1, 3 (1952).

sponse, two-thirds of a page long, which said, "Respondents waive the right to file a brief in opposition . . . and urge that if petitioners' petition . . . is granted this Court schedule the above entitled cases for argument following argument in No. 8 [Kansas], 101 [South Carolina], and 191 [Virginia], for the reason that the issues involved are closely related." We passed up the opportunity to file a cross-petition claiming that segregation was unconstitutional. If we had, the state would have thirty days to answer our brief and the case might not be heard with the others. That waiver would later prompt argumentative questions when, at oral argument, I challenged the constitutionality of segregation—why hadn't I cross-petitioned? Eleven days after Delaware's petition, the Supreme Court granted *cert,* and set all five cases down for argument together. Delaware was allowed until three weeks *after* argument to file its brief, following which we might reply. But we wanted the Court to understand the case fully as it heard oral argument so we rushed and filed our brief before argument.

The chancellor refused to stay his desegregation order. Black children immediately began attending school in Claymont and Hockessin on a non-segregated basis.

Getting Ready for the Supreme Court—Our Cast of Characters

Apart from the excitement of the work, the pleasure in this regimen was found in frequent dinners with Thurgood, other staff members, and out-of-town lawyers at the Blue Ribbon, a German restaurant on Forty-third Street. In what once was a townhouse, with heavy wooden furniture, leaded-glass windows, and small, dark paneled dining rooms hung with autographed pictures of stars of the opera and theater, the Blue Ribbon served great dark Munich beer on tap, black bread, various wursts, and one of Thurgood's favorites, pigs' knuckles. He made a ceremony of ordering the dish and, indeed, enjoyed talking about food, about his own she-crab soup, which was delicious, and about his Aunt Meenie's "sad cake." As soon as it started rising she'd open the oven and slap it down; as it tried to rise again, she'd spank it gently until it succumbed and lay almost flat until baked through.

Sometimes we lunched at the Algonquin, where visiting lawyers stayed and some staff lawyers stayed overnight when they worked into the wee hours. When we lunched there Thurgood focused on scrambled eggs, brought to him by the maitre d', Raul, with whom he had a relationship of bonhomie.

Brief writing was aided by frequent conferences among the staff, local counsel, and professional and academic friends. We consulted most often with Bob Ming, Louis Pollak, Bill Coleman, Charlie Black, and Jack Weinstein. William R. (Bob) Ming, Jr., a brilliant lawyer who taught at the University of Chicago, was the first black appointed to the faculty of a major white law school. He had great imagination and, in addition to his teaching, developed a successful practice in Chicago, representing, among others, the leading Polish Roman Catholic organization in the city.

Louis H. (Lou) Pollak had gone to Yale Law School, been clerk to Supreme Court Justice Wiley Rutledge, worked for the State Department and then had taken a job in New York in the legal department at the Amalgamated Clothing Workers Union. There was no question that he would employ his considerable talents at something other than getting rich. Tall, thin, ascetic looking, but rarely without a smile, he came to civil rights not only by conviction but by descent and marriage. Lou's father, Walter Pollak, had argued one of the Scottsboro cases in the Supreme Court. His wife, Cathy, was the daughter of Louis Weiss, one of the leading liberal lawyers in New York, a founder of the firm Paul Weiss Wharton and Garrison and later chairman of the LDF National Legal Committee.

One day as we worked together on an early phase of the school cases, Lou and I met at the Columbia law library and took a walk outside and speculated about how we hoped to spend our careers. We agreed that we would be happy if we could work at matters we cared about so long as we could earn five or six thousand dollars a year. Not long thereafter, he was appointed to the Yale faculty and later became dean of the law school there. Years later he became dean of the University of Pennsylvania Law School and then a United States District Court judge.

William T. (Bill) Coleman had been first in his class at Harvard Law School, and law clerk to Justice Frankfurter, the first black to become a Supreme Court law clerk. No Philadelphia firm would give him a job because he was black, and so he tried New York and found work at Paul, Weiss, where he shared an office with Lou Pollak for a time. Bill continued to live in Philadelphia, making the more than two-hour commute to and from New York. Ultimately Bill was offered a job at one of Philadelphia's leading firms, the Dilworth firm, where he became a partner. He was later the secretary of transportation in the Ford administration. After that he became a top partner at O'Melveny & Myers, one of the country's largest and most prestigious law firms, as well as a member of the boards of Pan Am, Chase Bank, IBM, and other corporations, and chairman of the LDF board.

Charles L. (Charlie) Black was a Texan, with a pronounced drawl, whom we met when he taught at Columbia. He soon moved to Yale to become the Henry Luce professor of law. His twin legal specialties were constitutional law and admiralty. A thorough intellectual, who sometimes quoted the classics in Latin, Charlie always followed his heart. He played the trumpet and harmonica, painted, and published poetry, and was a great teacher and prolific scholar. In the 1960s he stopped off in Iceland for a brief look, fell in love with the country, learned its language, and returned there to lecture on American constitutional law in Icelandic.

Charlie tells of when he was sixteen having heard Louis Armstrong play in Austin. Armstrong was in "the dazzlingly inventive small-band period of the Hot Five and Hot Seven, and the first period of improvisation around popular melodies—Stardust, Chinatown, When Your Lover Has Gone. . . . It is impossible to overstate the significance of a sixteen-year-old Southern boy's seeing genius, for the first time, in a black. We literally never saw a black then, in any but a servant's capacity." A good old boy from Charlie's high school had "pronounced judgment of the time and place: 'After all he's nothing but a God damn nigger!'" Charlie further observed that "it was just then that I started walking toward the *Brown* case, where I belonged." When some scholars theorized abstractly about the constitutionality of segregation, arguing that though it treated blacks and whites separately, it treated them equally, Charlie responded with a healthy dose of reality. He *knew* the purposes and effects of segregation firsthand.

Jack B. Weinstein was my law school classmate. His stamina was boundless and his encyclopedic knowledge of procedural law and evidence later was embodied in the leading treatises and encyclopedias. Not long after Jack began working with us he joined the Columbia law faculty.

Councils of War

We worked in a conference room in the basement of Freedom House or, after we moved to Forty-third Street, in the library in the rear of the office. Thurgood's way of presiding was to listen a lot and challenge virtually everything everyone said, often fiercely. If someone suggested that a certain course of action *had* to be taken, he'd often respond: "There's only two things I have to do: stay black and die." Or to one who argued that "we" should do this or that, he might say, quoting an old Bert Williams song, "I may be mistakin', but I think that you're makin' that 'weeeeeee' too long."

I did the first draft of the *Brown* brief, for Kansas, and sent it to Bob Carter, who was on vacation on Martha's Vineyard. Such differences in the briefs as there were came about because of the different factual circumstances of each case, or were adventitious, not the result of a planned strategy of different emphases for different cases. But whatever their differences, each brief called for an end to segregation in education.

The briefs for each case cited pure legal doctrine. For example, the claim that "the State of Kansas has no power . . . to use race as a factor in affording educational opportunities" called for applying *Sweatt* and *McLaurin* to lower schools, and argued that where there was physical inequality the trial courts "should have enjoined enforcement of the segregation laws." As to *Plessy*, the briefs argued that it had no relevance to education; the governing authority was *Sweatt* and *McLaurin*.

We filed an innovative appendix to the Kansas, South Carolina, and Virginia cases (Delaware had not yet arrived in the Court and

Jim Nabrit, Jr., for the District of Columbia case, made a pure legal attack), signed by many of the country's leading social scientists, entitled: "The Effects of Segregation and the Consequences of Desegregation: A Social Science Statement."[3] Its preface stated that it had been "drafted and signed by some of the foremost authorities in sociology, anthropology, psychology and psychiatry who have worked in the area of race relations." The appendix asserted that segregation imposes on individuals a distorted sense of social reality; leads to blockage of communication, which increases mutual suspicion, distrust, and hostility; perpetuates rigid stereotypes and reinforces negative attitudes; and leads to violent outbreaks of racial tensions. It drew heavily on the report of the Mid-century White House Conference on Children, for which Kenneth Clark had done a report on race.

The appendix might accurately be characterized as a compilation of the views of enlightened scholars who had studied racial issues as deeply as existing resources permitted. But this made the appendix no less valuable for a Court that, after all, had to make a decision based on the best information available.

As in other major civil rights cases, Truman's solicitor general filed an amicus brief. It turned to the conflict with the Soviet Union: "It is in the context of the present world struggle between freedom and tyranny that the problem of racial discrimination must be viewed." The brief quoted Dean Acheson, the secretary of state, extensively, referring to Soviet attacks on the United States for our racial practices and to the hostile reaction among otherwise friendly peoples to how America treated its black citizens.

---

[3] Kenneth B. Clark, *Effect of Prejudice and Discrimination on Personality Development,* Fact Finding Report, Mid-Century White House Conference on Children and Youth, Children's Bureau, Federal Security Agency, 1950, Columbus University, Social Work Library, New York, N.Y. Some of the findings of this report are updated in Kenneth B. Clark, *Prejudice and Your Child* (Middletown, Conn.: Wesleyan University Press, 1988). Among the well-known signers were Floyd Allport, Gordon Allport, Jerome Bruner, Hadley Cantril, Kenneth Clark, Allison Davis, Otto Klineberg, Robert MacIver, Robert Merton, Gardner Murphy, and Arnold Rose. The appendix was reprinted as *Effects of Segregation and the Consequences of Desegregation: Social Science Statement,* 37 Minnesota Law Review 427 (1953).

The amicus argument urged, as we did, that the physical inequalities in South Carolina, Virginia, and Delaware, as well as the psychological harm done by segregation irrespective of the equality question, as found by the court in Kansas, warranted prohibiting segregation in the defendant school systems. But then the brief went even further, arguing that the Court should reach the conclusion that "compulsory racial segregation is itself, without more [that is, even in the absence of tangible inequalities], an unconstitutional discrimination." It quoted extensively from *Strauder* and other cases in which racial distinctions were held unconstitutional. As to social scientific considerations: "The facts of every-day life confirm the finding of the district court in the Kansas case that segregation has a 'detrimental effect' on colored children; that it affects their motivation to learn; and that it has a tendency to retard their educational and mental development and to deprive them of benefits they would receive in an integrated school system."

The government's most significant innovation was uncoupling the question of whether segregation was unconstitutional from the practical question of how desegregation might be accomplished. The strategy, of course, was to allay fears some justices might have about provoking violence and about issuing orders that might be disobeyed, thereby undermining the authority of the Court, which might constitute a constitutional crisis. The headnote of the final section of the amicus brief advised: "If in any of these cases the Court should hold that a system of 'separate but equal' public schools is unconstitutional, it should remand the case to the district court with directions to devise and execute such program for relief as appears most likely to achieve orderly and expeditious transition to a non-segregated system."

The brief "recognized that racial segregation in public schools has been in effect in many states for a long time," asserting that "the practical difficulties which may be met in making progressive adjustment to a non-segregated system cannot be ignored or minimized." It called however, for expeditious settlement of problems by district courts within a "specified period." It did reveal a willingness in effect to sacrifice some black children's access to non-segregated education throughout the remainder of their educational careers by proposing the possibility of "integration on a grade basis, i.e., to integrate the first grades immediately, and to continue such integration until completed as to all grades in the elementary schools," or to "integrate on a school-by-school basis."

In 1987, in a highly controversial article in the *Harvard Law Review*, Philip Elman, who as assistant solicitor general wrote the U.S. brief, reported that this section on relief was his idea as a "way to end racial segregation without inviting massive disobedience, a way to decide the constitutional issue unanimously without tearing the Court apart." It grew out of Elman's conversations with Justice Frankfurter over a period of many months.

John W. Davis represented the state of South Carolina and was the leading advocate for the other side. Davis was seventy-nine, had been Democratic candidate for president of the United States in 1924, and headed one of the largest, most prestigious law firms in the country. He had been solicitor general and had argued hundreds of cases in the Supreme Court. He was an active practitioner and by all accounts had lost none of his prowess as an advocate. The other school districts had their own counsel, but everyone looked to Davis as the spokesman for the segregationist side.

The states' briefs boiled down to reliance on precedent; the concept of federalism, which, under the Constitution, arguably allocated control of internal matters to state authority, so that education and the running of schools were in the power of individual states, not in the federal government; and separation of powers, in support of the contention that school segregation was an issue for legislatures, not courts. They attacked our social science evidence as inconsistent and unpersuasive. They stressed that the defendants had already equalized schools or were in the very process of doing so.

Washington, D.C., had begun to relax a few segregation barriers in 1952, although there was no meaningful desegregation until the Supreme Court, in 1953, decided the *Thompson* case,[4] which resurrected two Reconstruction public accommodations laws for the District and made it a crime to discriminate in certain public

---

[4] District of Columbia v. John R. Thompson Company, Incorporated, 346 U.S. 100 (1953).

accommodations. While it had been possible to stay at the Statler or the Wardman Park over the previous year or two, rooms often weren't available (we had to wonder whether we were being told the truth or if the hotel preferred not to admit blacks) and most of us often stayed at the black hotel, the Charles. But now, for the first time while arguing before the Supreme Court, we stayed at the Statler. Unfortunately, over the years, the exercise of this choice, replicated many times over by others who had formerly stayed at black-only hotels, spelled doom for marginal black enterprises. In later years, blacks set up a few hotels and other businesses in the District of Columbia and elsewhere. LDF lawyers made a pass or two at patronizing them, but for a variety of reasons we, like other black groups, continued to use the big downtown hotels.

Before the argument, as we did prior to all Supreme Court cases, we conducted a "dry run" in a classroom at Howard Law School, which was then housed in the basement of the university's Founders' Library.

On Monday, December 8, 1952, Thurgood moved my admission to the bar of the Supreme Court. The brief ceremony announces the qualifications of the applicant, supported by a sponsor.

Every once in a while a sponsor strays from the script and waxes eloquent about the candidate, usually in moving the admission of a son or daughter; veteran Supreme Court lawyers cringe and make little jokes. According to tradition, it is considered a "class act" when one moves the admission of one's own child and makes no mention of the relationship. I couldn't wait to move the admission of my wife Debby and son Josiah, when Thurgood was sitting on the Court. After the ceremony, in Thurgood's chambers, we joked knowingly about my insider's "sophistication" in not mentioning the relationships. When Thurgood moved the admission of his own son, Thurgood, Jr. (Goodie), while the Court was in session, he stepped down from the bench, removed his robe, went to the podium, and made the motion in the prescribed terms for Goodie and Goodie's wife, Colleen.

Well before we appeared in court, we anticipated that *Brown* might be a historic case. We weren't alone in this perception. Long lines of spectators formed far in advance, some arriving in front of the courthouse as early as 5:30 A.M. and standing in line for admission as if for a rock concert. The crowds attested that many sensed that the Court might be ready to write *finis* to an institution that had existed in parts of the country since soon after the end of the Civil War. None of us recalls that any of the plaintiffs in the cases from the states were in court, possibly because of the expense of travel, although some from the District of Columbia were present.

There were no animated discussions about hopes or fears or possibilities. We were there to do the best we could, and that's all we could think about. Reaching back and using the only analogy I can find out of my own experience, I recall that as my ship approached the battles of Iwo Jima and Okinawa, turning points in the Second World War, no one talked very much about what might happen if we succeeded or if we failed. We had undertaken a job, set out to do it, and focused on doing what we had been trained to do.

Court officers allowed spectators to observe the arguments for about twenty minutes, then ushered the group out and seated another batch. A privileged few, guests of the lawyers presenting argument, were permitted to sit through the entire day. But if they left to go to the bathroom or to the cafeteria, they would forfeit their seats. Jim Nabrit, Jr., gave his son, Jim Nabrit III, then a law student, one of the precious all-day passes. He sat next to Mordecai Johnson, president of Howard University, who surreptitiously munched peanuts while Jim watched enviously, racked with hunger pangs. Every seat was filled.

Oral Argument Number One

Arguments in the School Segregation Cases commenced at 1:35 P.M. The conventional wisdom is that oral argument makes little difference for the outcome of most cases, particularly those of great importance, which are largely shaped by the times and by what lawyers have done before they find themselves standing before the Court. Once, after I had lost by a vote of five to four the appeal of Martin Luther King, Jr.'s conviction of contempt for having marched in Birmingham on a Good Friday to protest that city's racial policies in violation of a court order, I met Justice Douglas at a reception. "What did I do wrong?" I asked. "Nothing," he replied. "Once the case reaches us the record is made and we look at it and decide what to do." Still, lawyers do not, should not, and had better not approach oral argument with the mindset that it doesn't matter. Argument is an opportunity to answer questions, large and small, that the submitted papers may not have answered for one or more of the justices. It also offers a chance to smoke out their concerns, which then may be addressed. Some of the justices may be unsure about what story the facts of the case really tell, and argument may tip them one way or the other. In the school cases, perhaps oral argument also served to build confidence in us as partners in a venture into uncharted waters.

Any description of the oral arguments must make clear how dull they often are, relieved only rarely by a probing question or two and marked even more rarely by one of those conflicts of personality dramatic writers love to introduce into the retelling of legal proceedings. Bob Carter led off in Topeka in a style typical of mainstream appellate argument—conversational, not terribly loud, not very aggressive, perhaps even a little softer than ordinary. He did not leave any doubt that we were going all the way: "Here we abandon any claim, in pressing our attack on the unconstitutionality of this statute—we abandon any claim—of any constitutional inequality which comes from anything other than the act of segregation itself."

Not far into the arguments, Justice Burton asked Paul Wilson, assistant attorney general of Kansas, the key question: "Don't you recognize it as possible, that within seventy-five years the social and economic conditions and the personal relations of the nation may have changed so that what may have been a valid interpretation of them seventy-five years ago would not be a valid interpretation of them constitutionally today?"

Wilson recognized the possibility, but denied that conditions had changed.

During Bob's rebuttal Justice Black turned to the Kansas District Court's findings, which were based on our social scientific evidence: "Do you think that there should be a different holding here with reference to the question involved, according to the place where the segregation might occur, and if not . . . why do you say that it depends on the findings of fact at all?" Justice Black challenged the social science evidence from another viewpoint: was it specific to Topeka alone? Bob, not very responsive, replied that the trial court merely had used the same approach that the Supreme Court had used in *Sweatt* and *McLaurin*.

Thurgood was next up to argue *Briggs v. Elliott*. He hovered imposingly over the lectern as he addressed the justices familiarly, but respectfully. He had been before the court many times and the justices knew him well and trusted him. Some had had dealings with him over the years in political or professional roles, and some may well have considered this appearance a continuation of dialogues they had had over the years. While the case was specifically *Briggs v. Elliott*, the subject was a long-standing one between Thurgood and the Court—the status of blacks and the role of the Constitution in defining, perhaps advancing that status to one of full equality. Thurgood spoke slowly, for him, on this occasion, making sure to articulate his words in an educated Southern way, rather than in the country style he often used.

Justice Frankfurter showed great interest in how a decree would be implemented if we were to win: "What would happen if this Court reverses and the case goes back to the district court for the entry of a decree?"

After a bit of give and take Thurgood replied that the details would have to be worked out by the district court, which might allow some time:

> It would be my position that the important thing is to get the principle established, and if a decree were entered saying that facilities are declared to be unequal [note, again, not giving up victory based on unequal facilities] and that the appellants are entitled to an injunction, and then the District Court issues the injunction, it would seem to me that it would go without saying that the local school board had the time to do it. But obviously it could not do it overnight, and it might take six months to do it one place and two months to do it another place.

Just before Thurgood sat down, Justice Jackson turned to whether his argument would affect American Indians, a number of whom lived in upstate New York, Jackson's home. Thurgood replied that he thought that it would, but that Indians had not had the "judgment or wherewithal to bring lawsuits." In a bantering exchange, Jackson suggested, "Maybe you should bring some up," to which Marshall responded, "I have a full load now, Mr. Justice."

The colloquy was important because, in its casual good-naturedness, it showed a kind of rapport and confidence that might well have predisposed some justices in Thurgood's favor. Thurgood later told me that during the argument he flashed the Masonic secret distress signal to Jackson, who signaled back.

The legendary John W. Davis arose to reply. Of medium height, with white hair, thoroughly at home in the Court, having argued there more than any living lawyer, he came dressed in a club coat, exciting a fair amount of comment. (The things lawyers talk about even when matters of such high moment are at issue!) Many years before, lawyers who argued in the Court wore cutaways, also called morning coats, though the Court sat only in the afternoons, and striped trousers. In modern times, however, while lawyers from the solicitor general's office continued to wear cutaways, private attorneys, with the rarest of exceptions, have worn conservative business suits. Davis split the difference. The club coat, something none of us had heard of before, was a black suit jacket, which Davis wore with striped trousers.

Though styles of dress have changed to some extent, a certain code of formality continues. Lawyers who argue, and all others within the rail, must wear a vest or keep their jackets buttoned; if they don't, the marshal will tap them on the shoulder and request that they button up. A TV show about the *Brown* case depicted Thurgood arguing with his hands in his pockets. Unthinkable.

The justices had interrupted Thurgood's argument scores of times. Davis at first argued almost without interruption, commencing on Tuesday afternoon and arguing until 4:30 when the Court adjourned, resuming on Wednesday, December 10, shortly after noon. The schools were now equalized, he said. As to the Fourteenth Amendment and school segregation, Judge Parker, who had heard and decided the case in South Carolina, was right. Moreover, the same Congress that adopted the amendment voted for separate schools in the District of Columbia, "and from that good day to this, Congress has not wavered in that policy."

But Davis ran into heavy weather when Justice Burton asked the question he had earlier asked Wilson of Kansas, about whether constitutional standards might change over time: "What is your answer, Mr. Davis, to the suggestion mentioned yesterday that at that time the conditions and relations between the two races were such that what might have been constitutional then would not be constitutional now?"

Davis answered that "changed conditions cannot broaden the terminology of the Constitution." He agreed, however, that "many things have been found to be interstate commerce which at the time of the writing of the Constitution were not contemplated at all. Many of them did not even exist."

Justice Frankfurter then jumped in: "Mr. Davis, do you think that 'equal' is a less fluid term than 'commerce between the states'?"

Davis replied, "I have not compared the two on the point of fluidity."

Frankfurter rejoined, "Suppose you do it now."

Davis fenced a bit and then responded: "I should not philosophize about it. But the effort in which I am now engaged is to show how those who submitted this amendment and those who adopted it conceded it to be, and what their conduct by way of interpretation has been since its ratification in 1868."

When Frankfurter asked whether Davis meant that "history puts a gloss upon 'equal' which does not permit . . . admixture of white and colored in this aspect to be introduced," Davis agreed.

In rebuttal, Thurgood responded to Justice Reed's questions as to whether the legislature might consider the disadvantages of segregation to blacks against the advantages of maintaining law and order. It might, although "I know of no Negro legislator in any of these states." He added that, while some might say it was and is necessary, "it is not necessary now because people have grown up and understand each other."

They are fighting together and living together . . . in other places. As a result of the ruling of this Court, they are going together on the higher level. . . . I know in the South where I spend most of my time, you will see white and colored kids going down the road together to school. They separate and go to different schools, and they come out and they play together. I do not see why there would necessarily be any trouble if they went to school together.

Spotts Robinson was up next. He argued *Davis,* the Virginia case, with the careful, literal precision of the real property lawyer that he was. He attacked segregation, but argued also that the Virginia plaintiffs should have been admitted to white schools under the reasoning of *Gaines:* if the state did not have equal accommodations to offer the blacks, then they must be admitted to the better white schools. Of course, once they were admitted, he argued, they couldn't thereafter be re-segregated should physical equality be attained—another example of the conservative yet ambitious advocacy. As part of the response to Spotts, one of Virginia's lawyers, Justin Moore, a partner in Richmond's leading law firm, disparaged the social scientific material we had presented, declaring, "You might as well be talking about the Sermon on the Mount or something like that." To which Frankfurter replied, "It is supposed to be a good document." Jackson, in a series of questions, suggested that perhaps Congress, not the Court, should solve the problem—an outlook we had feared he held.

George Hayes and Jim Nabrit argued the District of Columbia case. They would have none of our modulated, less than all-or-nothing approaches. They argued that segregation was impermissible as a matter of constitutional principle, without regard to physical or psychological evidence. George argued too that Congress never had explicitly required segregation and, therefore, it was prohibited. But while Congress never had used the language of Southern segregation laws, its understanding seemed quite clear: it was prepared to accept it in the District of Columbia, an area under its own control. It regularly appropriated money for separate black and white schools that functioned in plain view of the Capitol, as some of the justices pointed out.

Justice Frankfurter brought up the "M" word (miscegenation): "Would [you] say, right off from your analysis of the Constitution, that marriage laws relating to race are ipso facto on the face of things, unconstitutional?"

George replied that "legislation based upon race is immediately suspect." To which Frankfurter replied, with satisfaction: "Well, that is a very candid and logical answer. That simply means that it can be valid. It is not an absolute prohibition, that good cause must be shown or great cause must be shown for the rule."

Jim Nabrit's argument began on Wednesday afternoon, was interrupted by the 4:30 recess, and resumed on Thursday. He largely devoted his time to trying to show that Congress had never required school segregation in the District of Columbia. But it appeared that he convinced nobody. He then, briefly, turned to the Constitution: school segregation in Washington was unconstitutional, he urged, because it violated the due process clause of the Fifth Amendment. Then Jim brought up the subject of bills of attainder, the legislative pronouncement that a convicted felon has forfeited all of his property and civil rights. Such bills often included a corruption of blood, meaning the felon's heirs would inherit his guilt. Bills of attainder are specifically proscribed by the Constitution. If the statutes were interpreted to require segregation, he said, "They have done it without a trial . . . merely because for some undisclosed crime, some status, some position, some matter of birth . . . or something else in the past, these Negroes are unfit to associate with whites, and under the definition of a bill of attainder . . . there would be another danger that these acts would be unconstitutional."

It was an innovative but too imaginative argument. Everyone knew that attainder referred to a specific historical practice. No justice was interested enough to ask a question.

Milton Korman, assistant corporation counsel for the District of Columbia, had a big belly, wore a morning coat, and made an incredibly bad argument. Everything he said was overshadowed by his startling quotation from the *Dred Scott* case, an infamous decision that had helped precipitate the Civil War by requiring the return of a runaway slave and declaring that a black man had no rights that whites were bound to respect. Korman's point was that constitutional interpretation should be immune from changes in public opinion. But *Dred Scott* was best known for having said that blacks were "beings of an inferior order, and altogether unfit to associate with the white race, either in social or political relations," an interpretation of the Constitution surely no longer held in any quarter, not even by the most ignorant. Heads shook in wonderment.[5]

Jim Nabrit arose for rebuttal. In a peroration that he had prepared the night before, he wrapped himself in the flag, as he had promised he would:

> The Negro should not be viewed as anybody's burden. He is a citizen. He is performing his duties in peace and war, and today, on the bloody hills of Korea, he is serving in an unsegregated war. . . .
>
> In the heart of the nation's capital, in the capital of democracy, in the capital of the free world, there is no place for a segregated school system. This country cannot afford it, and the Constitution does not permit it, and the statutes of Congress do no authorize it.

His stirring words mesmerized the courtroom.

The Delaware cases began at 1:27 on Thursday afternoon. From the beginning they were different. The Court is generally reluctant to overturn state court judgments and for once we had one in our favor. The Delaware attorney general, H. Albert Young, was trying to reverse his own Delaware Supreme Court and he had a rough time. He attacked the relief the courts ordered, integration rather than equalization. But several of the justices asked him whether the relief wasn't something to be left to the discretion of the judge. Justice Frankfurter responded to Young's assertion that the chancellor misunderstood the governing law: "If I may say so, a chancellor who shows as much competence as this opinion shows, probably can read the opinions of the Court with understanding."

Lou Redding got into a series of exchanges with Justice Frankfurter, who asked whether the Court might not simply affirm and leave the case alone: "If we just affirmed this decree below without

---

[5] Dred Scott v. Sandford, 60 U.S. 393, 407 (1857).

an opinion, that would be an end of the matter, and the plaintiffs in this case would get all they asked, would they not?" Lou replied that the attorney general had threatened that "the moment he has shown to the court that facilities are equalized they [the black students] would then be ejected from the schools."

I concluded the argument in the Delaware case, which was also the end of the arguments for all five cases. I was eleven days short of my twenty-eighth birthday. Was I nervous? Strangely, I wasn't. I knew the case inside out and had a detailed notebook on the lectern in front of me, which contained my argument, with marginal notes to guide me back if I lost my way. I had been in the trial and appeal and had done a dry run. I had listened to other LDF lawyers argue before the Court over two days and then heard Lou. I felt as well prepared as possible. Even if I did terribly the others already had made many of the points I planned to present.

The questions focused on two issues: was the chancellor right in ordering *immediate* integration; and how should the Supreme Court treat the social science evidence? I argued that if the state had presented evidence warranting delay, then the courts below might have considered it. But, in fact, "the decree of the Supreme Court of Delaware came down, I believe on August the 28, at which time both counsel for the respondents were on vacation, and before we could even return from vacation, the children who had read about the decree in the newspaper had applied to the school and had been admitted, and there was no more administrative problem involved than admitting anybody else."

Justices Black and Frankfurter explored whether the social science testimony was significant only for Delaware. I replied that a great deal had been presented by social scientists from Delaware, but that segregation generally was unconstitutional. Frankfurter observed that "if a man says three yards and I have measured it, and it is three yards, there it is. But if a man tells you about the inside of your brain and mine, and how we function, that is not a measurement, and there you are."

I argued that the testimony was uncontradicted and that the chancellor had been persuaded and then I concluded, "We urge that this Court affirm the judgment below, and assure that the respondents' stay in the schools to which they have been admitted and which they are now attending will be one unharassed by future litigation and attempts to segregate them once more."

With that the arguments ended. Each day, after the arguments, we would return to the hotel, dead tired, and try to read the tea leaves of the questions asked by the justices. Since Justice Frankfurter asked more questions than all the others combined, and Bill Coleman had been his law clerk, everyone hoped that Bill might shed some light on Frankfurter's mind and perhaps that of the other justices as well. But he was of little help.

After the last day, we just scattered. Neither following *Brown*, nor after other cases, did we hold post-mortems. About the only surprise questions from the bench had been those that Justice Jackson put to Thurgood about the education of Indians. No one had been prepared for that, but it didn't matter. Our side had ranged across all the possible styles of advocacy, from Spotts's meticulous, dry, complete coverage of the issues to Thurgood's vivid imagery about children playing together and then separating to go to school— everyone presented our arguments well.

I felt that I was particularly favorably situated in a case that we already won in the Delaware courts, because our plaintiffs actually were in the formerly white schools, and I could argue that there was no reason to postpone desegregation; it had already occurred without incident. John W. Davis had said all there was to be said in favor of keeping the status quo. He certainly had a cool, commanding presence, yet the most persuasive factor in his favor was not the legal argument, but rather the fear in the minds of the justices about what might happen if the law were to change.

CHAPTER 7

BACK TO THE DRAWING BOARD

Five Questions

All we could do was wait. In controversial cases the Court tended to delay deciding until near the very end of the term. At an April 1953 executive committee meeting, Thurgood reported that he thought we would win at least three of the school cases—which three he didn't say. This suggested the victories might come on grounds short of holding segregation unconstitutional—perhaps finding physical inequalities in some of the cases, as in Delaware, and upholding segregation where the bricks, mortar, and books were equal, or maybe, ducking deciding the others.

We were all astonished when, on June 8, 1953, the Supreme Court ordered that the cases be re-argued, setting re-argument for October 12, but later postponing it to December. The Court asked both sides to answer five questions.[1]

First, what was the understanding of the Congress that adopted, and the state legislatures that ratified, the Fourteenth Amendment as to whether it would proscribe segregation in public schools?

Second, if neither Congress nor the states understood that the Fourteenth Amendment would require immediate abolition of school segregation, did they nevertheless understand that Congress in the future might have the power to abolish it or that the Court in construing the amendment might abolish it in the light of future conditions?

---

[1] Brown v. Board of Education of Topeka, 345 U.S. 972, 973 (1953).

The third question addressed whether, without regard to the understanding of the framers, it was within the power of the Court to construe the amendment to abolish school segregation.

The final two questions suggested to the South that it had better start thinking the unthinkable, for they addressed how desegregation should be brought about, no longer merely whether or not segregation was constitutional. Question four asked, "Assuming it is decided that segregation in public schools violates the Fourteenth Amendment, would a decree necessarily follow that, within limits set by normal geographic school districting, Negro children should forthwith be admitted to schools of their choice," or might the Court permit an "effective gradual adjustment"?

The final question assumed that gradual change might be permitted and inquired who should work out the transition—the Supreme Court, a special master, or the district courts. The United States attorney general was invited to submit a brief and participate in the oral argument.

Materials made public subsequent to the *Brown* decision indicate that following the first argument the Court was divided, perhaps with our side getting five, six, or maybe even seven justices if the vote had been taken at that time. The only certain, or near certain, dissenters seem to have been Reed and Vinson, with Jackson and Clark open to persuasion to join the majority. Justice Frankfurter, however, feeling that unanimity would be highly important in so emotionally and politically controversial a decision, wanted to hold off deciding the cases for a year. He drafted the five questions and persuaded the Court to issue them along with its call for reargument. Among his reasons in proposing the questions about remedy was that "it is not undesirable that an adjustment be made in the public mind to such a possibility." He offered his belief that "the ultimate crucial factor in the problem presented by these cases is psychological—the adjustment of men's minds and actions to the unfamiliar, the unpleasant."

I took the five questions as a favorable omen, as did some of the other lawyers, including Spotts and Oliver. Why, after all, would the Court have put questions about remedy if it weren't seriously contemplating ordering a remedy? Bill Coleman was sure we would

BACK TO THE DRAWING BOARD • 113

win—everyone suspected that he had an inside line to Frankfurter, but he didn't. Jack Weinstein also was sure we would win. Putting all the legal issues aside, he believed that following the Second World War and all the horrors that had come out of Nazi racial doctrines and laws the Court would have no alternative but to come down on the side of full equality for all citizens. Bob Carter, on the other hand, remembered being less optimistic, recalling that the Court's questions "shook us—not completely—but they shook us. Where we had been 75 percent confident, we now were down to 50 or 55 percent confident."

Logistics

After the brief was filed, Arnold De Mille, who handled our public relations, issued a press release on November 11, 1953, in which he got somewhat carried away. While everything in the release, in any public relations release, should not be taken entirely at face value, De Mille did convey to the general public, with some exaggeration, the spirit of what the previous twenty-two weeks had been like for us:

> By midsummer some staff workers were going two and three days without sleep, taking time out only to eat. [I doubt it.] By the end of October, no one was getting more than three or four hours sleep at a time. [No one? Hardly.]
>
> Enough coffee was consumed by the workers in the Legal Defense office to supply a regiment for a full week. [How much coffee does a regiment drink in a week?] . . .
>
> The secretaries and volunteers put in shifts of fifteen to twenty hours a day, seven days a week, without requesting extra pay. [Almost true.]
>
> All members of the NAACP legal staff gave up their vacation time. [True.]
>
> The staff has used 1,000,600 sheets of copy paper, 6,000,225 sheets of manifold, 2,700 stencils, more than twelve million sheets of mimeographing paper and 115,000 sheets of carbon paper [I didn't count, but almost 20,000,000 sheets of paper? I can't believe it.] . . .

Some 325,000 miles were covered by lawyers who shuttled back and forth across the nation. [Probably true.]

We also had to engage in serious fund-raising. The Fund's income, at best, covered only ordinary expenses, but we estimated that the re-argument would cost an addition $39,000 (remember, this was in 1953 dollars). Today, any one of a number of large foundations and a handful of wealthy individuals would readily make such a contribution. Then, $39,000 was not so easy to come by. Marshall Field had given $75,000 of his $200,000 anonymous pledge in 1952, but in 1953 he gave only $50,000. The Field Foundation gave $15,000, but no other really big gifts were in the offing. In any event, those large gifts were budgeted to cover only the ongoing program, which did not count unanticipated expenses for the re-argument.

The black press started a campaign that produced $14,000. The *Pittsburgh Courier* called it "EE" (Equality in Education), the *Afro American* named it "Dollar or more will open the door," and the *Birmingham World* labeled it "Put up or shut up." In September, Walter Reuther of the CIO contributed $2,500, and the black American Teachers' Association (Southern black teachers weren't permitted in the National Education Association, the national teachers' guild) gave $5,000. Charles Buchanan, a black impresario who owned the Savoy Ballroom in Harlem, gave $500 for law books (over the years he supported our library generously). Churches (the Second Baptist Church of Los Angeles gave $1,500), black businesses (Rose Morgan, who owned a large beauty salon raised $5,000), and others gave amounts of similar magnitude. The Prince Hall Masons continued to contribute about $20,000 per year in gifts ranging from $100 to several thousand dollars from lodges all over the country. The South Carolina and Virginia state conferences of branches of the NAACP contributed $5,000 in September and $5,100 in December, respectively.

To bring in such income, Thurgood or some other staff member often would have to go out and speak to the potential donors. We appeared at branches, universities, and churches, before fraternal associations, veterans' groups, labor unions, professional associations, and other organizations. Rarely did we appear at fewer than ten meetings in a month and often we spoke at well over twenty, with Thurgood speaking far more often than anyone else. Besides being greatly in demand, Thurgood was the only staff member permitted into the Masons' inner sanctums. So a heavy travel schedule burdened everyone's, but especially Thurgood's, ability to do other work.

By September Thurgood reported that we were still $25,000 short in paying for the extra expenses generated by the re-argument, although "many of the research people are working just for carfare and lunch money." But before the brief was filed in November, the $39,000 shortfall was in hand, 70 percent of it raised from black people of no great means.

On July 13, Thurgood reported preparations for the re-argument to the National Legal Committee. He had assembled a team and placed the historical research under John A. Davis, a political scientist at Lincoln University, his alma mater, assisted by Mabel Smythe, another political scientist, who later would teach at Brooklyn College and in 1977 became American Ambassador to the United Republic of Cameroon. With Davis, Thurgood had recruited Howard Jay Graham, law librarian of the Los Angeles County Bar Association Library, an authority on the history of the Fourteenth Amendment, and Horace Mann Bond, president of Lincoln and a historian of early education for blacks. They later enlisted C. Vann Woodward, of Johns Hopkins, and John Hope Franklin, of Howard, both of whom had studied and written extensively on Reconstruction. Davis asked social scientists and educators, including Kenneth Clark, Otto Klineberg, and Dean William O. Penrose, of the University of Delaware—situated near the newly integrated Delaware schools—as well as staff member June Shagaloff, to study those and other recently desegregated schools "with the idea of devising an administratively sound plan under which integration can be accomplished without undue delay."

Connie Motley was given the task of researching the power of Congress to outlaw segregated schools under Section 5 of the Fourteenth Amendment; Bob Carter was asked to study cases in which the Court had overruled prior decisions; staff member Elwood

Chisolm to study the debates and early cases concerning the contemporary understanding of the terms *civil, political,* and *social* (words used in *Plessy* to distinguish matters controlled by the Fourteenth Amendment from those left untouched by it); staff lawyer Dave Pinsky to analyze cases where constitutional rights were defined as immediate, in contrast to antitrust cases where gradual adjustment sometimes was ordered; and Spotts Robinson to study cases where special masters had been appointed by the Supreme Court. I got the task of defining the equity powers of federal courts (and Delaware state courts) and was asked particularly to study and report on the reluctance of federal courts to supervise the performance of state administrative functions.

Other scholars joined our effort, including Alfred H. Kelly, of Wayne State University in Detroit, who had written a book on constitutional history, and who came to play a large part in the final drafting of the historical argument. Some scholars refused to participate. The noted historian Henry Steele Commager declined because he thought that our position on the history was wrong. He wrote: "The framers of the amendment did not, as far as we now know, intend that it should be used to end segregation in schools. . . . I strongly urge that you consider dropping this particular argument as I think it tends to weaken your case."

Bill Coleman recruited friends from law school and former Supreme Court clerks to research ratification of the Fourteenth Amendment in thirty-six states. He requested information about states immediately preceding submission of the Fourteenth Amendment for ratification and also at the time of submission: Whether there were provisions referring to segregation in the state constitutions that the secessionist states were required to submit to Congress after the Civil War before they could be readmitted to the Union; whether schools were unsegregated in those states between 1865 and 1877; and what the legislative history of segregation laws was after adoption of the Fourteenth Amendment.

Some of Bill's friends in the Deep South helped him with his research at considerable personal risk to themselves. Truman Hobbs in Montgomery, Alabama, son of the congressman who had argued to retain segregation in dining cars in the *Henderson* case, researched

Alabama, and James Wilson of Atlanta researched Georgia. Hobbs became a federal judge in Alabama and Wilson a partner in one of Georgia's leading firms; if their roles had been known then their careers most assuredly would have been ruined.

This foray into original intent posed seemingly unanswerable questions. How do you allocate weight to the differing expressions of different framers, to those who voted proposals up or down and the many members of the many ratifying state legislatures across the country? Most had said nothing about schools; a few had occasionally, but hardly systematically. Some may have changed their positions between the time of a recorded statement and the vote. Expressions about formal education were particularly sparse, because it didn't play the role it does today. But the most important factor in examining "intent" is the level of generality at which one chooses to address the question. If the question were "What did the Congress and the ratifying legislatures intend specifically with regard to schools as they then existed?" there might be one answer. This might be called the micro level of inquiry. But if the question were taken to be "What did the framers and ratifiers intend with regard to activities essential to full citizenship?" an inquiry, so to speak, at the macro level, the question of intent might elicit another answer. For, in the mid-twentieth century, a list of prerequisites essential to full citizenship certainly had to include equal access to good education.

Justices Burton and Frankfurter's questions to John W. Davis posed this dichotomy. As advocates, however, we felt we had to answer both versions of the question.

As we went about our labors, on September 8, Chief Justice Vinson died. President Eisenhower appointed Earl Warren to succeed him at the commencement of the new term. The change had no discernible effect on our work; I can't recall any speculation about what difference the new chief justice would make. If we had reflected, we would not have been encouraged, for we would have remembered that Warren had been a prosecutor in his native state of California and that he had played a supporting role in the relocation of Japanese Americans from the West Coast during the Second World War. Philip Elman has written, however, that Felix Frankfurter remarked at

Vinson's death, "This is the first indication I have ever had that there is a God."

Our massive effort culminated in a meeting of more than one hundred participants at the Overseas Press Club on West Fortieth Street in September. It divided into seminars to consider all the major problems and made recommendations for the final product. Then, in October, Thurgood, Bob, Connie, Spotts, Lou Redding, Bob Ming, and I met with Alfred Kelly over a period of five days to struggle with the history, which concluded in a drafting session between Ming and Kelly. Finally, that draft was redone in November by Kelly and John Frank.

Our battle over the history of the Fourteenth Amendment was finished and nothing would be gained by rehearsing the contending positions. While we came up with a highly persuasive argument at the level of the general purposes of the amendment, when we got down to specifics about education there were difficulties. For that reason our brief led off with the answer to the third question, the one in which the Court asked whether, without regard to the understanding of the framers, it was within the power of the Court to construe the amendment to abolish school segregation? We pointed out that "normal exercise of the judicial function calls for a declaration that the state is without power to enforce distinctions based upon race or color in affording educational opportunities in the public schools," and set forth the arguments that had worked so well for us in *Sweatt* and *McLaurin*.

On the history, one difficulty was that the same Congress that had enacted the Fourteenth Amendment appropriated funds specifically for segregated schools in the District of Columbia (indeed, as did all Congresses after that one), suggesting at the very least that it wasn't hell bent on ending segregated education. As to this uncomfortable circumstance, a Committee on Historical Development, which included John Frank, Horace Mann Bond, Mabel Smythe, and Buell Gallagher, wrote:

> We feel that here we are at the heart of one of our most important difficulties. It is imperative that we so analyze the District of Columbia material as to show that this is not indicative of a belief

that the Constitution condones segregation. We believe that the material can be analyzed to show the exact opposite. To show a widespread expanse of the conviction that segregation was incompatible with equal protection.

The way to do this, the memorandum suggested, would be to point out that the Thirty-ninth Congress inherited an "institutionalized system of segregation in the District, which was begun immediately upon the termination of slavery in the District," and that "early action came from a background of separate and discriminatory treatment of free Negroes in the District in the late 1850's." The congressional legislation was "permissive only" with regard to segregation and did not compel it. At the same time, the "Freedmen's Bureau was running non-segregated education in the District, and . . . private organizations were also running non-segregated education. . . . Sometimes colored students were, in fact, introduced into the white schools by action of the District of Columbia School Board."

The memorandum proposed taking the position that failure to eliminate segregation in the District was "not . . . a matter of constitutional judgment" but a "yielding to financial and political pressure which in no wise reflects a constitutional judgment." It included the following caveat: *"It is the firm consensus of the group that we shall not attempt to make too much of the foregoing lest it may boomerang."*

Indeed, the brief heeded the caveat so well that it did not discuss education in the District of Columbia at all. But when the segregating states' briefs made much of school segregation in the District of Columbia, we proceeded down the line of the memorandum, and in our reply responded that "the 39th Congress considered the District of Columbia school situation perfunctorily, as routine business, with little debate and practically no discussion of note. There is nothing in any of the debates on these measures to indicate that Congress contemplated or understood that the Fourteenth Amendment did not prohibit segregated schools."

The history of the Civil Rights Act of 1866 presented an equally prickly problem. An earlier version of the bill commanded "no discrimination in civil rights or immunities . . . on account of race, color, or previous condition of servitude." The "no discrimination" clause became immensely controversial; some opponents claimed that it would confer equality with regard to real property, punishment for crime, and require the abolition of separate schools, all of which they regarded as unthinkable. Others contended that Congress had no authority under the Constitution to adopt such legislation. As enacted, however, the 1866 act omitted the "no discrimination" clause. That would be bad enough for our position, but the excision was made on the motion of John Bingham, the very person who later drafted the Fourteenth Amendment. He advocated the amendment for the purpose, at least in part, of placing the 1866 act beyond the possibility of congressional amendment or repeal, should conservatives gain control of the Congress. This lent support to an argument that the framer of the Fourteenth Amendment had no intention that the act, and, inferentially, the amendment, would prohibit school segregation.

We decided to deal with the problem by arguing that Bingham's amendment to the Civil Rights Act of 1866, which removed the "no discrimination in civil rights" clause, was adopted "simply because a majority of the members of the House believed that so sweeping a measure could not be justified under the Constitution as it stood. They accepted Bingham's argument that the proper remedy for removing racial distinctions and classifications in the states was a new amendment to the Constitution."

It was also arguable that Bingham, who moved to remove the sweeping "no discrimination" clause from the 1866 act, saw the Constitution as not yet ready to support it, and that he saw the Fourteenth Amendment as curing this defect. Though this was not something we could prove with certainty, it did beat saying nothing on the point.

We were able to argue even more forcefully that proponents of the Civil Rights Act of 1875, among whom were many supporters of the Fourteenth Amendment, understood that it would prohibit segregated schools. Michael W. McConnell, whom President George W. Bush appointed Judge to the U.S. Court of Appeals for the Tenth Circuit, in an exhaustive examination of the legislative history of the amendment and the 1875 act, concluded that "a very substantial portion of the Congress, including leading framers of the Amendment, subscribed—often passionately—to the view that school segregation violates the Fourteenth Amendment." Bills prohibiting school segregation failed because of "procedural obstacles, including super-majority vote requirements and filibuster tactics."

The principal difficulty in researching the question of what went into the ratification debates was that virtually none of the state legislatures kept records of them, although something about intentions might have appeared in the newspapers and could be inferred from contemporaneous actions. But the researchers also found much better stuff than we ever expected. Nevertheless, we had to recognize that school segregation was widespread even in the North. On October 5, Horace Mann Bond, still in the midst of his research, wrote to Mabel Smythe:

NOW THE WONDERFUL THING ABOUT THESE TWELVE STATES—NEBRASKA [which, while not a secessionist state, was admitted to the Union during the life of the Thirty-ninth Congress, which prepared the Fourteenth Amendment], TENNESSEE, ALABAMA, ARKANSAS, FLORIDA, LOUISIANA, NORTH CAROLINA, SOUTH CAROLINA, MISSISSIPPI, TEXAS, VIRGINIA, GEORGIA IS THAT NOT A SINGLE ONE WAS ADMITTED, OR READMITTED, TO THE UNION, WITH ANY PHRASE IN THE CONSTITUTIONS (CONSTITUTIONS DRAWN AND REDRAWN TO MEET THE SCRUTINY OF THE 39 AND SUCCESSIVE CONGRESSES, AND TO BE IN CONFORMITY WITH THE CONSTITUTION AND WITH THE FOURTEENTH AMENDMENT)—*that sanctioned segregation, or mentioned race, in connection with the public school system. I do not know at this time what the Statutes, on final check, and recheck would show; but I think the rule is perfectly unanimous.*

The point was that these States *knew,* that if they put anything defining or restricting rights of any kind, into their constitutions and statutes, in terms of race, *prior* to readmission, that they would not be readmitted.

What better proof do you want, of the intent of the 39th Congress, or of the contemplation or understanding of the ratifying States?

The segregating states' eventual response to this argument was that prior to readmission to the Union these states' legislatures were controlled by blacks and carpetbaggers; following admission and return to conservative white control, eight of these states instituted school segregation, which, the states argued, would not have been done if they had understood it to be prohibited.

Other memos were not so encouraging. A preliminary memorandum from a New York team concluded: "It is apparent that New York's official position was that segregation was still legal as long as 'equal' facilities were furnished to Negroes." But, as the memorandum pointed out, white school appropriations were about three times more per capita than those for blacks during that period. California had segregated schools both before and after adoption of the Fourteenth Amendment. Connecticut, and other New England states, sometimes within a decade or more following ratification, prohibited school segregation. It was impossible to tie what the states did conclusively to the Fourteenth Amendment, but surely we were able to make a lawyer-like case concerning ratification. Lawyer-like, yes, but far from airtight. In our reply brief we printed elaborate pull-out charts detailing states' laws and practices before and after readmission and before and after ratification.

But if our argument at the micro level was difficult, at the macro level, that is, concerning the overall ambition of the framers of the Fourteenth Amendment, we were in wonderful shape. Howard Jay Graham wrote a ninety-eight-page paper, which we distilled into a thirty-six-page appendix and used elsewhere. His paper began:

> The Thirteenth and Fourteenth Amendments are fully intelligible and can be correctly understood only in the broad perspective of the anti-slavery movement of which they were the consummation. . . .
>
> Ethical and religious opinions were here molding and remolding constitutional doctrine. Moral premises were being translated into legal and constitutional premises—i.e., *enforceable rights*. This was being done, if you please, by a "due processing" and "equal protecting" of the law of nature. . . .
>
> In short, the Fourteenth Amendment, in Professor ten Broek's phrase, marked a "reconsummation" of the anti-slavery movement, and of that movement's broad purpose to root out the "badges and

incidents" of slavery. It was drafted by the Joint Committee of Fifteen on Reconstruction. Ten members of that Committee are known to have grown up in states where they were exposed for years to the old anti-slavery constitutional theory.

But the question then arose: how does one account for later interpretations of the Fourteenth Amendment that not only ignored these origins but condoned the opposite in, for example, *Plessy v. Ferguson?*

We turned to a paper C. Vann Woodward had written for us, "The Background of the Abandonment of Reconstruction" (a distillation of his great work, *Reunion and Reaction*), which described how Rutherford B. Hayes acceded to the presidency in 1877 even though "Tilden received over a quarter of million votes more than Hayes." Congress created an electoral commission to rule on disputed vote counts in several states and to assign electoral votes. Woodward's paper demonstrated that a deal was struck and that in exchange for a promise to take certain economic steps beneficial to the white South, Hayes gained enough disputed electoral votes to be elected. As Woodward wrote:

> The Reconstruction policy was quickly abandoned, radicalism was renounced, Federal troops were withdrawn from South Carolina and Louisiana, future use of force was disavowed, and the conservative governments that replaced the Carpetbaggers were publicly informed that responsibility for the disposition of the freedman's status was thenceforth in their hands. Acquiescence in the abandonment of Reconstruction and the adoption of the new policy of laissez faire accumulated in the form of endorsements by the press, by public opinion, by administrative rulings, and eventually by decisions of the courts.

We distilled Woodward's twenty-seven-page paper into a part of the brief concerning early decisions that treated the Fourteenth Amendment in strongly egalitarian terms, like *Strauder v. West Virginia,* the Slaughter House Cases, and, of course, Justice Harlan's dissent in *Plessy.*

In our Summary of Argument, we encapsulated the historical argument in a couple of sentences:

> The Fourteenth Amendment was actually the culmination of the determined efforts of the Radical Republican majority in Congress to incorporate into our fundamental law the well-defined equalitarian principle of complete equality for all without regard to race or color. The debates in the 39th Congress and succeeding Congresses clearly reveal the intention that the Fourteenth Amendment would work a revolutionary change in our state-federal relationship by denying to the states the power to distinguish on the basis of race.

The government's brief took essentially the same position.

The segregating states hit hard on school segregation in the District of Columbia, the amendment to the Civil Rights Bill of 1866, and the retention of school segregation in many of the ratifying states.

The stubborn problem remaining at the end of the historical exercise was how the justices would reconcile the two versions. One told of the framers embracing abolitionist idealism, committing generally to full equality, and, in debates on the 1875 act, expressing the belief that the amendment prohibited school segregation; the other presented examples of less than full commitment to complete equality—amending the 1866 bill and sustaining segregated schools in the District, for example. When there was original intent of several different sorts the choice of which intent to follow came down to the values of the justices, and on that count we felt vastly stronger than the other side.

Alfred Kelly, one of our principal consultants on the Fourteenth Amendment, addressed the American Historical Association in 1961 and angered some of the lawyers who had been with us in *Brown* by saying he had faced a "deadly opposition between [his] professional integrity as a historian and [his] wishes and hopes with respect to a contemporary question of values." He referred to "bearing down on facts, sliding off facts, quietly ignoring facts and, above all, interpreting facts in a way" that would "get by" the justices. He would have preferred a scholar's paper that set forth "on the one hand" and "on the other hand," without marshaling facts to support a particular conclusion. He seemed to be unaware of the nature of legal advocacy, in which the other side is given both the opportunity and responsibility for presenting the conflicting view, and for pointing out errors, omissions, and misinterpretations, if any, in the first side's presentation. Ultimately, he conceded that while the conclusions we had offered to the Court had not been, in his view, "hammered out with . . . historical truth as our [only] objective, [they] nonetheless contain[ed] an essential measure of historical truth."

Kenneth Clark's research team had the assignment of suggesting how desegregation might be best achieved. It conducted a massive study, not merely in education, but across American society of churches, the armed forces, housing, interstate transportation, public accommodations, organized sports, employment, politics, higher education, prep schools, and elementary and secondary public schools. It considered instances where desegregation had been brought about by population changes, the pressure of public opinion, referendums, community action, legislation, and law-suits. It concluded that to desegregate with a minimum of social disturbance there should be:

A. A clear and unequivocal statement of policy by leaders with prestige. . . .
B. Firm enforcement . . . and persistence. . . .
C. A willingness to deal with violations . . . by . . . strong enforcement action. . . .
D. A refusal of the authorities to . . . tolerate subterfuges. . . .
E. An appeal . . . in terms of . . . religious principles . . . and acceptance of the American traditions of fair play and equal justice.

The *Journal of Social Issues* published the study in full.

In our 1953 brief we made no reference to the study or its underlying materials. (However, in 1954, in a brief dealing with implementation only, we made considerable use of it.) As for time to comply, we hung tough and in a handful of pages set forth the straight legal proposition that the children should be admitted to integrated schools "forthwith." We agreed that time might be taken to make administrative changes, but not to deal with threats of violence, to fire black teachers, or to close public schools. We attacked the United States' last brief's grade-a-year and school-by-school plans as "intolerable": many plaintiffs would never obtain relief. Defendants should offer reasons for delay; we would respond and the courts could decide.

Before the brief was put in final form Thurgood sent the Summary of Argument to lawyers outside the staff for comment and editing, including to Lou Pollak, who was then in the State Department. Thurgood had taught that the Summary of Argument was the most important part of a brief; most justices read it first, some don't read beyond it. Lou thought it wasn't clear and didn't argue forcefully enough. Lou, who writes beautifully and with great precision, self-deprecatingly recalls that he painstakingly rewrote the section and brought it down the hall for a secretary to type. When she returned it she asked whether she might ask a question: "Mr. Pollak, the brief was so interesting. I really enjoyed typing it," she said. "It was clear and well written. But, I have one question. Do you want the little colored children to go to school with the little white children, or don't you?"

The states' briefs argued that courts might allow time for transition. The United States agreed on the need for a transition period, but backtracked from its first brief by not repeating suggestions about grade-a-year and school-by-school, arguing that there should not be delay of more than a year, although a school district might ask for more time.

Reargument

The first reargument began December 7, 1953, a year after the original argument. Thurgood and Spotts decided it would be best to combine the arguments in Virginia and South Carolina, assigning to Spotts the history and to Thurgood the argument about judicial power, obviating the need to repeat each argument in each case. Virginia, South Carolina, and the Court agreed; those cases were combined. From the beginning, the arguments were different from last year's. Spotts led off with a meticulous, dull, historical presentation and spoke for perhaps forty minutes before he was asked a question by, of course, Justice Frankfurter, about the weight to be given individual utterances by congressmen or senators. Not a terribly important issue, and a question to which everyone knew the answer. Justice Reed asked several questions about the power of Congress, and that was all. Had they made up their minds? Didn't they care about the history? I wondered and others did too.

Thurgood's presentation was equally uninspiring, eliciting unedifying questions about the basis of decision in *McLaurin*: had it been decided under separate-but-equal or was it a tacit rejection of segregation per se? Law professors' questions. Of course, the decision in *McLaurin* could be described either way. Thurgood was thrown a bit off base when he got questions about the history, for which Spotts had specially prepared, but segued back to his prepared presentation. Thurgood made clear that we rejected segregation in any shape, manner, or form.

John W. Davis, representing the State of South Carolina, and lead advocate on the opposition's side, argued for close to an hour, also with only a couple of questions. His peroration survives as one of the grand rhetorical errors of advocacy:

> I am reminded—and I hope it won't be treated as a reflection on anybody—of Aesop's fable of the dog and the meat: The dog, with a fine piece of meat in his mouth, crossed a bridge and saw the shadow in the stream and plunged for it and lost both substance and shadow.
>
> Here is equal education, not promised, not prophesied, but present. Shall it be thrown away on some fancied question of racial prestige? . . .
>
> I entreat them to remember the age-old motto that the best is often the enemy of good.

As he closed, tears ran down his cheeks. I later expressed my surprise to my classmate Marvin Frankel, who was in Court that day, having argued a case for the government just prior to ours. He said that one of his colleagues had whispered, "That sonofabitch cries in every case he argues."

Justin Moore for Virginia received the same largely silent treatment as Spotts. A hint of things to come emerged when he suggested that Virginia might desegregate by setting up three sets of schools: black, white, and non-segregated.

Thurgood's rebuttal was his best argument ever. First he picked up on John W. Davis's reference to "prestige":

> As Mr. Davis said yesterday, the only thing the Negroes are trying to get is prestige.
>
> Exactly correct. Ever since the Emancipation Proclamation, the Negro has been trying to get what was recognized in *Strauder v. West Virginia,* which is the same status as anybody else regardless of race.

And, building on an argument he made the year before, Thurgood concluded with passion:

> I got the feeling on hearing the discussion yesterday that when you put a white child in a school with a whole lot of colored children, the child would fall apart or something. Everybody knows that is not true. Those same kids in Virginia and South Carolina—and I have seen them do it—they play in the streets together, they play on their farms together, they go down the road together, they separate to go to school, they come out of school and play ball together. They have to be separated in school.
>
> There is some magic to it. You can have them voting together, you can have them not restricted because of law in the houses they live in. You can have them going to the same state university and the same college, but if they go to elementary and high school, the world will fall apart. And it is the exact same argument that has been made to this Court over and over again, and we submit that when they charge us with making a legislative argument, it is in truth they who are making the legislative argument.
>
> They can't take race out of this case. From the day this case was filed until this moment, nobody has in any form or fashion, despite the fact I made it clear in the opening argument that I was relying on it, done anything to distinguish this statute from the Black Codes, which they must admit, because nobody can dispute, say anything anybody wants to say, one way or the other, the Fourteenth Amendment was intended to deprive the states of power to enforce Black Codes or anything else like it. . . .
>
> The only thing can be is an inherent determination that the people who were formerly in slavery, regardless of anything else, shall be kept as near that stage as possible, and now is the time, we

submit, that this Court should make it clear that that is not what our Constitution stands for.

Assistant Attorney General J. Lee Rankin, a dry, uninspiring Nebraskan, whose presentation, nevertheless, perhaps for that reason, was highly effective, argued for the United States and after a few minutes of clear sailing it was questions every inch of the way. The Court had invited the United States to participate. The government's brief for the first argument (a Truman administration product) attacked segregation head-on. This time (under Eisenhower), it was a bit vague; although called a "supplemental brief," it only implicitly embraced the earlier position. Justice Douglas pushed Rankin, asking what was the position of the government. Rankin replied, "It is the position of the Department of Justice that segregation in public schools cannot be maintained under the Fourteenth Amendment." We breathed sighs of relief.

On implementation, Rankin introduced "handling the matter with deliberate speed." On another occasion he said "diligent speed." He urged sending the cases to the lower courts and placing the burden on the defendants as to how much time they would need to adjust, suggesting a year for presentation and consideration of plans. Nothing more specific was offered.

The argument on the District of Columbia case was punctuated with many questions about its segregation policy. A majority of the school board now consisted of new members who were opposed to segregation. A number of the justices wanted to know whether there still was a lawsuit or whether the District had capitulated. (By this time Delaware had integrated somewhat, and Topeka was no longer resisting integration.)

Justice Black asked Milton Korman: "Will you let us know in the morning, when the case comes up, whether the Board wants you to defend this case?"

The next day, in a rather confused set of exchanges, Korman took the position that the school board had not *officially* changed its position and he was permitted to continue.

Jim Nabrit, Jr., once more made a patriotic appeal, with tremendous effect:

America is a great country in which we can come before the Court and express to the Court the great concern which we have, where our great government is dealing with us, and we are not in the position that the animals were in George Orwell's satirical novel, *Animal Farm*, where after the revolution the dictatorship was set up and the sign set up there that all animals were equal, was changed to read "but some are more equal than others."

Our Constitution has no provision across it that all men are equal but that white men are more equal than others.

Under this statute and under this country, under this Constitution, and under the protection of this Court, we believe that we, too, are equal.

Bob Carter, whose argument preceded Jim's, and I, following Jim, ran into similar problems for similar reasons: we were arguing that defendants should integrate the Topeka and Wilmington schools, but in each case integration was under way. In Topeka, the school board had abandoned its policy of segregation; in Wilmington, the chancellor's decree was being implemented. Justice Frankfurter badgered Bob with the proposition that since his clients were getting what they had asked for, he no longer had any case. Bob, after perhaps ten minutes, said, "I certainly have no real desire to proceed with an argument," and sat down.

In my own argument, I tried to raise the point that the Delaware case remained alive because defendants claimed the right to re-segregate once blacks got equal schools. But Frankfurter pounced on me with the assertion that I should have cross-appealed if I wanted a ruling on the constitutionality of segregation. Of course, we hadn't cross-appealed, because we wanted our case to be heard right away, along with the others. A cross-appeal would have had to await the other side's answer, defeating our purpose in waiving response. I argued that the Court should affirm the chancellor, not on the grounds he gave—desegregate because the black schools were physically inferior—but because segregation was unconstitutional. (That's what the Court ultimately did.)

But I felt that I was in a cul-de-sac and couldn't get off that issue into anything else I wanted to talk about. At the mid-afternoon break we hastily conferred and agreed that Thurgood could use the balance of my time more profitably by concluding the Delaware argument and folding all the cases together. He rushed to the clerk's office to ask permission to change the batting order. The clerk, Harold Willey, who had been in the bathroom, came running out, his suspenders dangling, and hastened to convey word to the justices that Thurgood would wrap up.

It all seemed rather curious. They had turned our world upside down with a demand for the most exhaustive historical research ever conducted for a Supreme Court case, and with inordinately difficult questions about implementation. Then they gave most of their attention to whether we had live lawsuits or issues. Even if they were to get rid of Topeka, Wilmington, and the District on mootness grounds, South Carolina and Virginia would continue to stare them in the face. Did they, perhaps, not care about the history? Or were the questions at oral argument just a game justices play?

Most of us assumed that we would win, but with the exception of Spotts Robinson and Jim Nabrit, who spent a long evening analyzing the Court, none of us concluded that we would win unanimously. The rest of us vacillated in our predicted outcomes from five to four, to six to three, to seven to two. The general view was that Justice Jackson was opposed to segregation (not least because he just had returned from prosecuting the Nazis at Nuremburg), but was leaning toward deciding that Congress should end it, not the Court. Douglas and Black in many ways had shown that they were on our side—they had opposed sending the South Carolina case back for findings about equalization as not relevant—and would be safe votes. As to Frankfurter, we followed Bill Coleman's intuition. Frankfurter had hired him as the first black law clerk on the Supreme Court. He always voted right in civil rights cases involving blacks, with the arguable exception of not having joined the dissenters in the second *Sipuel* case, going along with calling for a further hearing. He had been on the NAACP National Legal Committee. Bill thought he would vote with us. Tom Clark, although a Texan, had always voted right in civil rights matters. Thurgood knew him personally and felt good about his vote. But personal relationships were not always good predictors of how a justice might come down.

A case in point had been Oliver Hill's optimism about Vinson, who had written the opinions favoring us in *Sweatt* and other cases. Oliver's wife's brother, Armistead Walker, had been Vinson's chauffeur, and when Vinson moved from the Senate to the Supreme Court, he made Armistead his bailiff there. Armistead was so close to the Vinson family that Oliver, his wife, and son became friendly with them too. So much so that Oliver once seated his son Oliver, Jr. (Dukey), in the chief justice's chair in the Supreme Court, hoping that some day he would attain that position on his own. When, much later, records of the Court's conferences revealed that before his death Vinson had been against us, Oliver was dismayed—personal friendship and official positions about blacks were not necessarily related.

There were no clear views about Minton, who was perceived as possibly negative, or Burton, who seemed to be a possible favorable vote. Reed was counted by everyone as pretty much against us. There was general optimism that we would win by some margin, however, because we were on a roll. Until then we hadn't lost any case, although at times the victory had been empty, as in *Sipuel,* where the Court ducked facing up to Oklahoma's refusal to integrate.

At Davis, Polk, John W. Davis's law firm, the lawyers saw things differently. Davis assigned two young lawyers to the case, Sydnor Thompson, a 1950 Harvard Law School graduate, who sat next to him at the oral argument, and William C. Meagher, as well as Taggart Whipple, who supervised the younger lawyers. Nothing at all like the immense army we assembled. Thompson, who came from Lynchburg, Virginia, recalled that he spent 322 hours, 15 minutes, on the case, writing the principal part of the brief, including the history of the Fourteenth Amendment, which Davis touched up. Meagher wrote the part dealing with the history of ratification in the states. Thompson's research absolutely convinced him that Congress had no concept of abolishing school segregation. When he read our brief he couldn't see how we could have reached the opposite conclusion.

As Davis and his colleagues counted the votes, they believed they had Reed and Jackson on their side at the very least. They had reason to be optimistic about Frankfurter, because they thought he wouldn't want the courts to become involved in administering school desegregation. There was a chance at Clark and maybe, out there, another vote or two to make a majority for their side. Davis did not contemplate the possibility that they could lose unanimously.

We hadn't been too far off in guessing, but not exactly right either. Speculation, particularly that based on personal factors, often is off base. While we weren't wildly inaccurate following the first argument, we didn't have it exactly right. Notes of the Justices, taken before the second argument indicate that Chief Justice Vinson told the conference that he believed *Plessy* had been decided correctly. It was not clear, but it appears that only Justices Black, Burton, Minton and Douglas would have voted to hold segregation unconstitutional. Justice Frankfurter's vote was uncertain. So the vote would have been 5–4 to reverse or to affirm.

When Earl Warren became Chief the picture changed dramatically. A summary of the notes indicates that the conference began with Earl Warren asserting that Plessy had relegated blacks to second class citizenship. The conference ended with six votes for prohibiting segregation; only Justices Jackson, Clark and Reed were opposed. The first two, however, indicated that they were open to persuasion.

The Time Has Come

Once, when Sydnor Thompson was in the library, Stuart Marks, another young associate at Davis, Polk, pointed a finger at him, looked him in the eye, and asked, "Do you ever think you're on the wrong side?" At the time, Thompson had difficulty understanding this challenge. Eventually Thompson went on to practice in Charlotte, North Carolina, and became a friend of Julius Chambers, who succeeded me as head of LDF. Thompson ultimately said, "I thank God every day we lost the case. It was an idea whose time had come."

PART III

BROWN DECIDED:

EYES ON THE FUTURE

CHAPTER 8

A HISTORIC TURN

Victory

Thurgood got a tip that the School Segregation Cases would be decided on May 17, 1954, the last day of the Court's term, and went to Washington to hear Earl Warren read the opinion in *Brown v. Board of Education*,[1] a name now instantly recognized by almost every American. In what may well have been the most important Supreme Court decision of the century, maybe ever, we won unanimously. Though the opinion itself was relatively brief and simple (there was a separate and even shorter one for the District of Columbia),[2] it touched on all the stubborn points that had bedeviled civil rights lawyers over the years: the history, the precedents, and harm done by segregation. The historical sources "at best . . . are inconclusive," the Court held. Moreover, because public education was rudimentary at the end of the Civil War, "it is not surprising that there should be so little in the history of the Fourteenth Amendment relating to its intended effect on public education." We had fought the opposition to a draw on the history.

The history, however, deserves an additional word. While the Court could not conclude that the amendment or its framers and ratifiers "intended" that there be either segregated or nonsegregated schools, in effect it accepted our way of looking at the question of intent, embracing the view that there was a clear intent to prohibit

---

[1] Brown v. Board of Education of Topeka, 347 U.S. 483 (1954).

[2] Bolling v. Sharpe, 347 U.S. 497 (1954).

state discrimination that might stigmatize black people as inferior. It did not matter whether or not the framers had been thinking of education at the time. This was the moral and religious notion of equality that, we had argued, the Fourteenth Amendment constitutionalized.

The precedents? The Court adopted our view again: *Plessy* was a travel case and didn't pertain to education; other school cases based on *Plessy* were irrelevant. *Sweatt* and *McLaurin* found inequality in the fact that segregation inhibited the plaintiffs' "ability to study, to engage in discussions and exchange views with other students, and, in general, to learn [their] profession," and that "such considerations apply with added force to children in grade and high schools."

Quoting the Kansas District Court, which had adopted the God-given eloquence of Louisa Holt, the psychologist who testified for us, the Supreme Court cited the harm that segregation inflicts on black children—that it denotes a sense of inferiority and retards their educational and mental development. *Plessy*, it will be recalled, had made a contrary social scientific assertion that "the underlying fallacy" of the defendant's argument was the assumption that segregation "stamps the colored race with a badge of inferiority," but if so, it would be "solely because the colored race chooses to put that construction upon it." To this, the Supreme Court replied: "Whatever may have been the extent of psychological knowledge at the time of *Plessy v. Ferguson*, [the finding that segregation is harmful] is amply supported by modern authority. Any language in *Plessy v. Ferguson* contrary to this finding is rejected."

Here the Court placed a footnote, footnote 11, at the bottom of the page, citing works by Kenneth Clark, other social scientists, and Gunnar Myrdal's *An American Dilemma*. The footnote became tremendously controversial, giving rise to charges that *Brown* was based on social science, not law. But, of course, *Plessy's* contention that no real harm comes about from the stigma of forced segregation was based on the then-current understanding of social science factors.

The questions the decision did not address were those dealing with relief, making no determination about how segregation might be dismantled. It scheduled the cases for another argument on the last two of its five questions, in which it had asked for comments and ideas on how the change might be brought about if the Court were to decide as it eventually did.

There remained the District of Columbia case. Because the Fourteenth Amendment applies only to the states, and the District of Columbia is not a state, it is governed by the Fifth Amendment's provision, which prohibits the United States from denying life, liberty, or property without due process of law. Liberty, the Court held, "extends to the full range of conduct which the individual is free to pursue. . . . In view of our decision that the Constitution prohibits the states from maintaining racially segregated public schools, it would be unthinkable that the same Constitution would impose a lesser duty on the Federal Government."

That the *Brown* decision was unanimous is universally attributed to Earl Warren's political skills in bringing along some of the doubters, including Jackson and Reed, likely the strongest dissenter. Bill Coleman says that Frankfurter also worked on Reed, telling him that a dissent is written for the future, but that there was no future for segregation.

Thurgood rushed to a telephone and called me with the news. I immediately called Roy Wilkins and Walter White. Walter White was the Secretary of the NAACP, its highest executive officer. He was a Negro as defined by the law of Georgia, his original home. But, in fact he had a fair complexion and by appearance was white. He used his appearance to infiltrate racist groups. He was a highly influential public figure, friendly with leading political figures including Eleanor Roosevelt. He wrote important books and articles on race, including its role in international affairs. Roy Wilkins, who succeeded White as head of the NAACP when White died, not long after Brown was decided, was an urbane, sophisticated black journalist who then led the NAACP during most of the years that I was at LDF. Thurgood also called Kenneth Clark, who was teaching a class, which he left to receive the news. The switchboards at the Association and LDF began lighting up. Walter called a press conference, which he dominated while Thurgood sat quietly. After every other Supreme Court victory, we had celebrated with a raucous, boozy party. But after *Brown* there was quiet. It was all so awesome. We still didn't know what it meant or where it would lead. Besides, if the decision were not to become merely a moral victory, we had to prepare for the argument on the relief questions.

Two days after the decision we had a dinner for the lawyers and leading witnesses at the Roosevelt Hotel. Kenneth Clark recalls that Thurgood asked Bill Coleman and Bob Ming to bow down to him and admit they were wrong.

John W. Davis refused to take a fee from the state of South Carolina and in lieu of payment, Governor Byrnes sent him a silver tea service, which was displayed in the law firm's library. On it was an inscription stating that it was a gift from the people of South Carolina. Stuart Marks notes that despite the donor identification, the gift givers did not likely include the black people of South Carolina.

First Reactions

A week later, the Court summarily vacated, for reconsideration in light of *Brown,* judgments in two university cases and a junior college case.[3] The order said, in effect, that now that we were into the next step, desegregation at elementary and high school levels, the Court would tolerate no more fooling around in higher education. Significantly, in the Louisville City Amphitheatre case,[4] which presented the state action question of whether a lessee of the city could exclude blacks, the Court vacated the judgment of the court of appeals "for consideration in the light of the Segregation Cases . . . and conditions that now prevail." While *Brown* may have seemed to

---

[3] Florida ex rel. Hawkins v. Board of Control, 342 U.S. 877 (1951), *motion denied,* 60 So. 2d 162 (Fla. 1952), *vacated,* 347 U.S. 971 (1954), *cert. denied and vacated,* 350 U.S. 413 (1956); Board of Supervisors of Louisiana State University and Agricultural & Mechanical College v. Tureaud, 202 F.2d 807 (5th Cir. 1953), *vacated,* 347 U.S. 971, *on rehearing,* 225 F.2d 434 (5th Cir. 1955) and 228 F.2d 895 (5th Cir. 1956), *cert. denied,* 351 U.S. 924 (1956); Battle v. Wichita Falls Jr. College, 101 F. Supp. 82 (N.D. Tex. 1951), *aff'd,* 204 F.2d 632 (5th Cir. 1953), *cert. denied,* 347 U.S. 974 (1954).

[4] Muir v. Louisville Park Theatrical Association, 102 F. Supp 525 (W.D. Ky. 1953), *aff'd,* 202 F.2d 275 (6th Cir. 1953), *vacated and remanded,* 347 U.S. 971 (1954).

have nothing to do with that issue, the order illustrated that its power reached beyond the question of segregation in schools.

Florida enacted a complex procedural scheme, known as "pupil placement," soon adopted across the South. Districts assigned black children to black schools and required them to apply for transfer, virtually always finding a basis to turn them down. Criteria included the effect of admitting children upon "orderly and efficient administration," "effective instruction," and "health, safety, education and general welfare." Louisiana made its contribution to legal anarchy by adopting a constitutional amendment, soon copied elsewhere, that provided that "all public elementary and secondary schools in the State of Louisiana shall be operated separately for white and colored children."

Equally disturbing, mobs took their cue from their political leaders and a movement of massive resistance was born. In September 1954, to protest enrollment of eleven black high school freshmen in downstate Delaware Milford High School, fifteen hundred whites met at the American Legion hall. The superintendent closed the schools. The state board ordered them reopened with the black children in attendance, and criticized the local board for not having consulted the state before taking action. The local board resigned and the state took over. Four thousand whites then rallied at an airport meeting led by Bryant Bowles, president of the National Association for the Advancement of White People. Schools reopened, surrounded by reporters, cameramen, and hundreds of white protestors. Police escorted the black children into school, but a new local board expelled them. I went with Lou Redding to the edge of the demonstration, observing the mobs. We drew up a complaint and won a court order requiring that the black kids be readmitted.

H. Albert Young, the Delaware state attorney general, a Republican, backed us, saying that the court order would be enforced even if it takes "the governor of Delaware and our two United States senators to lead these Negro children by the hand back into the Milford school." But he was immediately repudiated by Republican Senator John J. Williams and Delaware's other senator, a Democrat. The state supreme court stayed the chancellor's order and the black children remained out.

Lou lost the appeal, the court holding that although segregation was unconstitutional, the local school board had not followed proper procedure in admitting the blacks.[5]

In West Virginia, partial integration took place in over half the state's districts. But Milford was followed by similar demonstrations in White Sulphur Springs, West Virginia, in Washington, D.C., and in Baltimore. Milford led to smashing Republican defeats in Delaware elections and destroyed Young's political career—he had hoped to run for senator. The lessons were clear for demagogues and politicians alike: violent opposition could intimidate courts and political disaster might attend support for the law.

The Philip Murray Foundation, named after the late president of the CIO, gave us $75,000. We put half into educational materials, including a film, the other half into field work. We hired three new workers to assist June Shagaloff and Dan Byrd in urging the black community to seek desegregation and advising how best to accomplish it. Thurgood hired Dr. John W. Davis, a great black educator, once president of West Virginia State College, formerly an all-black school, which he led toward integration even before *Sweatt,* and at that time head of United States aid missions in West Africa, to head up a department of Teacher Information and Security to protect black teachers.

Joining the backlash against our victory, the Internal Revenue Service threatened our tax exemption. In September 1954, Thurgood distributed to the executive committee a Treasury Department letter requesting information about our activities between 1951 and the first half of 1954, for the purpose of determining whether we would continue to be tax exempt. At a later meeting he reported, "There is a strong possibility that our tax-exempt status might be taken away. . . . One of the rumored regulations would prohibit participation in any social reform program of a controversial nature."

We retained Adrian W. (Bill) DeWind, the tax partner at Paul, Weiss, who waived any fee and represented us. Bill reported that the Treasury officials told him frankly that they needed a result that would satisfy Southern congressmen and senators.

---

[5] Steiner v. Simmons, 111 A.2d 574 (Del. 1955).

Changes

As we prepared for the second reargument Walter White died; Roy Wilkins succeeded him as secretary of the NAACP.

In February 1955, Vivian (Buster) Marshall died of cancer, Thurgood having been at her bedside, almost without interruption, for months. During this period he lost so much weight that he became cadaverous in appearance. In March, the board voted to "make available (to him) the sum of $600 . . . for the purpose of a short cruise at the expense of the Corporation during this interval between now and the argument of the school cases . . . as a necessary precaution to preserve Mr. Marshall's health as a result of the great strain he has been under both personally and with respect to his official duties."

In fact, Thurgood went to Mexico, where he visited with my cousin in Mexico City and stayed at a spa in San Jose Purua. At the end of the year he married Cecilia (Cissy) Suyat, who had been a secretary at the Association, at St. Philip's Episcopal Church on 134th Street. Shelton Hale Bishop, St. Philip's rector, performed the ceremony. Later there was a party at the Roosevelt Hotel, where we had often held board meetings.

The Implementation Brief

The urgent task at hand was to prepare a brief on how to implement *Brown*. In June, the executive committee resolved: "While recognizing the need for administrative adjustments from a segregated to a desegregated school system in any community, we are opposed to any time beyond the actual time needed for such administrative adjustment."

Our opening brief was short and pointed: in the normal course of events, the decision would be put into effect "forthwith" or by September 1955. Should the states desire postponement, "the affirmative burden must be on them" to state what they propose and to justify it, in light of the fact that black children were suffering serious injury. The brief reviewed data that Kenneth Clark had gathered on experience with desegregation and asserted that "gradualism, far from facilitating the process, may actually make it more difficult. . . . This, like many wrongs, can be easiest and best undone, not by 'tapering off,' but by forthright action." The brief argued that the local conditions that might be taken into account should include only "variations in administrative organization, physical facilities, school population and pupil redistribution," and should not include "need for community preparation" and "threats of racial hostility and violence." It suggested that whatever "the reasons for gradualism . . . if the Court decides to grant further time . . . September, 1956, [should be] the outside date by which desegregation must be accomplished."

While briefs often are a joint effort and a particular writer's product often is unknowable, the conclusion to our reply brief displays Charlie Black's unmistakable style:

> Appellants recognize that the problems confronting this Court as it turns to the implementation of its decision in these cases are of primary magnitude. Their high seriousness is enhanced by the fact that sovereign states are in effect, though not formally, at the bar and the evil to which the Court's decree must be directed is no transitory wrong but is of the essence of the social structure of a great section of our nation.
>
> Yet, it should be borne in mind that the very magnitude of these problems exists because of the assumption, tacitly indulged up to now, that the Constitution is not to be applied in its full force and scope to all sections of this country alike, but rather that its guarantees are to be enjoyed, in one part of our nation, only as molded and modified by the desire and customs of the dominant component of the sectional population. Such a view, however expressed, ignores the minimum requirement for a truly national constitution. It ignores also a vast part of the reality of the sectional interest involved, for that interest must be composed of the legitimate aspirations of Negroes as well as whites.

The government's position in many respects was unexceptionable: Time might be allowed for administrative, procedural, fiscal, regulatory, and related changes. We wouldn't deny that. It also maintained that "general community hostility cannot serve as justification for avoiding or postponing compliance." Our position, too. But the government adopted a yielding tone that delivered a message encouraging accommodation, not resolve. One passage, said to have been drafted by President Eisenhower himself, counseled:

> The Court's decision in these cases has outlawed a social institution which has existed for a long time in many areas throughout the country—an institution, it may be noted, which during its existence not only has had the sanction of decisions of this Court but has been fervently supported by great numbers of people as justifiable on legal and moral grounds. The Court's holding in the present cases that segregation is a denial of constitutional rights involved an express recognition of the importance of psychological and emotional factors. . . . In similar fashion, psychological and emotional factors are involved—and must be met with understanding and good will—in the alterations that must now take place in order to bring about compliance with the Court's decision.

The defendants, along with the six other Southern states, filed briefs offering grounds for delay: "sustained hostility," withdrawal of white children from public schools, racial tensions, violence, loss of jobs for black teachers, the loss of legislative support for, or even the destruction of, the school systems. Virginia argued that blacks scored far lower on IQ tests than whites and had higher levels of tuberculosis, venereal disease, and illegitimacy than whites. North Carolina argued that in some counties one-third of the black children were retarded, and to integrate them would create "more numerous and more serious administrative and instructional difficulties" than it would to integrate in counties with few black children.

The Second Reargument

The second reargument took four days, beginning April 11, 1955. The Court invited every state with school segregation laws to submit briefs and argue. Topeka, Delaware, and the District of Columbia purported to have desegregated, or to be well on the way. Yet, each allowed transfers or grandfather clauses that permitted both black and white children to attend schools where their own race was in the majority, continuing a large measure of segregation. The

Deep Southern states were downright defiant. I. Beverly Lake, one of the leaders of the resistance in North Carolina, told the Court that his state had appointed a commission that concluded: "The mixing of the races forthwith in the public schools throughout the state cannot be accomplished and should not be attempted."

Lake argued that the state, by forcing integration, "could abolish the public school system." When Justice Frankfurter countered, "It could bring up its children in ignorance if it wanted to," Lake responded, "It could do that also."

John W. Davis had died since the May 17 decision and the local school board lawyer, S. E. Rogers, argued for South Carolina. He told the Court: "I am frank to tell you, right now in our district I do not think that we will send—the white people of the district will send their children to the Negro Schools."

Earl Warren asked, "You are not willing to say here that there would be an honest attempt to conform to this decree, if we did leave it to the district court?"

Rogers replied, "No, I am not. Let us get the word 'honest' out of there."

Warren, restraining his fury, responded, "No, leave it in."

But Rogers persisted, "No, because I would have to tell you that right now we would not conform—we would not send our white children to the Negro schools."

The Atlanta Declaration

Less than a week later, the NAACP met in Atlanta and announced in the "Atlanta Declaration" that "we approach the future with the utmost confidence." It proposed to "resist the use of any tactics contrived for the sole purpose of delaying desegregation," and to "accelerate our community action program to win public acceptance." It insisted that there be no discrimination against teachers. At the annual convention in June, the Association called on Southern branches to get "signatures of as many parents of children in public schools [as possible] on petitions," and to "engage local counsel immediately."

Nothing could better illustrate the gap between successful litigation to secure rights and the actual enjoyment of those rights than the difficulties that beset our office messenger shortly after *Brown II.* Two police officers came to the office and arrested him on a charge of grand larceny. Everyone was astonished—he was such a nice young man. One of the lawyers who knew his mother called her. She seemed to know what it was all about, but wanted nothing to do with it. We reached our young messenger by phone at the police precinct, but he politely declined our assistance. The next morning he returned to work as if nothing had happened. A legal aid lawyer had arranged his release. The charges had been lodged by his former girlfriend, to whom he had given a ring. When he took the ring back she reported it to the police as a larceny, although it was a run-of-the-mill lover's quarrel. I said, "Ronnie, I don't understand. Here, you've been working with us for years. We are the lawyers who won *Brown v. Board of Education* and all sorts of other cases in the Supreme Court. Yet, instead of allowing us to help, you turned to the Legal Aid Society." He replied, "Mr. Greenberg, I didn't want to go to the Supreme Court. I just wanted to get out."

"With All Deliberate Speed"

On May 31, 1955, in a virtually unprecedented opinion, the Court sent the School Segregation Cases back to the district courts. Having decided in 1954 that blacks had constitutional rights, it then paradoxically announced that they might continue to be denied the exercise of those rights for an indeterminate time. For how long? The Court spoke with forked tongue: under one interpretation, hardly any time at all, under another, perhaps indefinitely. At the outset the Court made clear that "constitutional principles cannot be allowed to yield simply because of disagreement with them." It required that school districts "make a prompt and reasonable start toward full compliance" with the Court's ruling. It then allowed more time to comply—but "at the earliest practicable date." To warrant allowance of additional time courts might take into account problems related to "administration, arising from physical condition of the school plant, the school transportation system, personnel, revision of school districts and attendance areas into compact units to achieve a system of determining admission to the public schools on a non-racial basis, and revision of local laws and regulations which may be necessary in solving the foregoing problems."[6]

It would be difficult to argue that systems shouldn't be allowed time to accomplish such major changes. What nullified any sense that desegregation should proceed with dispatch, with only brief delays for administrative adjustments, was the final paragraph of the Court's opinion, which called for district courts to "enter such orders and decrees consistent with this opinion as are necessary and proper to admit to public schools on a racially nondiscriminatory basis with *all deliberate speed* the parties to these cases" (emphasis added).

---

[6] Brown v. Board of Education of Topeka, 349 U.S. 294, 300–01 (1955).

CHAPTER 9

THE SPIRIT OF BLACK REVOLT STIRS AND JIM CROW FIGHTS BACK

The Community Mobilizes: The Montgomery Bus Boycott

In the Margold Report Nathan Margold had argued in favor of the litigation campaign in part because "the psychological effect upon Negroes themselves will be that of stirring the spirit of revolt among them." How right he turned out to be. Soon after the decision in *Brown* was reported, in December 1955, Rosa Parks, who was secretary of the Montgomery, Alabama branch of the NAACP, refused to move to the back of the bus when a white person demanded her seat.

A dozen years earlier, Rosa Parks had engaged in a similar act of defiance, which had been pretty much ignored, and she resumed obedience to the Jim Crow law. However, in the post-*Brown* South the reaction to her refusal to yield her seat was different. Her impulsive act of defiance was the impetus behind the 1955 Montgomery bus boycott led by Martin Luther King, Jr. The entire black community refused to patronize the bus lines until they reformed their discriminatory seating practices. Dr. King was catapulted into world prominence.

Indicating how modest their demands were at that early stage of the movement, the Montgomery protestors didn't seek non-segregated seating. At first they only wanted not to be forced to give up seats when there weren't enough for whites. What was most important about the boycott was that the community organized and stuck together. Car pools and ride-sharing plans were devised. An over-whelming majority of the black community participated in the boy-cott, so that businessmen who depended on the buses to bring them their black customers, as well as the bus lines themselves, were fi-nancially hurt by the boycott.

Bob Carter, assisting Arthur Shores and two newly admitted law-yers, Fred Gray and Orzell Billingsley (the three were perhaps half the black bar of Alabama), defended Parks and King against pros-ecution for leading the boycott. Both were convicted, but lost the right to appeal because their Alabama lawyers filed their papers late. But, before Alabama could carry out their punishment, we won an-other case in the Supreme Court in November 1956 holding segre-gation on Montgomery buses unconstitutional—a rejection of *Plessy,* which also had been an intrastate transportation case.[1] That ended the boycott; there was nothing left to boycott and there was no way to prosecute the former boycotters successfully.

Still, segregation on buses died hard. In 1958, we had to file another bus case in Memphis, which the district court dismissed because it was a test case. The Supreme Court reversed.[2]

Backlash and Default at the Top

Among those who might have had some positive influence, Presi-dent Dwight Eisenhower expressed his antipathy in refusing to en-dorse the Court's decision or to provide national leadership beyond saying that "I think it makes no difference whether or not I endorse it. The Constitution is as the Supreme Court interprets it; and I must conform to that and do my very best to see that it is carried out in this country." He also said, "It is difficult through law and through force to change a man's heart," which hardly encouraged compliance.

But if the executive branch was derelict, Congress was down-right antagonistic. In 1956, 101 congressmen—19 senators and 82 house members—all from states of the former Confederacy, signed

---

[1] Gayle v. Browder, 352 U.S. 903 (1956).

[2] Evers v. Dwyer, 358 U.S. 202 (1958).

the Southern Manifesto (among Southerners, only Lyndon Johnson, Estes Kefauver, and Albert Gore, Sr., refused to sign) denouncing *Brown* as having "substitute[d] naked power for established law."

Senators and representatives introduced numerous Court-bashing bills. Senator Strom Thurmond of South Carolina declared that the Court was "a great menace to this country" and called for the impeachment of justices who had voted to curtail the anti-communism campaigns of Congress. In 1958, pro-segregationists, states rights advocates, and anti-Communists launched the most serious assault against the authority of *Brown,* the Jenner-Butler bill. It would have deprived the Supreme Court of jurisdiction over the practice of law in state courts (responding to a decision that prohibited disbarring an alleged Communist); over the conduct of congressional committees (to counteract a decision that had required a committee's questioning of a witness before it pass a "test of pertinency to legitimate legislative powers"); over programs concerning executive employee loyalty and security; over state regulation of subversive activities; and over school board regulations dealing with subversive activities among teachers. The proposals came quite close to passing. Only adroit parliamentary maneuvering, led by Lyndon Johnson, defeated the whole lot at the last minute.

The nation's legal and judicial establishments were hardly supportive of the supremacy of the Supreme Court in determining the law of the land. The Conference of State Chief Justices criticized the Supreme Court for decisions in cases involving subversion (the Communist issue) and the rights of defendants in criminal cases. A *U.S. News & World Report* survey of federal judges reported that a majority of those responding agreed with the state judges and believed that the Supreme Court "too often has tended to adopt the role of policymaker without proper judicial restraint." The National Association of State Attorneys General debated a resolution attacking the Court for decisions in cases involving the rights of criminal defendants. The resolution was defeated, but opponents used the opportunity to get off some serious criticisms of the high court. The American Bar Association House of Delegates adopted resolutions recommending passage of legislation that would overturn recent Supreme Court decisions, especially those limiting the prosecution of Communists. The assault went beyond attacking the Court to assailing those who brought cases to it.

The federal government prosecuted Louis Redding for income tax evasion, but a Delaware jury acquitted him. I was a defense witness and knew, as was widely believed, that the prosecution really stemmed from his role in the School Cases. Virginia commenced disbarment proceedings against Sam Tucker, one of the state's few black lawyers, who had also been involved in the School Segregation Cases. But after a vigorous defense, charges were dropped.

Meanwhile, the John Birch Society splashed "Impeach Earl Warren" across billboards all over the country, attempting to foment a constitutional crisis at the very least, and national anarchy at the most. I saw pickets try to club Earl Warren with their signs as he entered the Association of the Bar of the City of New York for a meeting. While these were the acts of know-nothings and yahoos, often part of a calculated strategy to intimidate anyone who might want to implement *Brown,* they acquired a sort of respectability when highly regarded scholars and jurists expressed criticism of *Brown* in a more intellectual cast.

Learned Hand, then retired, but a man who had earned a special reputation as a federal appellate judge and legal scholar, gave a series of lectures that chastised the Court for having become a "third legislative chamber" and for having exceeded "its proper scope in some recent cases." Senator Albert Jenner used Hand's 1958 lecture series at Harvard Law School to promote his court-curbing bill. In a celebrated article, *Toward Neutral Principles of Constitutional Law,* Herbert Wechsler, while personally opposed to segregation, took the Court to task for what he characterized as unprincipled decisions, mainly in civil rights, and *Brown* in particular.[3]

Edmond Cahn, a highly regarded legal philosopher, in an article that expressed opposition to segregation, argued that *Brown* had come to the right result, agreed that segregation harms black children, asserted that the decision had not turned on the social scientific testimony and brief, but then excoriated Kenneth Clark and

---

[3] 73 Harvard Law Review 1 (1959).

other social scientific witnesses, though he did so in polite language: "Merely translating a proposition of 'literary' psychology into the terms of technical jargon can scarcely make it a scientific finding."

Cahn refused to review my book *Race Relations and American Law* for the *New York Times* because, he told me, while he thought highly of the book, his review would be discredited by the fact that his son had married a black woman. That's how convoluted thinking became when race was the subject.

In Alabama, Georgia, Louisiana, Mississippi, North Carolina, South Carolina, and Virginia lopsided majorities in state referenda and constitutional ratification elections (in which blacks, still limited by violence, arbitrary officials, and all sorts of other strategies, had a hard time voting or couldn't vote at all) adopted laws and constitutional amendments that threatened to abolish public education whenever courts might require integration. These measures prohibited integration outright; required or permitted abolition of public schools; authorized sale of public schools to private groups (so that defendants could claim there was no state action); authorized public funds for segregated schools only; and made grants for private education. Related provisions in these states and in Arkansas repealed or modified compulsory attendance laws. Alabama, Florida, Louisiana, North Carolina, and South Carolina changed teacher employment laws to frighten black teachers away from supporting desegregation, and, they hoped, to enlist them in the effort to retain Jim Crow schools.

James Kilpatrick, editor of the Richmond *News Leader,* touted declarations of "interposition" and "nullification," in which eleven Southern states joined "to interpose their sovereignty between the Federal government and the object of its encroachments upon powers reserved to the States." If it weren't so serious, the orotund language would be grist for an H. L. Mencken-style lampoon of Southern pomposity. Most Southern states set up State Sovereignty Commissions or committees to study segregation that whipped up sentiment against desegregation. A Joint Legislative Committee for the Preservation of Segregation in the State of Louisiana placed an advertisement in the New York *Herald Tribune,* paid for from a public appropriation of $100,000, to attack segregation and defend the state's opposition to integration. When the NAACP protested, the *Tribune* asserted that it had published the advertisement in the "best tradition of a free press."

White citizens councils, states rights councils, the National Association for the Advancement of White People, and similar groups developed throughout the South. By mid-1957, they claimed as many as 80,000 members in Mississippi; 100,000 in Alabama; 40,000 in South Carolina; 20,000 in Texas; and 15,000 to 20,000 in North Carolina, Georgia, and Virginia. Membership included leading political figures, such as Senators Strom Thurmond of South Carolina, Herman Talmadge of Georgia, James Eastland of Mississippi, and Governor Marvin Griffin of Georgia. These groups propagandized about school desegregation, intermarriage, and "mongrelization;" boycotted and harassed whites and Negroes who got out of line; and socially ostracized whites who seemed to be soft on segregation.

This widespread resistance to the Court's authority fueled and validated uglier efforts. Ku Klux Klan activity and cross burnings erupted across the South. In Hoxie, Arkansas, white citizens councils tried to block the integration of twenty-five blacks into a school with one thousand whites. The school board, aided by the Justice Department, obtained a court order enjoining them. Behind the scenes we drafted the legal papers for the school board. In Clinton, Tennessee, a mob led by John Kasper of the white citizens council gathered at a school where twelve blacks had been admitted to a student body of more than eight hundred, picketed, and threw rocks and tomatoes. Though the governor called out the highway patrol and National Guard, a mob of fifty whites and adults chased black students and beat one of them. Members of the football team rescued the blacks, but attendance at the school dropped sharply. The principal, D. J. Brittain, Jr., brought suit against Kasper and, in a proceeding in which the Justice Department took part, the court sentenced him to one year in prison for contempt. In Texas, following a court order that Mansfield schools admit blacks, a mob of more than 250 persons threatened violence. Governor Allan Shivers announced that he would not "shoot down or intimidate Texas citizens who are making orderly protest against a situation instigated and agitated by the N.A.A.C.P." When blacks registered to attend white schools in

Clay and Sturgis, Kentucky, riots erupted that required calling in the National Guard. Similar mob scenes and boycotts developed in South Carolina, on the mere rumor that blacks would be admitted to a white school, as well as in Maryland and Little Rock, Arkansas, in what developed into a national crisis. There were bombings and bomb threats in Tennessee, Alabama, Georgia, North Carolina, and elsewhere.

In April 1959, in Poplarville, Mississippi, whites broke into the local jail and lynched a black man, Mack Charles Parker, who was being held for trial on the charge of raping a white woman. The local paper saw the connection between the lynching and the broader attempt to intimidate blacks out of asserting the rights they had won in court: "Reprehensible as the act of lynching is, it served to emphasize again the fact that force must not be used in pushing revolutionary change in social custom. Every action produces an equal and opposite reaction." As if they hadn't been lynching blacks before the Court upheld their rights!

Southern Legal Efforts to Destroy LDF

There was no doubt whom the South saw as the mastermind behind it all. In a coordinated effort, virtually every Southern state passed laws and started legislative investigations, criminal prosecutions, suits for injunction, and disbarment proceedings against lawyers to put the NAACP and LDF out of business.

By 1964, it became clear that the South's drive to crush the Association had failed. At the peak of the civil rights movement, membership was up to 455,839 and income was $1,143,426. Nevertheless, the NAACP paid a price. The partial vacuum created by its membership losses contributed to the growth of the Southern Christian Leadership Conference (SCLC), the Student Non-violent Coordinating Committee (SNCC), and the Congress of Racial Equality (CORE) as alternative centers for civil rights activities.

The troubles the NAACP and LDF endured during this time should not obscure the real progress that was made during this post-*Brown* period. Despite the furor over the decision, some border states began to comply, though always haltingly. Within the Eisenhower administration Attorney General Herbert Brownell helped bring about passage of the Civil Rights Act of 1957, which created the Civil Rights Commission and the Civil Rights Division in the Justice Department, giving it a little more power to enforce voting rights. But a proposed provision that would have allowed the Justice Department to enforce school desegregation was deleted.

Even the campaign of vilification against Earl Warren failed to engender grassroots support anywhere but in the South. Following Eisenhower's heart attack in 1955, when there was some question as to whether or not he would stand for reelection, public opinion polls indicated that Earl Warren was so popular he could have beaten Adlai Stevenson in a presidential election.

Charlie Black and Lou Pollak, among others, wrote powerful articles defending *Brown* against attacks from the legal academy. In a *Yale Law Journal* article entitled *The Lawfulness of the Segregation Decisions*,[4] Charlie responded to Herb Wechsler's *Neutral Principles* article: "If a whole race of people finds itself confined within a system which is set up and continued for the very purpose of keeping it in an inferior station, and if the question is then solemnly propounded whether such a race is being treated 'equally,' I think we ought to exercise one of the sovereign prerogatives of philosophers— that of laughter." At a level of visibility so low that even most scholars of constitutional law are not aware, in 1969 Wechsler gave a lecture that appeared as an article in an obscure journal, *Texas Quarterly*. He wrote: "The decision is, however, more acceptable when its principle is seen to be that any racial line, implying an invidious assessment, may no longer be prescribed by law or by official action."[5] This was Charlie's argument, too. But by then it was too late to undo the harm that flowed from the justification that defenders of segregation had found in *Neutral Principles*.

Lou's article offered a proposed rewrite of *Brown* that addressed Wechsler's concern about freedom of association: "To the extent that implementation . . . forces racial mingling on school children . . . this

---

[4] 69 Yale Law Journal 421 (1960).

[5] Herbert Wechsler, *The Nationalization of Civil Liberties and Civil Rights*, 12 Texas Quarterly No. 2, at 10, 23 (Supp. 1969).

consequence follows because the community through its political processes has chosen and may continue to choose compulsory education. . . . Parents . . . are presumably entitled to fulfill their educational responsibilities in other ways."[6]

The Internal Revenue Service Attacks

The Internal Revenue Service's challenge to our tax exemption continued unabated. In March 1956, Thurgood met with the general counsel of the Bureau of Internal Revenue, who elaborated its dissatisfaction with our relationship with the Association. He complained, as Thurgood reported, that:

> a great many things point to the interlocking of the two corporations. (1) The fact that we have NAACP before our name; (2) in the past we have given money to NAACP branches in law suits; (3) we were not operating as a legal aid society because we were helping people who could afford to pay their own legal fees. He further remarked that if these corporations are so separate why is it we are defending the NAACP in North Carolina and Louisiana [against efforts to compel it to register and to enjoin it from functioning]?

To defend the Association without risking our tax exemption Bob Carter took a leave of absence for the balance of the year, which later became permanent. Bob's leave enabled him to become the Association's lawyer at the Association's expense and to defend it against Southern efforts to put it out of business, so that LDF no longer subsidized the Association by providing free legal counsel. Thurgood resigned as special counsel of the NAACP. Later, in November, we adopted a resolution codifying our policy on taking cases, making clear that we decided *ourselves* which cases to take. The resolution said:

> [We will] give . . . legal aid only when requested to do so . . . by the party involved. . . .

---

[6] Louis H. Pollak, *Racial Discrimination and Judicial Integrity: A Reply to Professor Wechsler*, 108 University of Pennsylvania Law Review 1 (1959).

All members, officers, employees and employed and retained lawyers of this corporation are specifically prohibited from soliciting . . . anyone to be a party to litigation. . . .

The relationship between the lawyer involved and the party in interest continues to be controlled by the Canons of Ethics of the American Bar Association.

When requested by the N.A.A.C.P. or any organization to act . . . we enter cases only when requested to do so by the parties in interest. . . . Each case is considered on its individual merits.

The resolution concluded with a reminder that we were not permitted to engage in political action or propaganda or to influence legislation.

The purpose was, of course, to protect us from charges that we stirred up litigation and that non-lawyers solicited our cases, which were then violations of law. It also answered IRS claims that we were a tool of the NAACP, making clear that we were not under its domination and not obligated to take cases it might refer to us.

CHAPTER 10

LUCY AND LITTLE ROCK:
WAR OF ALL MEN AGAINST ALL MEN

Inching Ahead

In June 1955, Thurgood acknowledged, referring to *Brown* and the subsequent "deliberate speed" decision, that "we may have to go from district to district but that was inevitable . . . and we knew that. . . . But the May 17th and May 31st decisions give us the tools with which we may secure compliance at the lower court level. . . . We would tackle the difficult states with one or two cases and then go to the more easy ones." That notion was soon frustrated by reality. Thurgood reported to an executive committee meeting almost a year later, "There appears to be a feeling taking root among the good people that we should not be pushing so hard in the Black Belt Counties [loosely, black soil areas of South Carolina, Georgia, Alabama, and other states]." By "good people," Thurgood meant Southern whites sympathetic to civil rights. Nevertheless, at the same time he proposed filing cases in Norfolk, Newport News, Charlottesville, and Arlington County, as well as farther south in Sumter, Charleston, and another town in South Carolina.

The Autherine Lucy Case

A defining case of the period was not an elementary or high school suit. Rather it was Autherine Lucy's effort to enter the University of Alabama. After Connie Motley, Thurgood, and Arthur Shores litigated up and down the courts for three years, they finally got a court order under which Lucy registered at the University of Alabama at Tuscaloosa in February 1956.[1] (Her co-plaintiff, Polly Ann Myers, was rejected because of her "marital record.") Mobs surrounded and invaded the university, chanting "Where is the nigger?" "Keep 'Bama white," "Lynch her," and so forth. Those who were less uncouth (or, indeed, feigned a certain refinement) objected that she had arrived at the school in a Cadillac (in fact, it was a Buick), driven by an undertaker friend, paid her tuition in new $100 bills, and sat in the front row of her geography class.

The university expelled Lucy after three days of classes, allegedly in response to a statement in our pleadings that it had intentionally permitted an atmosphere of mob rule to develop. In February 1957, the judge who had ordered her admission held that the university was justified in expelling her because of our allegation. The stress of the situation proved too much for Lucy, and in March she dropped her effort to enroll.

In 1989, Lucy reported, "Recently the university wrote me a letter that said I'm no longer an expelled student. I can now enroll. . . . It's very late. Thirty-two years." That year she re-enrolled at the same time that her daughter registered and both graduated in 1992, two of 1,755 blacks on a campus of more than eighteen thousand students.

The Lucy experience was traumatizing. While Thurgood reported the intention to file a motion for relief in another case, he raised the question of whether we should not be "re-examin[ing] strategy" with a view to revising it and considering "what we should do . . . to *prevent another Lucy case* so that we can arrive at the point that when the Court stated a plaintiff goes in she will be permitted to enter." But Roy Wilkins responded that while there was indeed great resistance in the Black Belt, we had a moral obligation to proceed there. The meeting arrived at a "consensus": "Since we have the Supreme law of the land on our side we are obligated morally and legally."

---

[1] Lucy v. Board of Trustees, 213 F.2d 846 (5th Cir. 1954); Lucy v. Adams, 134 F. Supp. 235 (N.D. Ala. 1954), *modified*, 350 U.S. 1 (reinstating injunction in part), *aff'd per curiam*, 228 F.2d 619 (5th Cir 1955), *cert. denied*, 351 U.S. 931 (1956).

Political and social circumstances more or less resolved this dilemma. While we did file in areas of high resistance, courts rarely ordered extensive desegregation in the face of physical resistance. In most of the worst places we did nothing because there were few, if any, plaintiffs prepared to face the very real risks involved. Carsie Hall, our lawyer in Mississippi, reported, "There is not one town ready for a school segregation case." Thurgood informed the board, "We must realize that as far as school cases are concerned, there will have to be a delay in Mississippi."

Forcible Resistance: Kentucky

In 1956, when a handful of blacks registered, unnoticed, for admission to public schools in Clay and Sturgis, Kentucky, and arrived to attend class they found a mob of five hundred angry whites blocking their entry. Another mob ran newspapermen and photographers at the scene out of town. The governor, A. B. "Happy" Chandler, who had been the commissioner of major league baseball when Jackie Robinson broke the color barrier, called out the National Guard, which arrived at the school with tanks. Chandler said, "The tanks were taken along for the proper psychological effect. Some men won't let a soldier with a gun push them. No man is going to argue with a tank." Then, twenty-five hundred whites, including some white teachers, boycotted the schools. The Kentucky attorney general, who was opposed to the governor, issued an opinion that justified expelling the black children on the grounds that parents were not allowed to enroll children without school board approval. The board then removed the children and the mob went home.

Thurgood assigned me to work with James Crumlin to get the children back in school. Crumlin was a soft-spoken, jowly, black country lawyer, not at all a firebrand, who had just begun to practice in Louisville after having been graduated from Terrell Law School in Washington, D.C. Altogether there were about seven or eight black lawyers in Kentucky, of whom only two or three handled civil rights cases. Typically, they barely made a living. Someone had to pay them or they couldn't afford to file a case. Crumlin said of one of them, he "would sit in the white section of the bus station, but would not file civil rights cases. He was more interested in preaching."

In September 1956, we filed cases to integrate the Clay and Sturgis schools. As the cases proceeded, segregationists harassed the plaintiffs, fired on their homes, and cut off the water to one plaintiff's house. I traveled a half-dozen times to Kentucky for meetings with Crumlin, black parents, and the local NAACP, and for court hearings before Henry Brooks, a lanky, laconic federal judge. In December 1956, Brooks entered an order that required both school boards to file desegregation plans. The Clay plan, filed in January 1957, proposed complete desegregation commencing September 1957. Sturgis proposed desegregating the high school by 1959 and offered no plan regarding the elementary schools.

Neither plan, however, contemplated truly integrating the systems; they would merely allow blacks to enroll in white schools. The result would be a continuing dual system—of all black schools and formerly all-white schools attended by some blacks—rather than one in which students were assigned to schools without regard to race. Judge Brooks accepted Clay's plan, but rejected the too-long-deferred nature of the Sturgis plan. To our complaint that it did not include grade schools, he replied that our plaintiffs were high school students and grade schools were, therefore, not part of our case.

Little Rock

For a while it looked as if desegregation would develop peacefully in Arkansas. The university had desegregated its professional schools in February 1948, even before *Sipuel,* after Wiley Branton threatened suit. Following discharge from the army, Branton went to the University of Arkansas Law School, from which he graduated in 1953. By the time he began practicing in Pine Bluff, there were perhaps nine black lawyers in the state, not all with active practices and even fewer who handled civil rights. Following *Brown,* as state chairman of the Arkansas NAACP legal committee and an LDF cooperating lawyer, Wiley wrote to every school district in Arkansas with more than a few blacks, asking them to adopt integration plans. Some did.

Wiley was about five feet eight, with black wavy hair, and spoke with the Southern accent of the gentry of his hometown, Pine Bluff, Arkansas. His father was a small businessman who owned a taxi company, and the family was well-to-do. Wiley was sufficiently light complexioned to be mistaken for white, a circumstance he sometimes exploited. He delighted in telling and retelling of the time he drove from Arkansas to Florida with another black man to represent the son of a Pine Bluff woman who had been falsely accused of impregnating a woman. The defendant was the target of local ire because, according to the prosecutor, he was a "high steppin' nigger." The prosecutor got the notion, which Wiley did nothing to dispel, that Wiley was a "Colonel" Branton of Little Rock. When the prosecutor asked why the colonel would take the trouble to travel all the way to Florida, "hemmed up in a car with a nigger," for such a minor case, the "Colonel" swallowed his pride and improved the illusion by explaining that the defendant's mother worked for Wiley's family. The prosecutor added to the insult by attempting to bond with Wiley, offering the view that a "good nigger woman" was hard to find. Wiley won the release of his client by agreeing to compensate for the hospital costs of, as the prosecutor put it, birthing a "nigger baby." Paying the money to the prosecutor, Wiley bit his tongue, and as they drove back to Little Rock he and his newly freed client chortled over their Uncle Remus story, the racist, who thought he was colluding with a fellow white supremacist, undone by his racism.

One week before the 1955 *Brown* opinion the Little Rock school board approved a desegregation plan. Its first stage provided for desegregating grades ten through twelve, commencing in 1957, with completion by 1963. Wiley, with U. S. Tate, LDF Southwest regional counsel, sued in early 1956 because the plan was too slow and uncertain. But the courts, in April, 1957, upheld the board, although they retained jurisdiction, perhaps to move things along faster later on. We decided not to go to the Supreme Court, fearful it might place its imprimatur on so gradual a scheme. As well, we thought it wise to let the plan begin in September and see what would happen, rather than risk stalling it for a year or more by a dragged-out lawsuit. As the 1957 school year approached, Georgia's governor, Marvin Griffin, came to Arkansas and made a speech about how he would not tolerate school integration in Georgia. His remarks were so enthusiastically received that Arkansas Governor Orval Faubus apparently decided to reap some of the same political advantage for himself.

Faubus is a strange case in Southern segregation politics. Until the late 1950s, he had been seen as somewhere between a moderate and a liberal, according to Wiley. Labor, blacks, and liberals assumed he shared their values. The white citizens council must have seen him the same way, for they attacked him. Faubus was midway through his second term in 1957, and ordinarily that would have been the end of it: The term for governor was only two years and only one person in the history of the state had ever been elected for a third term. It soon became clear that whenever Faubus attacked integration his support broadened and deepened. According to Wiley's analysis, this created too great a temptation for a governor facing imminent unemployment, and Faubus quickly made the desegregation issue the centerpiece of his stump speech. Time bore out his political judgment if not his moral rectitude: He ultimately served six terms.

Under the school board's plan, more than three hundred black children would have been eligible for admission to Little Rock's Central High School. The board first screened that number down to seventy-five, and ultimately approved only about twenty-five for admission. But even this small number would not be admitted without a fight. A white woman sued in late August to enjoin integrating the schools. The suit was probably brought at Faubus's instigation; he testified in her case that revolvers had been taken from Negro and white pupils. The local judge prohibited integrating the schools.

The school board then went to federal court and requested an order permitting it to proceed with the desegregation. Wiley, with LDF, joined the school board. The judge, Ronald N. Davies of Fargo, North Dakota, who happened to be sitting in Little Rock by special assignment, forbade the state court to interfere with the desegregation. However, on September 2, 1957, the day before school was to open, Faubus went on radio and television and announced that he had called out the Arkansas National Guard with instructions to block the admission of black children to Central High School because, if the black children were admitted, he said, "Blood will run in the streets."

In fact, there had been no evidence to support this fear of violence. The mayor and police believed they could cope with any problems that did arise and hadn't asked the governor for help. Nevertheless, the school board asked the black children not to attempt to enter the school.

On September 3, the board asked the federal district court for instructions. Judge Davies ordered it to proceed with the plan. But of the twenty-five children scheduled to enter Central, the parents of only nine agreed that their children would try to run the gauntlet of the civilian mob and the National Guard who were trying to keep them out. The next day, September 4, Elizabeth Eckford and Terrence Roberts, proceeding alone, and seven other black children, accompanied by two white and two black ministers who had been enlisted by Daisy Bates, president of the local NAACP, tried to attend the school. Jostled and shoved by a growing mob of segregationists attracted by the publicity and the governor's fiery speeches, the children made their way to the line of National Guardsmen who, shoulder to shoulder, blocked their entrance. A captain announced that they would not be admitted, pursuant to Governor Faubus's orders. When informed of what had occurred, Judge Davies ordered the United States attorney to investigate and fix responsibility for interference with the desegregation order.

The school board decided to capitulate to Faubus and the mob, and on September 5, went into district court to ask Judge Davies to suspend the desegregation order. By now Thurgood was virtually in full-time residence in Little Rock. He and Wiley, with George Howard, another young black lawyer in Arkansas, later to become a United States district judge there, opposed the delay. Judge Davies refused to postpone desegregation. Now, as Thurgood said, there was a lot of "fast play around second base."

On September 9, Judge Davies requested the United States attorney general and the United States attorney in Little Rock to enter the case as "friends of the court." He directed that they file a petition seeking an injunction against the governor to prevent interference with the integration order. The very next day, September 10, the United States filed a petition. It asked that Faubus and the National Guard officers be made parties to our original case "in order to protect and preserve the integrity of the judicial process of the Courts of the United States and to maintain due and proper administration of justice." It asked also that they be enjoined from "obstructing or interfering with the carrying out and effectuation of" the court's orders in the case. The same day, Judge Davies made Faubus and the guard officers defendants in our case and set a hearing for September 20. Faubus responded by making a motion to disqualify Judge Davies as prejudiced against him. He obviously would have preferred a good old Little Rock judge.

The next day, though Davies had already done so, Thurgood and Wiley filed our own motion to make Faubus and the National Guard officers defendants and to enjoin them from interfering with the integration plan—we wanted to keep control and not concede the power of deciding how to proceed to the government. If we had not sued Faubus and Justice had decided to withdraw or settle, we might have been without standing to urge a different position. There was also a real question of whether the United States had the authority to participate as a friend of the court and make motions, put on evidence, and otherwise act as a party to the dispute. Our motion would serve as a backup if it were held later that the Department of Justice had overstepped its bounds.

Following the September 20 hearing, on that same day, Judge Davies enjoined Faubus and Arkansas National Guard officers from obstructing black children from attending Central High School. The order carefully preserved the governor's power to use the guard to maintain peace and order. But Faubus decided to withdraw the Guard and leave the school at the mercy of the mob.

Although some police officers sympathized with the segregationists, the chief of police, who himself didn't favor desegregation, was devoted to upholding law and order. But the mob completely overran his forces, pulling black citizens from their cars near Central High School, and venting its wrath on Northern journalists, beating three members of the *Life* magazine staff, who, ironically, were then arrested for inciting a riot. Daisy Bates's husband, L.C., sat up nights with a shotgun cradled in his arms.

Woodrow Mann, the Little Rock mayor, and Harry Ashmore, editor of the Little Rock *Gazette,* and other influential people called

President Eisenhower, as well as senators and representatives who in turn called the White House, asking for federal troops. On September 23, President Eisenhower issued a proclamation entitled "Obstruction of Justice in the State of Arkansas" that "commanded all persons engaged in such obstruction of justice to cease and desist therefrom, and to disperse forthwith." The next day he issued another proclamation authorizing the secretary of defense to order the Arkansas National Guard "into the active military service of the United States . . . and to use such of the armed forces of the United States as he may deem necessary." The secretary federalized the National Guard and also sent to Little Rock one thousand paratroopers of the 101st Airborne Division from Fort Campbell, Kentucky.

Soldiers were on the Central High School campus every day to keep the peace, until November 27 when the Defense Department removed the army and left the federalized National Guard in charge.

For the first few months of that school year, the Little Rock Nine, as they became known, gathered at Daisy Bates's house every morning. From there National Guard troops escorted them to school.

On their first day they reported that some of the white pupils had been friendly and had even invited them to lunch, some were indifferent, and only a few showed open hostility. But soon a pattern developed in which groups of whites harassed, insulted, and attacked the Nine, not enough to force them from the school, but enough to make their lives unpleasant. The school suspended Minnijean Brown, one of the Nine, for six days, after she emptied her tray on the heads of two boys who shoved chairs in her path in the cafeteria. Afterwards, the boys said that they "didn't blame her for getting mad." On another occasion a white boy dumped soup on her head, following which the principal suspended Minnijean and the boy for the remainder of the term. Rather than fight the suspension, during which Minnijean most likely would have been out of school for months, she moved to New York, where she lived with Kenneth Clark and his family, and attended private New Lincoln High School, from which she graduated in 1959.

During that school year Thurgood, Connie Motley, and I shuttled between New York and Little Rock, taking depositions, gathering facts, preparing further proceedings. Segregationists kept up their harassment of the children and continuously threatened Daisy and the parents and families of the Little Rock Nine. But on May 27, 1958, when the school year ended, Ernest Green became the first black graduate of Central High School.

On several occasions over the year school board lawyers approached us to ask whether we would put school integration on hold, pending an improvement in the political and racial climate in Arkansas. Of course, we said no: A "yes" would have invited violence elsewhere and would have forced us to go through the Little Rock experience all over again.

Judge Davies returned to North Dakota and was replaced by Harry J. Lemley, an Arkansan. In February 1958, the school board, unable to gain a postponement by agreement, tried the courts again. Citing "pupil unrest, teacher unrest, and parent unrest" the board alleged that

> the principle of integration runs counter to the ingrained attitudes of many of the residents of the District. For more than eighty years its schools have been operated on a basis of segregation. . . . The transition involved in [the] gradual plan of integration has created deep-rooted and violent emotional disturbances. . . . The concept of "all deliberate speed" should be re-examined and clearly defined by the Federal Courts.

In May the board elaborated on its earlier plea and asked that desegregation be postponed until January 1961, that is for two and a half years. Judge Lemley then held a trial from June 3 to 5. School board witnesses testified to "chaos, bedlam and turmoil," racial incidents, and vandalism. On June 20, 1958, Judge Lemley granted the board's petition and suspended school integration in Little Rock until mid-semester of the 1960-61 school year.

The fast play around second base got faster. On June 21, we filed a notice of appeal to the Eighth Circuit Court of Appeals and simultaneously asked Judge Lemley for a stay of his order suspending integration, which he promptly denied. The next day we asked the Eighth Circuit to stay the order and docketed the appeal there.

In the normal course of events the Eighth Circuit would have taken some months, maybe even more, to hear and decide the appeal. Whatever its decision, the case would go to the Supreme Court and, therefore, integration of the Little Rock schools could have been delayed at least for a semester, perhaps longer. The best course would be to skip the court of appeals and go to the Supreme Court first—a technique we had encountered in *Bolling v. Sharpe,* the District of Columbia school segregation case. To move that fast, however, required some cooperation from court clerks, because cases can't be appealed to higher courts without having filed the records in the courts below, and ordinarily that takes time. Wiley loved to tell the story of how he moved the record rapidly from Little Rock to Washington:

> I talked with Thurgood and a decision was made that we would seek to bypass the Eighth Circuit and go straight to the Supreme Court of the United States. But Thurgood told me, he said Cullinan [E. P. Cullinan, chief deputy clerk of the United States Supreme Court] . . . had told him you've got to have a transcript certified as the record in that case before they could do anything at all. At that time, the Eighth Circuit had a very peculiar rule which I understand was different from the other circuits. They didn't want any records sent up to them, any transcripts sent up to them unless they requested it.
>
> So I had a problem there. I asked the clerk in Little Rock to certify it as the transcript and they said we can't do that because we're under instructions pursuant to Eighth Circuit rules not to send up any transcript unless the court requests it. And I didn't tell them what I wanted to do with it, I really wanted to bypass the Eighth Circuit, although Thurgood had told me that I had to come through there.
>
> And I said, "Well I need to take it up."
>
> And they said, "Well, you can't take it. When the Court sends for it, then we will send it up there."
>
> So I got on the phone and called Judge Lemley who was down in Hope, Arkansas. And he said, "What do you want, Wiley?"
>
> I said, "Well, Judge, I want to appeal your order."
>
> He said, "Oh, I knew you were going to do that. What's the problem?"
>
> I told him about this transcript and all and he said, "Oh, hell, put the clerk on." And he said to the clerk, "Listen, give Wiley that

transcript. I trust him quicker than I would the United States mail and if they don't want to take it up there at the Eighth Circuit, he'll just bring it back to you all. Fine."

So I left there then, without any certification, and go to the Eighth Circuit and tell them I don't want to do anything in the Eighth Circuit, but I want to come through there and let them certify that at least they have seen it. And the Eighth Circuit was already on vacation.

The clerk said, "Mr. Branton, if you give me that I'll have to file it and if you file it I cannot release it without a court order, and I don't know how soon you can get a court order." And he said, "Or I can give it back to you and you can do whatever you want to do." So it was agreed that I would take it back. This was, I think, on a Monday morning. So I caught a plane then and came on to Washington with full knowledge that Cullinan wanted something that said, "this is the record."

So, I go there and we present it and Cullinan starts thumbing through it and he says, "Where is the certificate?" So I start telling him my problem and he said, "I can't do a damn thing without a certificate. I want a certificate either from the Eighth Circuit, but preferably from the District Court." And he said, "Today is really the last day, if I hope to get this Court back in any way at all." And he had somebody checking airline schedules to see if there was a plane going out to where I had to go and come back, and that was going to push it. He was willing to accept it even late at night. But, it didn't look like I'd get back until too late.

I think I went to Frank Reeves's law office. And I said let me try something else. I don't even remember the lady's name now but in the South it is customary to call women by their first name so long as you put Miss in front of it. I'll just call her Miss Ellen, who was the deputy in the clerk's office. So I tried to use my Southern charm and the conversation went something like this:

"Miss Ellen, this is Wiley Branton up here in Washington."

And here Wiley raised his voice half an octave to imitate Miss Ellen:

"In Washington, I thought you just left here going to St. Louis."

"Yes ma'am, but they couldn't take care of what I needed there so I came on up here to the Supreme Court of the United States.

And guess what Miss Ellen, I got that transcript and they tell me that I should of had you put on a certificate on there coming to them that this is the record."

She said, "Well, that's what we put on it going to the Eighth Circuit, but we can't do that until the Court wants it."

I said, "Yeah, but they wouldn't take it up there. The Supreme Court wants it and they want that certificate on there, and they claim that we made an error down there in not putting it on there. I said I know ya'all know what ya'all are doing Miss Ellen. They just got things all screwed up. You know how technical they can be." So I got her on my side on that.

I said, "Now they tell me I got to get on a plane, come all the way back out there and get you to just stamp that thing, attach a certificate saying this is the transcript and record, and then bring it back to them." I said, "You know, I don't get up to a place like Washington very often and while I'm up here I sure would like to spend a couple of days. But I told them, shucks, ya'all don't know how we get along down there. I told them I don't need to get on no plane go all the way back down there. All I got to do is call down to Little Rock and they'll put the thing on a plane and send it up here to me."

"Well you know we'll do that, Wiley."

I said, "Yes, ma'am." I said, "Here's where it needs to be sent to and here's what it needs to say."

She took all that down and she said, "Now, I got one little problem."

I said, "What's that?"

She said, "Well, everything we send out with franking privileges is just regular mail and we don't have any airmail postage on things like that." She said, "Even if we send it out it will be late." She said, "You really need to put it on the plane."

I said, "Yes, ma'am, that's what I was talking about."

Finally, she said, "I'll tell you what I'll do. I will advance the money out of my pocket and take it out to the airport."

And in those days you didn't have Federal Express and stuff like that; you'd go out and make arrangements with the people at the desk to put something on the plane as long as somebody met the plane and took it. So she paid for it out of her pocket and that's how we got the certificate in time to file a record.

In the meantime, Thurgood, Connie, Irma Feder, an LDF staff lawyer, and I worked day and night preparing a petition to file with the record requesting the Court to hear the case. Perhaps as much time had to be spent in printing the petition (with hot lead type), proofreading among rackety Linotype machines all through the night at the printshop in downtown Manhattan, and hand-carrying the petition to Washington, as in actually writing it. We filed it on June 26, only four days after docketing the appeal in the Eighth Circuit.

The petition focused on the reasons the Court grants review, the caption of the petition's main section stating, "The Decision Below Conflicts With Applicable Decisions of This Court." It cited two NAACP and LDF cases—*Buchanan v. Warley,* which held residential apartheid unconstitutional against the claim that it would promote public peace, and the School Segregation Cases, which held that "it should go without saying that the vitality of these constitutional principles cannot be allowed to yield simply because of disagreement with them." Less than a week after Lemley's decision, on June 30, 1958, the Supreme Court denied our petition but entered an order almost as good as granting it. It referred to our appeal in the Eighth Circuit and wrote, "That court is the regular court for reviewing orders of the District Court here concerned." It made clear to the Eighth Circuit that it should treat the case as an urgent matter: "We have no doubt that the Court of Appeals will recognize the vital importance of the time element in this litigation, and that it will act upon the application for a stay or the appeal in ample time to permit arrangements to be made for the next school year."[2]

We had successfully impressed on the Court the urgency of the issue and primed it to hear the case again if necessary.

The court of appeals gathered in St. Louis en banc, that is with all of the seven judges of the Eighth Circuit sitting on the case, rather than the ordinary panel of three. On August 18 it reversed Judge Lemley, stating that "an affirmance of 'temporary delay' in Little Rock would amount to an open invitation to elements in other dis-

---

[2] Aaron v. Cooper, 357 U.S. 566, 567 (1958).

tricts to overtly act out public opposition through violent and unlawful means."

And, in italics, the court emphasized that *"the time has not yet come in these United States when an order of a Federal Court must be whittled away, watered down, or shamefully withdrawn in the face of violent and unlawful acts of individual citizens in opposition thereto."*[3]

But Archibald Gardner, the nearly ninety-year-old chief judge, dissented. He argued that:

> for centuries there had been no intimate social relations between the white and colored races in the section referred to as the South. . . . It had become a way of life in that section of the country and it is not strange that this long-established, cherished practice could not suddenly be changed without resistance. Such changes, if successful, are usually accomplished by evolution rather than revolution, and time, patience, and forbearance are important elements in effecting all radical changes.[4]

Then the court of appeals did something we found unintelligible as well as intolerable. On August 21, without allowing us the five days provided in the rules to reply to the board's application, it granted a stay of its own order reversing Judge Lemley, at least until the school board could file a petition in the Supreme Court. School was scheduled to open September 2, and although the board advanced the date several times to await the outcome of the legal wrangling, a stay would delay integration beyond the opening of school. The board won on procedural grounds what it had lost on constitutional grounds.

On August 23, we filed an application with the United States Supreme Court to vacate the Eighth Circuit stay and to stay Lemley's judgment. (The procedural nicety—addressing what had occurred in Lemley's court as well as in the court of appeals—stemmed from

---

[3] Aaron v. Cooper, 257 F.2d 33, 40 (8th Cir. 1958).

[4] *Id.* at 41.

the fact that if the Supreme Court vacated only the Eighth Circuit stay, Lemley's judgment would remain in effect until the Eighth Circuit judgment could be transmitted to him, following which he would have to implement it—which would take time. Given his frame of mind, he could have stalled, dissembled, or refused to obey).

Applications to vacate stays and other motions ordinarily are presented to a circuit justice, a member of the Supreme Court with responsibility for such matters in the region comprising his circuit. So we addressed our papers to a new Eisenhower appointee, Charles Evans Whittaker, who was attending the American Bar Association meeting in Los Angeles, with Chief Justice Warren and Justices Tom Clark and William J. Brennan. As often happens with important motions, Whittaker referred this one to the entire Court. Warren consulted with the justices who were with him in Los Angeles and, by telephone, with the others. On August 25 the Court scheduled a special term and set a hearing on the motions for August 28. In one of those judicial invitations that amount to a command, the Court requested that the government enter the case as a friend of the court. Warren, Clark, and Brennan took the train to Washington; Justice Douglas, vacationing in the state of Washington, drove to Portland, Oregon, and flew to Washington, D.C. Justice Burton was in Europe and wasn't expected to attend. The last special term had been in 1953 and dealt with the Rosenberg spy case. The one before that, in 1942, decided the fate of Nazi saboteurs who had been captured during the Second World War.

The political waters became even more turbulent. President Eisenhower disclosed at a press conference that at the time of the *Brown* decision he had told friends that he preferred "slower" progress toward integration. Roy Wilkins denounced the statement as "incredible," pointing out that seven states had not made "a single move" toward integration and only 770 school districts out of some 3,000 in the South had "done anything toward integration." On the other hand, notwithstanding his sentiments about school segregation, Eisenhower supported the courts. He believed that the law must be enforced and stated also that in the Little Rock case his views would not diverge materially from those of the Justice Department. His attorney general, William P. Rogers, in a major address to the

American Bar Association meeting in Los Angeles, said that racial segregation in public schools, transportation, and recreation "must be considered a thing of the past." Senator Richard Russell of Georgia, one of the most powerful Senate Democrats, sent a telegram to Rogers, demanding that the Justice Department not "flaunt [*sic*] the will of Congress." The Arkansas legislature passed its package of anti-integration, anti-NAACP legislation and Governor Faubus continued to excoriate the courts.

Arkansas Senator J. W. Fulbright's position indicates better than anything else the powerful hold that segregationist sentiment had on political figures who should have known better. Fulbright, whose name is honored in the academic community for the fellowships that bear his name, has written in his autobiography, published in 1989, that he disagreed with the Southern Manifesto as originally written, but he swallowed his objections and demanded as a price for his signature that "we would oppose the *Brown* decision only by constitutional means." He felt, however, "that there were issues fundamental to this nation as a whole in foreign policy that I wanted to focus on." "In those days in Arkansas my constituents were not about to be persuaded on civil rights." He adds, "I avoided taking a stand." While he subordinated the rights of blacks to foreign policy considerations, he didn't seem to realize the foreign policy implications of America's racial policies.

In fact, however, he *did* take a stand. He entered the Little Rock case against us by filing a friend-of-the-court brief that argued that it was a grave error not to realize that there was a "Southern mind." He urged that the integration problem in Arkansas "is more likely to yield to the slow conversion of the human heart than to remedies of a more urgent nature."

On August 28, we filed a short brief in the Supreme Court that argued that the procedural device of granting or denying a stay cannot be employed where the result will be to delay or nullify the exercise of clearly determined rights. The same day the Justice Department filed a brief—now the government was four-square behind us. The issue was no longer segregation or desegregation, but the integrity of the courts and, indeed, as in the Civil War, when the status of blacks was also the focus, whether the Union would hang together. It called upon the Court not only to decide our application to vacate the stay but to pass on the merits of the case, and, if the Court deemed it necessary, to require the school board to file a petition for review at once. It asserted that "there is no likelihood that the [school board] can prevail on the merits."

At oral argument that day all nine justices were present. Thurgood, described by Russell Baker in the *New York Times* as "having the hint of a scowl on his face, looking like Othello in a tan business suit," addressed the Court in his customary conversational manner, scarcely looking at his notes. He pushed the Court to decide the merits, not merely our application to vacate the stay. But the justices resisted because the board had not yet filed a petition for review. Richard Butler, a tall, soft-spoken Little Rock lawyer, argued in a quiet, controlled manner that integration at that time would "destroy the public school system of Little Rock." He asked that the two-and-a-half-year delay be affirmed to allow Arkansas citizens to learn "what the law is." In that time a "national policy could be established" and state laws designed to prevent integration could be "clarified," or tested in the courts.

From that point on the justices were all over him like "white-on-rice," to use a Southern black colloquialism. Frankfurter asked, "Why aren't the two decisions of this court a national policy?" Warren said, "Suppose every other school board in the South said the same thing." When Butler began a sentence, "Mr. Chief Justice, you've been the Governor of a great state," Warren, with scarcely controlled anger, replied, "But I never tried to resolve any legal problem of this kind as Governor." He went on sternly, "I thought that was a matter for the courts and I abided by the decision of the courts." And when Butler brought up Faubus's views, Warren interjected, "I have never heard such an argument made in a court of justice before, and I have tried many a case through many a year. I never heard a lawyer say that the statement of a Governor as to what was legal or illegal should control the action of any court."

The most powerful argument of the day—because he spoke for the United States—was that of J. Lee Rankin, the solicitor general. About five feet six or seven inches in height, dressed in the traditional morning coat of the solicitor general's office, he spoke in the flat tones of his native Nebraska. In essence, his argument was that "no court of law in this land, state or federal, can recognize that you can ever bow to force and violence. We have paid too great a price to come this far along the road of lawful action." But the major impact of his words was that he had discussed the government's position with President Eisenhower and had received his approval.

Russell Baker, reporting for the *New York Times,* described the scene in a remarkable passage: "The room momentarily looked like a crowded tableau in the rich deep colors of the Flemish masters— the justices in their black at the polished wooden bar, the deep maroon curtains draping the side walls, the lawyers and young assistant attorneys general in somber blues, grays and blacks and, here and there, a splash of bright color from the costumes of the women."

The Court recessed at about 3:30. The merits were on everyone's mind, but technically the only issue before the Court was whether to revoke the Eighth Circuit's stay. Following the rules meticulously, the Court declined to pass upon the merits at that time, but instead, at 5:00 P.M. the same day, entered an order that said that it agreed with the parties and the solicitor general that the Court had to consider the merits. In view of the fact that school was scheduled to open on September 15, and that Butler had said that he planned to file a petition for writ of certiorari, the Court ordered him to file by September 8. Both sides were required to file briefs on the merits by September 10. The Court set oral argument for September 11. To tie the loose ends up properly it deferred action on our application to vacate the court of appeals stay and to stay Lemley's order, pending disposition of the board's petition. In a case involving whether the law must be obeyed, the Court took pains to cut square corners.[5]

On September 8, the school board filed a short petition seeking review. It pleaded "not to simply return the school district to the bedlam, turmoil and chaos which has been destroying the school district and has emasculated the educational program." It argued, rather incomprehensibly, that to refuse delay "would discourage any further voluntary compliance by school districts." The next day the

---

[5] Aaron v. Cooper, 358 U.S. 27 (1958).

school board filed its brief on the merits, which, in its main thrust, argued that it had "not pursue[d] a plan of desegregation through choice and it should not now be placed in the position of being duty bound to quell defiance."

During another hectic week I worked on our brief along with Thurgood, Wiley, Bill Coleman, Lou Pollak, and other staff members. There wasn't a lot of time and there also wasn't a great deal to be said. The issue was basically whether the Court would tolerate Faubus's rebellion. If it did in any way, the idea of a national government would be damaged severely, perhaps fatally. We took a short cut around the ordinarily lengthy statement of facts by referring to the court of appeals description. We led off our argument by pointing out that the case involved "the very survival of the Rule of Law," and cited the cases in which the Court had rejected claims that rights should be denied because of violent opposition, many of them NAACP or LDF cases. At that point in the brief I took particular pleasure in quoting one of the great books I had read in my Columbia College Contemporary Civilization course, Thomas Hobbes's *De Cive* (1651). The brief asserted that if transient emergencies were a ground for denying rights, "then we have returned to a state prior to civil society, when there was the Hobbesian state of a 'war of all men against all men.'" We concluded by arguing that to suspend the integration plan would subvert the fundamental objective of public education and quoted Rankin's August 28 argument: "If you teach these children . . . that as soon as you get some force and violence, the courts of law in this country are going to bow to it . . . I think that you destroy the whole educational process then and there."

On September 11, the Court met to hear oral argument. For me, the argument offered a small personal thrill—Thurgood asked me to sit at counsel table with him. Nominally, a colleague seated at the counsel table is there to help argue the case, but there is relatively little one can do, maybe hand up a citation or find a page in the record. Essentially, a seat at counsel table in the Supreme Court is a form of recognition.

The argument was basically a rehash of the August 28 argument. But the Court asked Thurgood and Rankin only a single question each. On the other hand, the justices raked Butler over the coals.

Brennan distilled the essence of the questioning into his observation that the Constitution required every state official to take an oath "to support the Federal Constitution." He asked whether Butler was familiar with that. Butler said he was. Brennan went on to ask, was it not curious that the board should ask delay because of action by the governor and legislature opposed to the Constitution in "every way that the state can contrive?"

The next day the Court unanimously affirmed the Eighth Circuit. Judge Lemley's two-and-a-half-year stay was invalid. The justices wrote a short per curiam (by the Court) order, which stated that "in view of the imminent commencement of the new school year we deem it important to make prompt announcement of our judgment." President Eisenhower appealed for public support of the Supreme Court's decision. Governor Faubus retaliated by issuing a proclamation closing all four high schools in Little Rock. But from that point on the fantasy that violent resistance could succeed in undermining the law began to fade. On September 29, the Court issued a full opinion addressing more elaborately the issues in the case.[6]

The opinion, at the outset, listed as its authors each justice by name, something which had not been done before or since. The Court described the case as raising "questions of the highest importance to the maintenance of our federal system of government." Citing *Buchanan,* the Court wrote, "Law and order are not here to be preserved by depriving the Negro children of their constitutional rights." The Court then answered "the premise of the actions of the Governor and Legislature that they are not bound by our holding in the *Brown* case." It cited Article VI of the Constitution, which makes the Constitution "the supreme Law of the Land," and quoted John Marshall's 1803 opinion in *Marbury v. Madison,* which "declared the basic principle that the federal judiciary is supreme in the exposition of the law of the Constitution." The Court's opinion concluded, therefore, that "the interpretation of the Fourteenth Amendment

---

[6] The *per curiam* opinion is published as a footnote in the full opinion. *See* Cooper v. Aaron, 358 U.S. 1, 5 n.* (1958).

enunciated by this Court in the *Brown* case is the supreme law of the land."

The Court addressed another issue provoked by Faubus's actions—whether the state might turn public schools into private ones. Right after the Court's September 12 order to desegregate, Faubus closed the schools and, five days later, a group of Little Rock whites filed a private school charter. On September 23, the Little Rock school board asked the district court whether it might lease the public schools to the private group. The next day we were in court asking for an order restraining the school board from transferring school property to private corporations, and asking also that, if the transfer were permitted, that those schools be required to be nonsegregated. On the same day the attorney general filed a friend-of-the-court brief in support of our position. The Supreme Court's September 29 opinion demolished this attempt at evasion by stating, in passing, that segregation in schools was prohibited "where there is state participation through any arrangement, management, funds or property." This would include private schools that the state might subsidize.

The district court dismissed the board's petition inquiring about whether it might lease to private schools. On September 29 the board declared the public school properties surplus and authorized leasing them to the Little Rock Private School Corporation. We went to the court of appeals that same day and got an order prohibiting the leasing.

At the end of 1958, more than two thousand white and nine black students were attending Central High School; white Hall High School was closed and its 717 students had no school to attend; about thirteen hundred students were in private schools; and others were attending school outside the city or state, were out of school, or were being educated only part-time. State courts upheld a student transfer aid law that sent state aid to schools attended by displaced students. Little Rock residents, refusing to see the writing on the wall, voted overwhelmingly against school integration in a special election.

In June 1959, we got a federal court to hold the school closing and student aid transfer laws unconstitutional. That case went to the United States Supreme Court, where we won once more.[7] Then, under pupil assignment laws, which required black children to apply for transfer to white schools and permitted school boards to decide the merit of the applications according to vague criteria defining the suitability of children for transfer, the school board began registration in July for the 1959–60 school year. The school board granted only six of sixty applications from blacks who tried to transfer to white schools. Some white students attempted a protest walkout, but the school board suspended them. The board permitted sixty-eight whites who refused to attend class with blacks to transfer to whites-only classes. The Little Rock Private School Corporation announced it was broke and went out of business.

By spring 1960, pupil assignment was working in Little Rock pretty much as elsewhere. Central had 1,510 whites and five blacks. Hall High School had 730 whites and three blacks. That month the Little Rock school board assigned eight more black students to the two high schools for the September term. From that point onwards, punctuated by violence, real bombs, and bomb threats, the Little Rock case took the form of litigation elsewhere: The board continued to hold the line against integration by means of pupil assignment laws, and LDF lawyers fought to overturn them, winning admission to white schools for a few students at a time.

The Little Rock convulsion made clear once and for all that the federal government would not tolerate rebellion against the *Brown* decision. Only twice more did the federal government have to call on troops to quell resistance to school integration: when James Meredith entered the University of Mississippi accompanied by gunfire; and when Alabama Governor George Wallace stood in the schoolhouse door flanked by troops. Both incidents arose out of LDF cases. In each instance the outcome was preordained by Little Rock. Thereafter, violence and physical obstruction having failed,

---

[7] Aaron v. McKinley, 173 F. Supp. 944 (E.D. Ark.), *aff'd*, Faubus v. Aaron, 361 U.S. 197 (1959).

bureaucracy in the form of pupil assignment laws became the principal means of fighting integration.

What becomes of kids who have been through such an ordeal? In 1982, at its annual Civil Rights Institute, LDF celebrated the twenty-fifth anniversary of the Little Rock case. Seven of the Little Rock Nine attended the event. Ernest Green had been assistant secretary of labor in the Carter administration and was president of his own consulting firm, which dealt with employment and training. Minnijean Brown Trickey and her husband, a zoologist, and two children lived on an 880-acre farm in northern Ontario. She was active in antiwar, anti-nuclear, and conservation groups. Thelma Jean Mothershed Wair was a vocational counselor in the East St. Louis, Illinois, school system. Gloria Ray Kaarlmark was a manager at Philips Telecommunications Industries in Brussels, Belgium, and was founder and editor-in-chief of *Computers in Industry,* an international journal. Terrence J. Roberts, Ph.D., was director of Mental Health and Social Services at St. Helena Hospital and Health Center in Deer Park, California. Jefferson Thomas was in charge of employee training and contract reviews for the Defense Department in Los Angeles. Carlotta Walls LaNier was a real estate broker in Fresno, California.

Generalizations are always suspect, but examination of these seven veterans of the war in Little Rock, and of what they made of themselves, seems to suggest that being a civil rights pioneer need not interfere with a child's chances for a normal, or perhaps better than normal life.

CHAPTER 11

TRENCH WARFARE

Louisiana

Integrating schools in Louisiana, where "segregation forever" translated into "litigation forever," involved a tough, lengthy struggle. It was played out in *Bush v. Orleans Parish School Board*,[1] where, from early 1956 through late 1960, LDF fought an obstinate army of defendants' counsel, alone at first and later with the Justice Department at our side. Thurgood, Connie Motley, Jim Nabrit III (who had joined us in 1959), and I virtually commuted to the New Orleans district court and the court of appeals, where our every appearance was greeted by hordes of reporters, pickets, and, at times, pushing, shoving, and screaming mobs.

We stayed at the home of Dan and Mildred Byrd. Mildred regularly prepared a wonderful gumbo for me. Dan, who usually chomped an unlit stub of a cigar in a rubber holder, was one of the small number of LDF field workers who organized the black community and assured black teachers that we would defend their jobs. Like Thurgood, he was a serious Mason. He would pick us up at the airport, take us to court, and then home. Hearings went on late into the night after the judges' staffs left for the day. One night, the district judge, Skelly Wright, issued an order, and because his secretary had gone home, Jim Nabrit typed it out and the judge signed it.

Our lead lawyer in the New Orleans school case was A. P. Tureaud, at whose sparely equipped office we worked day and night.

---

[1] 187 F. Supp. 42 (E.D. La. 1960), 190 F. Supp. 861 (E.D. La. 1961).

A. P. stood for Alexander Pierre, but everyone called him Tureaud. Like many other black lawyers, he never used his given names. He was rotund, the crown of his bald head ringed by gray hair, very soft-spoken in style, and always calm, even in trying situations. Indeed, he often seemed to be on the verge of chuckling, amused by the shenanigans of the opposition. He had graduated from Howard Law School in 1925, returned to New Orleans in 1927, and worked in the customs house, a job he got through political connections. Like many other Southern blacks of this period, Tureaud was a Republican. He went into full-time practice in 1935.

For a while there had been two other black lawyers in town, graduates of Straight University in New Orleans, which had been set up as an integrated institution during Reconstruction, but which was defunct by the 1880s. Tureaud was the only black lawyer in New Orleans from 1937 to 1950, when he was joined by Earl J. Amadee, who did virtually no civil rights work. In 1952 or 1953 A. M. "Mutt" Trudeau (the similarity of names sometimes led to confusion) became the next black lawyer in New Orleans and devoted a great deal of his time to civil rights. In 1954, they were joined by Ernest Morial, who entered Tureaud's firm, and later became mayor, and by Robert Collins, the first black law graduate of Louisiana State University—the fruit of cases Tureaud and LDF had won.

Tureaud's office was in a modest walkup in a black neighborhood. Books, furniture, and office equipment were minimal. He also conducted a real estate business from the premises. These were the forces with which we confronted the assembled might of the state of Louisiana, its governor, mayors, legislature, treasury, corps of lawyers, and a hostile white population.

In early 1956, Tureaud, with "Mutt" Trudeau, Thurgood, and Bob Carter (who dropped out of the case following his resignation from LDF), presented the New Orleans case to a three-judge court, which referred it to a single judge, Skelly Wright.[2] Wright then presided over a litigation that by 1962 resulted in forty-one judicial opinions and many more trials and arguments. Wright had a straight

---

[2] Bush v. Orleans Parish School Board, 138 F. Supp. 337 (E.D. La. 1956).

back, held his head high, in a military manner, and spoke concisely, as if accustomed to giving commands.

Before he went on the bench, Wright was best known for having argued in the Supreme Court the case of Willie Francis, a black adolescent who had been sentenced to death for murder. The execution was bungled and the electric chair didn't kill Francis, though it burned and shocked him severely. Wright argued that to execute Francis at this point would amount to double jeopardy and cruel and unusual punishment, but in 1947 he lost five to four and the state was allowed to take a second shot at executing Francis, this one successful.

In 1948, Wright was among the few Louisiana Democrats who supported Truman, the majority having defected to Strom Thurmond's Dixiecrats. That, plus the fact that he had become a United States attorney and was reasonably well connected politically, got him the United States District Court judgeship in 1949.

For some time there were only two federal judges in New Orleans, Wright and Herbert W. Christenberry. While Christenberry was not a hard-line segregationist, his sympathies were not as much in tune with ours as were Wright's. At times, he permitted cases to linger interminably when we thought he should have ruled for us, so civil rights lawyers always preferred Wright. The method of assigning cases between Christenberry and Wright was for one to get the even-numbered cases, the other the odd-numbered ones. Those who preferred Wright would lie in wait near the clerk's desk. As soon as a case was assigned to Christenberry, a lawyer seeking Wright would step right up and file. It didn't take long for the clerk to catch on, and the system was changed.

Louisiana filed a slew of defenses: It had not consented to be sued; the court had not given permission to file a supplemental complaint; the newly appointed school superintendent should have been named in an amended complaint; plaintiffs had not stated a justiciable controversy and hadn't exhausted their administrative remedies. Wright entered a rather gentle temporary injunction. Segregation had to end "with all deliberate speed." He expressed sympathy for white Southerners: "It is a problem which will require the utmost patience and understanding, generosity and forbearance from all of us, of whatever race."

The defendants then began an interminable hegira of litigation from court to court that went on virtually daily for years. The bulwark of the Constitution in all of this became the United States Fifth Circuit Court of Appeals, the heroes of which were Richard T. Rives, Elbert P. Tuttle, John R. Brown, and John Minor Wisdom.

Rives, of Montgomery, belonged to the traditional Deep South culture of Alabama, but had developed a sympathy for the plight of Southern blacks. He had served as campaign manager for Hugo Black when he was elected to the United States Senate. Associates speculated that Rives's feelings derived from his son, who had been educated at Exeter and Harvard, served in the Second World War, and became committed to working against racial injustice. Rives had planned to practice with his son, but he was killed in an automobile accident while still in law school. One of the son's friends believed that "Rives wanted to live the new South his son talked to him about."

Tuttle had lived in Atlanta since 1923, but had grown up in Hawaii, where he had attended the elite, multiracial Punaho school, and went to college and law school at Cornell. Well over six feet tall, thin, with ramrod posture, he had been a war hero who engaged in bloody hand-to-hand combat with Japanese in the Pacific. He carried his military bearing while on the bench; lawyers felt they were in the presence of their superior officer.

John Minor Wisdom came from a traditional, well-connected New Orleans background, belonged to—and continued to after he went on the bench—the "right" clubs, even those that excluded blacks and Jews. He was outspoken, however, in his belief in absolute racial equality. One of his grandfathers, Wisdom proudly observed, came from "a Jewish, French background." Wisdom went to Tulane Law School and to Harvard as a graduate student. In the Second World War he worked in the office of legal procurement with a group of lawyers from all over the country who would later become part of the national legal elite. Wisdom returned to New Orleans to build a highly successful practice and developed a national, nonracial perspective.

John Brown grew up in Nebraska in a small town in which only one black person lived, a shoe shine man, with whom Brown was friendly. Abraham Lincoln was Brown's boyhood hero. He went to law school at the University of Michigan and then practiced with an admiralty firm in Galveston, Texas, where he became a partner. Southern traditions scarcely had touched him.

Tuttle, Brown, and Wisdom were Southern Republicans who had supported Eisenhower in 1952, indeed, helped assure his winning the Republican nomination. Like Skelly Wright, who was among the few Democrats who did not join the Dixiecrats, they were not part of the dominant segregationist Democratic oligarchy.

In the Fifth Circuit, which presided over the core racial issues of that time, the churning effect of the Second World War had weakened the sense of regional isolation and undermined many parochial perceptions about race. A growing number of people in the area began to view the racial status quo as neither right nor inevitable. This kind of re-orientation came to a focus in the persons of Rives (through his son), Tuttle, Wisdom, and Brown. Through them the broader values of places like Harvard, Michigan, Cornell, Washington, Hawaii, and Nebraska, aided and abetted by perspectives born of other experiences outside the South, would find their way into the Fifth Circuit decisions.

In the meantime, the Louisiana state legislature passed a mountain of ridiculous obstructionist legislation, and the schools continued to segregate, with the full encouragement of political leaders in all branches of Louisiana government. At one point the district court cited the state attorney general, Jack P. F. Gremillion, for contempt because he had called the district court "a den of iniquity" and a "kangaroo court." Gremillion defended, saying that he had been misunderstood: He really had said "a den of *inequity.*" He got sixty days in the custody of the United States attorney general, probated to eighteen months if he remained on good behavior.

As the end approached in 1960, the legislature passed twenty-five more acts crafted to prevent desegregation. In the meantime school officials began screening 137 black applicants for transfer to white schools under seventeen pupil assignment standards, including psychological and ability testing. Officials decided that five black children were qualified to transfer to white schools. But, on November 13, 1960, the eve of desegregation under the district court's de-segregation order, the state superintendent of education declared a school holiday.

Staying up all night to prepare the papers, Thurgood and Tureaud got an injunction against observing the holiday, and only then did the first, tiny step toward integration begin in Louisiana. The *New York Times* reported:

> Federal deputy marshals escorted four black girls into two white elementary schools, while angry crowds hurled jeers and insults. Many white parents withdrew their children from school. Marching youths sang "Glory, glory segregation" to the tune of the "Battle Hymn of the Republic" and legislators filled the capitol at Baton Rouge with threats and a flood of oratory.

Norman Rockwell painted a *Saturday Evening Post* cover of the event in which one of the girls entered the school, depicting all the radiant beauty of innocence Rockwell had long found in the faces of his young white subjects.

Mobs gathered and police restrained them; there was no violence. Two days later, however, mobs "surged through New Orleans streets . . . in demonstrations against school integration that were marked by sporadic rioting, assaults and vandalism." Blacks retaliated by throwing rocks and bottles and prepared Molotov cocktails. The Louisiana Citizens Council gathered a mob of five thousand shouting segregationists. White students boycotted the schools the blacks had entered. The state legislature called for Judge Wright to step down. Louisiana Senator Russell B. Long said, "I would personally vote to impeach the entire Supreme Court if I thought my vote would do it. But we simply do not have the votes." The Louisiana House of Representatives passed a resolution accusing President Eisenhower and the federal courts of "making common cause with the Communist conspiracy."

In two hearings in early 1961, in which the United States attorney appeared on our side, the district court knocked out some additional state laws.

The year 1961 marked the beginning of a new administration in Washington and, with it, a change in the composition of the federal judiciary in the South. Not long after desegregation began in Louisiana, John F. Kennedy named Skelly Wright to the United States Court of Appeals for the District of Columbia. Under any other circumstances Wright would have been promoted to the Fifth Circuit Court of Appeals. But sending him to the D.C. Circuit gave Wright a well-deserved promotion, while it served these segregationists in Louisiana as well, getting rid of a jurist who was dedicated to upholding the law in the face of all manner of challenges. Kennedy replaced Wright with Frank Ellis, his Louisiana campaign manager. While not as unfriendly to blacks as some other Kennedy-appointed Southern judges, Ellis went right to work cutting back on Wright's desegregation orders, limiting them to the first grade, and did little to enforce civil rights law.

Virginia and Maryland

Virginia's white public and politicians, though farther North, were right up there with those of Louisiana in the vanguard of the massive resisters of segregation. But the small group of black lawyers there, led mainly by Spotts Robinson, with Oliver Hill, Jim Nabrit III, Frank Reeves, and Otto Tucker, battered the state into some acquiescence, so that by mid-1960, 103 black children were in school with whites.

Much earlier, in November 1955, I had filed suit against Harford County, Maryland, and the school board there agreed to admit children without regard to race, beginning in September 1956. I therefore dropped the case, typing the order myself in the clerk's office, making clear that I was withdrawing the suit only because black children would be admitted to the white schools. But when four of the plaintiffs applied to the white schools, the board rejected them. Learning of this I tried to open the case but the Judge, Roszel Thomsen, held that we had to exhaust our administrative remedies before being allowed back into court, and then ordered the school board to reconsider the applications of only two of the four plaintiffs. I argued that the school board was bound by the representation on which I had dismissed the complaint. The Fourth Circuit upheld the judge.[3] The school board then announced that it would admit black students in all grades by 1963.

---

[3] Slade v. Board of Education of Harford County, 252 F. 2d 291 (4th Cir. 1958).

Pupil Assignment: The Defense In Depth

In the early years after *Brown,* only in Mississippi was the black community too intimidated to file even one case. Then, when across the South violence finally was beaten down, and outright defiance was subdued, blacks had to run the gauntlet of pupil assignment, which in the end became the South's most effective defense against desegregation. Pupil assignment statutes erected unknowable and insurmountable procedural barriers to desegregating and put a premium on lying; officials could exclude children because of race simply by giving false reasons for the exclusion, including adverse effects on health, welfare, and the effective administration of the schools.

The stratagem had its origins in the South Carolina case that had gone to the Supreme Court as part of *Brown.* Less than six weeks after the Supreme Court's implementation decision returned *Briggs* to the district court, Judge Parker, while declaring the South Carolina school segregation laws "null and void," merely enjoined the defendants from excluding blacks after they made the necessary arrangements "for admission . . . on a non-discriminatory basis with all deliberate speed." He added:

> If the schools which [the state] maintains are open to children of all races, no violation of the Constitution is involved even though the children of different races voluntarily attend different schools, as they attend different churches. . . . *The Constitution, in other words, does not require integration. It merely forbids discrimination.* It does not forbid such segregation as occurs as the result of voluntary action.[4]

Parker's opinion imposed no deadline, invited school boards to do nothing and placed the burden of change on blacks, enlisting black fear and white recalcitrance in the cause of the status quo. Applicants might have to learn how whites were assigned, something about their residence, grades, and conduct, or what went on during deliberations of the board—among an almost infinite num-

---

[4] Briggs v. Elliot, 132 F. Supp. 776, 777 (E.D.S.C. 1955) (emphasis supplied).

ber of possibilities. A simple matter of applying to a school would become, literally and figuratively, a big federal case.

The Parker opinion encouraged widespread adoption of pupil placement laws. The people who drew up the North Carolina law were said to have been good friends of Parker. Thurgood said he had learned that Parker had privately offered the opinion to state officials that such laws would meet the requirements of *Brown*. In any event, Arkansas, Florida, Louisiana, Mississippi, North Carolina, South Carolina, Tennessee, Texas, and Virginia all adopted such laws. They typically required that children might transfer from one school to another according to vague criteria, such as (in North Carolina) "health, safety and general welfare." They authorized local school boards to adopt rules for transfers and set up appeal procedures. Transfer forms were distributed only on certain days and had to be picked up in person (usually during working hours), returned in person promptly, and notarized. Appeals had to be in person, not through counsel. Every state with such laws first placed black and white children in the "school the child normally would attend."

Within pupil assignment some systems adopted grade-a-year plans, admitting black children to the first grade during the first year of the plan, to the second during the second year, and so forth, under which plan it would take twelve years to integrate the system. The rationale was that younger children take to integration better. But other grade-a-year plans admitted blacks to white schools in the twelfth grade during the first year, to the eleventh during the second year, and so forth, on the theory that older children integrate better.

Other districts enacted minority-to-majority transfer procedures, which made it sound as if they were dealing with both races equally: A white child assigned to a predominantly black school had the right to transfer, and a black child assigned to a predominantly white school also might transfer. The practical effect of such policy was that the education system remained totally segregated, or very nearly so.

We had to consider whether to attack pupil assignment head-on as unconstitutional, or whether to build a record of how it worked, to demonstrate that it was, in fact, a means of perpetuating segregation. If we were able to attack it head on, or on its face, and it was upheld, it might then be viewed as presumptively valid in later challenges based on how it was applied—or so we thought. We believed that the Supreme Court, having struggled through three years of *Brown,* and having observed the Southern uprising against it, would be reluctant to confront school segregation so soon again. We decided to forego the head-on attack and to build a record instead.

The slow, yet continuing, growth of the black bar proved to be a mixed blessing. Other lawyers had ideas different from ours and chose to attack pupil assignment head-on. They lost.[5]

One of the early cases was in Asheville, North Carolina, the birthplace of novelist Thomas Wolfe. High in the Smoky Mountains— the area had once been a favorite summer resort of the Vanderbilts, whose red-tile-roofed estates dominated the area—Asheville had a single black lawyer, Reuben Dailey. Its black population was small and those not engaged in agriculture worked in local mica mines, out in the "hollers" (hollows), as the locals called the area. Black kids had to make what was an eighty-mile round trip to the nearest black school.

I spent a lot of time in many hearings in Judge Wilson Warlick's court, watching him sentence moonshiners while I waited for my case to be heard. I finally won a court order requiring the local school board to admit some plaintiffs to a white school. This was the first court order in North Carolina requiring any desegregation. Courtroom skirmishes continued into 1963.

I brought my sons Josiah and David, then aged eight and six, to Asheville. We stayed in Reuben Dailey's house, and the boys came to court with me the next day. Then, with Conrad Pearson, we traveled to a nearby Indian reservation where I bought them a peace pipe and had their pictures taken with Indians in full headdress. Their clearest recollections are of the enormous quantities of fried chicken they consumed and of Reuben feeding his dogs chicken bones, which was supposed to be death for dogs in the North; Reuben's dogs ap-

---

[5] Carson v. Warlick, 238 F.2d 724 (4th Cir. 1956), *cert. denied,* 353 U.S. 910 (1957); Shuttlesworth v. Birmingham Board of Education, 162 F. Supp. 372 (N.D. Ala.), *aff'd,* 358 U.S. 101 (1958). In the Alabama case, the Supreme Court, in affirming, wrote that in some later case the law might be challenged as applied.

parently thrived on them. They have no memories of the historic drama played out in the courtroom.

We didn't have much luck with grade-a-year plans either. Shortly after *Brown II* Thurgood sued the Nashville, Tennessee, schools with local counsel—Avon Williams, Thurgood's cousin, who had graduated from Boston University Law School and begun practice in 1949, and Avon's partner, Z. (Zephaniah) Alexander Looby, who had graduated from Columbia Law School in 1925. Looby, as Thurgood called him—Avon referred always to "Mr. Looby"—spoke with a West Indian accent, walked with a bad limp, and, remarkably, was elected to the Nashville city council in 1964. Looby and Williams were the only lawyers handling civil rights cases in Nashville and most of eastern Tennessee at that time. There was another black lawyer in Knoxville, Carl Cowan, and a couple in Memphis, right on the Mississippi border.

Not long after *Brown,* the board submitted a plan to permit blacks to attend white schools in the first grade, which the federal district court held was an acceptable start. But it was a struggle every inch of the way. It later held unconstitutional a state law allowing segregated schools to exist with nonsegregated ones, and rejected the school board's argument that we had to exhaust administrative remedies. In 1958 the court ordered the board to present a plan to desegregate the entire system.[6]

In the meantime, John Kasper, a notorious segregationist, led riots to attack first-grade desegregation. A bomb destroyed a synagogue. Hattie Cotton School, where one black child was enrolled, was bombed. The school board then proposed that blacks be permitted to transfer to white schools one grade each year commencing in 1958, completing the process in 1968, actually a little faster than grade-a-year. The courts upheld the plan. We took the case to the Supreme Court, which refused to hear it.

Pupil assignment, grade-a-year integration, and minority-to-majority transfer accommodated to the violence, the political re-

---

[6] McKissick v. Carmichael, 187 F.2d 949 (4th Cir. 1951), *cert. denied,* 341 U.S. 951 (1951).

monstrances, and the threat of congressional retaliation. They allowed schools to claim they were desegregating, while actually doing nothing, or very little, and allowed courts to dismiss cases or enter minimal orders. The best remedy for this inertia would be a change in political climate.

The Extent of School Desegregation: 1960

By end of the 1950s LDF had commenced more than sixty elementary and high school cases, but only a few had been concluded. The issues under litigation included flat refusals to desegregate (Louisiana and Virginia), outright violence (Little Rock), lower courts' reluctance to enforce the law vigorously (Maryland, South Carolina, Texas, and Virginia), pupil placement rules (Maryland, North Carolina, and Tennessee), and other stratagems to subvert integration. Many cases involved a combination of resistance tactics. In June 1960, forty-six school cases were still pending in Arkansas, Delaware, Florida, Georgia, Kentucky, Louisiana, Maryland, North Carolina, South Carolina, Tennessee, Texas, Virginia, and West Virginia—virtually all LDF cases.

The LDF staff and board urged that something be done to spur blacks and whites to do more apart from litigation. Even before *Brown II*, June Shagaloff and Dan Byrd were already working with community groups. As early as January 1955 we had hired three educational specialists to work with NAACP branches, churches, labor groups, and school boards to bring about desegregation without legal action. We set up a committee of social scientists, including more than forty scholars, under the leadership of Alfred McClung Lee, a professor of education at Brooklyn College, and Kenneth Clark, to offer expert advice. Dr. John W. Davis, former president of West Virginia State College, set up a department of Teacher Information and Security at LDF to preserve jobs of black teachers. The idea was right. However, while the field workers and social scientists were able to promote desegregation in a few Northern and border areas, they were greatly underfunded and badly understaffed, which severely limited what they could accomplish.

What had all our efforts achieved? By June 1960, in five states of the Deep South—Alabama, Georgia, Louisiana, Mississippi, and South Carolina—not a single black child was in school with whites. In Arkansas, Florida, North Carolina, Tennessee, and Virginia the numbers of black children attending white schools ranged from 34 to 169. But in border areas the numbers were substantial: Delaware, 6,196; the District of Columbia, 73,290; Kentucky, estimated 12,000; Maryland, 28,072; Missouri, estimated 35,000; Oklahoma, estimated 10,000; Texas, estimated 3,300; and West Virginia, estimated 12,000. Little of this, however, was genuine integration, generally consisting instead of a few blacks in formerly white schools and not of whites in formerly black schools. Virtually no school districts were yet fully integrated, with all students assigned to schools on bases other than race.

States began improving the schools blacks attended. There were two basic motivations for this change. The first, of course, was that blacks might be less inclined to transfer from all-black schools if the schools available to them were of a higher quality. The states were, however, too late in coming to this understanding. The states' second reason for improving the conditions of black schools was that if any whites ended up having to go to black schools they would at least be decent schools. Of course, the prospect of lawsuits was no doubt the ultimate moving force.

Another important effect of the suits was that they kept the issue before the public: Blacks, especially, now knew they had rights that the majority population had an obligation to respect. This new awareness soon translated into the civil rights movement of the 1960s.

PART IV

THE MOVEMENT TAKES OFF

CHAPTER 12

CRUSHING JIM CROW

Out of the Courts and into the Streets

Although none of us knew it at the time, *Brown* marked the end of that phase of the civil rights struggle in which all our important victories were won in court. By 1960, six years after *Brown,* the "spirit of revolt"—Margold's phrase—was a nationwide phenomenon.

After *Brown,* and partly because of it, in 1960 the movement began a pervasive transformation of America with regard to race, not merely in constitutional law, but in the ways people treated each other, whether mandated by law or not. Black people, increasingly joined by whites, spoke up for racial equality in numbers so large and in protests so vigorous that they could not be ignored.

They refused to put up with back-of-the-bus treatment, not just in buses but in any of the many places where they daily interacted with whites. They would no longer be denied the right to try on clothes in department stores. They wanted to be served at the lunch counters of the dime stores where they bought soap and toothpaste. They claimed a share of the jobs in offices and factories and universities where previously the presumption had been that such jobs were the exclusive preserve of whites. They pressed volubly and openly for the vote. They couldn't be made to go away by harassment or by the threat of arrest, or even by the actual arrest of a handful of their swelling numbers.

In the late 1950s the idea of nonviolent protest in the form of sit-ins began taking root at various points in the South—it had earlier appeared only sporadically. In 1959 in Nashville, James Lawson, a black theology student at Vanderbilt University, who had been to India and studied Gandhi's nonviolent movement and who had been a conscientious objector in the Korean War, began conducting a series of workshops on nonviolent protest against segregation in downtown restaurants. The Nashville students soon became active in the movement, but before they could act, on February 1, 1960, four black freshman at North Carolina Agricultural and Technical College, all members of the NAACP Youth Council, took the lead by demonstrating at Woolworth's in Greensboro.

Franklin McCain, one of the original Greensboro four (and later a product development manager at Hoechst Celanese Corporation), recalled that his mother was concerned over his safety; she wanted him to withdraw from the demonstrations. His father, knowing that his son would continue on the road he had chosen even if told not to, said, "Do what you have to, but be careful." McCain says that there weren't many fathers like that. Parents of most of the other protesters wanted their sons to stop sitting in for fear they would be physically hurt. Their attitude was that they had sent their children off to college to get an education, not to protest. McCain recalls that *Brown* inspired these young students not as the vindication of a basic legal principle, but as an example of determined people setting out to accomplish something and succeeding. The synergy of law and social action was manifest. As one of the leaders of the Greensboro sit-in, Joe McNeil, put it: "I was particularly inspired by the people in Little Rock. . . . I was really impressed with the courage that those kids had and the leadership they displayed."

The four protesters entered the store, sat at the white lunch counter, and demanded service. They sat for an hour, until the store closed, but no one served them. Something about the quiet resolve of the four must have captured the imagination of the national press and television because the event was reported nationally the next day; after that things changed. The following day more students sat in. The third day well over a hundred protesters turned out. That number soon multiplied to about a thousand. The students were orderly, well dressed, and nonviolent.

Suddenly, it was as if a spark had been struck in an oxygen-filled atmosphere. The sit-ins spontaneously spread to neighboring cities in North Carolina and within two weeks they were all over the South. Blacks began demanding nonsegregated service at lunch counters, department stores, bus terminals, and all the places from which they had been excluded or segregated; supporters joined them at branches of the offending chain stores in the North as well. But not everyone saw what was happening the same way: Harry Truman, who had been a courageous civil rights pioneer when he was president, thought that the demonstrations were Communist-led.

The sit-ins spread like wildfire to other Woolworth's stores and to such establishments as S. H. Kress, W. T. Grant, Liggett's, Sears Roebuck, Belk's, Ivey's, and other stores, national and local. Amazingly, the thousands of demonstrators, part of no organized group, seemed all to have spontaneously signed on to the nonviolent credo, for the demonstrators were nearly universally peaceful. Their massive presence had the desired effect of preventing the stores from doing their normal business.

Connie Motley Marches Through Georgia

On January 6, 1961, Judge William A. Bootle ordered the University of Georgia to admit two applicants to college, Charlayne Hunter, later to become Charlene Hunter-Gault, an important TV personality, and Hamilton Holmes, now a distinguished physician in Georgia. Even though *Sweatt* had been decided in 1950, and Connie Motley had filed suit for Hunter and Holmes in 1959, the university rejected both, interposing one spurious justification after another.

Vernon Jordan, who became one of Washington and New York's great movers and shakers, was NAACP field secretary in Georgia in 1961. He took Hunter and Holmes to the registrar's office through a crowd of students shouting "Nigger go home." As they waited to register, a loud cheer arose from the crowd. Word had arrived that Judge Bootle had just granted the state's motion for a stay of his order and some white students looking in over the transom yelled, "The nigger lawyer ain't smiling no more."

But Georgia had not counted on Connie Motley's indomitability. Immediately, she raced to Atlanta to Judge Elbert Tuttle of the court of appeals, where she filed a petition to vacate Bootle's stay.

He did—then and there. A newspaper headlined the story, "Tuttle Boots Bootle." The political uproar intensified. Attorney General Eugene Cook went on television to announce that he would fly to Washington and petition the Supreme Court to reinstate Bootle's stay. Connie saw the broadcast, called me in New York—I had already gone home—and I called Jim Nabrit, who lived not too far away. He drove to my house and together we drafted a response to Cook's application.

There was, however, a problem: We had to prepare an answer to an application we had not seen. But we assumed that Cook would make the arguments one must, which would deal with the likelihood of success on appeal, and the relative harm that the parties would suffer if the stay were granted or denied. As to the first, certainly we would win on appeal. As to relative harm, Georgia could not demonstrate any legally cognizable injury to the university if Holmes and Hunter were to be allowed to enter while the appeal worked its way through the courts. Hunter and Holmes, on the other hand, would suffer considerable damage if their entry to college were delayed. As well, Little Rock had made clear that courts shouldn't bow to riots.

Late into the night Jim and I batted out the response. The next morning we flew to Washington on the earliest plane and arrived at the Supreme Court shortly after it opened. We went to the clerk's office to inspect Cook's petition, but Cook had not yet arrived. I asked E. P. Cullinan, the chief deputy clerk, whether he would take our response to papers that had not yet been filed, and he agreed. We left the papers and wandered around the corridors to kill time.

Later that morning Cook arrived, accompanied by assistant attorneys general, trailed by reporters and TV cameramen. As he strode down the hallways, he issued pronouncements, which I could not hear clearly. Then he reached the clerk's office and, with a flourish, handed his papers to the clerk, announcing, "Here is the application of the State of Georgia for a stay." At which point Cullinan, deadpan, handed him my papers and replied, "And here is Mr. Greenberg's response." That day the Court denied Cook's application.

Hunter and Holmes entered the university. At the same time, Connie continued to press her attack. That day she filed an application for a temporary restraining order (TRO) to restrain the governor and other officials from enforcing a law cutting off funds to schools that integrated pursuant to a court order. The court immediately issued the TRO and set the case down for hearing on January 12 to decide whether to issue a preliminary injunction, which would remain in effect until a full trial could be held.

At the hearing Connie got the preliminary injunction, but rioting broke out at the university and state officials hustled Hunter and Holmes off the campus. Georgia obviously was hoping for a replay of the Autherine Lucy case; once Autherine was removed from the campus she would not return until 1989. That same day Connie brought the suspensions to Judge Bootle's attention, and he ordered that formal pleadings be filed the next day to enjoin them. Connie got the papers into court the next day. Bootle held a hearing, and ordered that the suspensions be lifted and that Hunter and Holmes be readmitted on January 16.[1] They went back to school, Georgia appealed Bootle's orders, and the case bounced around the courts for a while.

I'm afraid I may be painting a picture of Connie as all grim devotion to the cause. That would be inaccurate, for she cared about some of the fun factors in life, about friends, family, and is recalled by many from those times for her more human side. Derrick Bell, who used to be an LDF lawyer, once said that if he ever were to write his memoirs about his days at LDF, half the book would consist of describing his trips to the drugstore to buy hair curlers and other articles for Connie.

Universities in Mississippi, Alabama, and South Carolina still held out, and we soon moved against them. On May 31, Connie filed *Meredith v. Fair,* for James Meredith, against the University of Mississippi; it would not come to a head for a good many months. Thurgood had pondered long and hard before ordering her to pro-

---

[1] Danner v. Holmes, 191 F. Supp. 385 (M.D. Ga. 1960), *permanent injunction granted,* 191 F. Supp. 394 (M.D. Ga. 1961).

ceed. He feared bloodshed and didn't want to proceed without being certain that Meredith really wanted to go to Ole Miss.

James Meredith Wants to Enter Ole Miss

In 1958, Clennon King, a black professor at black Alcorn State University, applied to Ole Miss; the state locked him up in a mental hospital. In 1959, Clyde Kennard, an African-American applied to white Mississippi Southern College and was prosecuted for a variety of criminal charges, culminating in a seven-year prison sentence for burglary for stealing chicken feed. R. Jess Brown twice took Kennard's case to the Supreme Court of Mississippi, which ruled against him, and then Thurgood and Connie petitioned the United States Supreme Court, which refused to hear the case.[2] We went to the United States District Court in December 1962, where we lost. As we prepared an appeal, the governor, in January 1963, released Kennard, citing his ill health.

Around the time the sit-ins and Freedom Rides began, James Meredith, a black air force veteran from Kosciusko, Mississippi, was thinking of attending the University of Mississippi. Meredith wrote to the university in January 1961 for an application to transfer from Jackson State (a black school) and received a form asking for character references from five alumni and a picture. He completed the application, but because as a black man he did not know any Ole Miss alumni who would support his application (the idea behind the requirement), he included recommendations of five blacks and attached his picture. Ole Miss countered by saying it was overcrowded and wouldn't act on applications received after January 25—although the following semester it admitted more than three hundred more students than before, evidence that there was plenty of room. It then adopted a rule restricting transfer admissions to students from schools whose programs it approved.

Around this time Meredith wrote to us for legal assistance: "I am making this move in, what I consider, the interest of and for the

---

[2] Kennard v. State of Mississippi, 242 Miss. 691, 128 So. 2d 572 (1961), *cert. denied*, 368 U.S. 869 (1961).

benefit of: (1) my country, (2) my race, (3) my family, and (4) myself. I am familiar with the probable difficulties involved in such a move as I am undertaking, and I am fully prepared to pursue it all the way to a degree from the University of Mississippi."

Thurgood called Meredith and concluded that he was serious. But starting a case to integrate Ole Miss had to be viewed with trepidation. Nevertheless, there seemed to be no alternative. If we didn't take the case someone else might, and violence might occur anyway. Moreover, the case might, if taken by a lawyer or lawyers lacking the Fund's expertise, be botched legally, making future applications to Ole Miss even more difficult. Thurgood assigned the case to Connie, who just had won Charlayne Hunter and Hamilton Holmes's case against the University of Georgia. But, as racist as Georgia was, it was mild compared to Mississippi when it came to a capacity for violent response.

Mississippi rejected Meredith, citing a new rule: Students might transfer only from accredited institutions, and Jackson State wasn't accredited. With R. Jess Brown, Connie filed our complaint in United States District Court on May 31, 1961, asking for a preliminary injunction so Meredith could attend the June 8 summer session. From that point onward, Meredith's case was in the news, often on front pages and on national television.

R. Jess Brown was one of the three black Mississippi lawyers on whom we relied. Slight in stature, hawk faced, with sunken cheeks, he quietly and unassumingly made it possible for Connie to accomplish what had to be done. But while Connie was all business, and admired Brown's courage, she could not restrain herself from occasionally chiding him for wearing red socks, which he often did. He showed some little irritation with the criticism, but got on with the job.

Judge Sidney C. Mize set the hearing for June 12, after school was scheduled to open, and Connie made her first of more than twenty trips to Mississippi for Meredith. In mid-hearing, in the first of a series of delays and obfuscations, Mize suspended the proceedings and reset them for July 10, after the end of the first summer session. On July 10 he announced he couldn't hear the case that day after all and reset it for August 10, past the start of the second summer session. He held hearings August 10, 15, and 16. Fall registration ended

September 28, but Mize didn't rule until December 12, when he denied a preliminary injunction. He found that Meredith had not been rejected because he was black.[3]

By this time, Thurgood had left LDF to take his seat on the United States Court of Appeals for the Second Circuit, and I was in charge.

Connie sped to the court of appeals, which, a month later, ruled against Meredith in form, although it was a victory in substance for us. Judge John Minor Wisdom's opinion rejected Mississippi's incredible claim that it did not segregate, ridiculed Ole Miss's argument that we had to establish the genealogy of its students and alumni to prove that they all were white, and concluded, "We take judicial notice that the state of Mississippi maintains a policy of segregation in its schools and colleges." But the court realized it had a highly controversial case on its hands and cut the squarest of square corners. It ordered a fresh district court hearing at which Mize was required to allow Meredith to introduce evidence that previously had been excluded. Wisdom wrote, "A man should be able to find an education by taking the broad highway. He should not have to take by-roads through the woods and follow winding trails through sharp thickets, in constant tension because of pitfalls and traps, and, after years of effort, perhaps obtain the threshold of his goal when he is past caring about it." Wisdom ordered Mize to decide promptly, in view of the fact that a new school term was scheduled to begin on February 6, 1962.[4]

Mize obeyed the instruction of the court of appeals but remained a pettifogger. He promptly held another hearing and on February 3, concluded, "The evidence overwhelmingly showed that the Plaintiff was not denied admission because of his race. . . . The proof shows and I find as a fact, that the University is not a racially segregated institution."[5] Connie went once more to the court of appeals in New Orleans for an injunction to order Meredith into Ole Miss immediately, while the appeal was going on. Once more, the court of ap-

---

[3] Meredith v. Fair, 199 F. Supp. 754 (S.D. Miss. 1961).

[4] Meredith v. Fair, 298 F.2d 696, 701, 703 (5th Cir. 1962).

[5] Meredith v. Fair, 202 F. Supp. 224 (S.D. Miss. 1962).

peals gave Mississippi more than its full measure of due process, this time by a vote of two to one. On February 12, Judge Rives and Wisdom wrote that the appeal should follow its regular course, but should be speeded up, so that if Meredith were to win he could be admitted before the beginning of the next term. The third member of the bench, Judge Tuttle, dissented, saying that enough was enough.[6]

While the appeal was pending, on June 6, Mississippi arrested Meredith, because he had registered to vote in Jackson, where he attended Jackson State, although his residence was in Kosciusko. We then got an injunction from the court of appeals restraining the prosecutor and the state's attorney general from prosecuting.

On June 25, the court of appeals reversed Judge Mize's rehearing decision and, in a scathing opinion, demolished all of Ole Miss's and Mize's lies: Wisdom called the defense "a carefully calculated campaign of delay, harassment, and masterly inactivity. It was a defense designed to discourage and to defeat by evasive tactics which would have been a credit to Quintus Fabius Maximus." Maximus was a Roman army commander known as a master of attrition and described as famed for "conducting harassing operations while avoiding decisive conflicts." Wisdom concluded that "what everybody knows the court must know." Meredith had seen a psychiatrist while in the air force (one of Ole Miss's arguments for rejecting him), from which Wisdom concluded that his "record shows just about the type of Negro who might be expected to try to crack the racial barrier at the University of Mississippi: a man with a mission and with a nervous stomach."[7]

Three weeks later, on July 17, in the normal course of events, the court's order went down to Judge Mize. The next day a new player entered the scene, prepared to break up the game rather than see his side lose. What followed was an unseemly challenge to the authority of the United States Court of Appeals by one of its own members. Judge Ben F. Cameron, a member of the court of appeals and a Mississippian, ordered a stay of the order his own bench had issued. It

---

[6] Meredith v. Fair, 305 F.2d 341 (5th Cir. 1962).

[7] Meredith v. Fair, 305 F.2d 343, 344–45, 358 (5th Cir. 1962).

was nearly unheard of for a judge who was not one of those who decided a case to stay its mandate. The court of appeals could not have been pleased and on July 27, vacated Cameron's order and, pending Mize's action, entered its own order against Ole Miss, requiring it to admit Meredith.

The next day Cameron once more stayed the court's mandate. The same day the court vacated his order, and on July 31, Cameron entered yet another stay. On August 4, the court overruled Cameron once more.[8] On August 6, Cameron reinstated his order. Apparently afraid they might be caught between conflicting court orders, or, more likely, to make matters more difficult for Meredith, Ole Miss's board of trustees adopted a rule that denied to university officials power "relating to action on the application of James Howard Meredith . . . and the same is reserved exclusively unto this Board of Trustees of Institutions of Higher Learning."

Ole Miss also petitioned the Supreme Court to hear the Meredith case. We waived the right to reply and, to put an end to Cameron's rebellion, asked Justice Black, who handled motions for the Fifth Circuit, to vacate Cameron's latest order. The Supreme Court's clerk asked the Justice Department for its views on Justice Black's power to vacate Cameron's orders. The department's brief argued that Black indeed had the power, that Cameron had acted improperly and that Ole Miss should be required to admit Meredith. On September 10, Justice Black announced that he had consulted all other members of the Court and that "there is very little likelihood that this Court will grant certiorari to review the judgment of the Court of Appeals which essentially involves only factual issues." He enjoined Ole Miss from "taking any steps to prevent enforcement of the Court of Appeals judgment and mandate."[9]

Connie went back to Mize for an injunction to get Meredith into Ole Miss. Now sitting alongside Mize was Harold Cox, a new Kennedy appointee, and possibly the most racist judge ever to sit on

---

[8] Meredith v. Fair, 306 F.2d 374 (5th Cir. 1962).

[9] Meredith v. Fair, 83 S. Ct. 10 (1962).

the federal bench. Mize, at an age that permitted him to enjoy senior status (meaning he had the option of sitting only on those cases he might choose), would soon give up the Meredith case to Cox, and was acquainting him with the case. Cox began indicating that he would deny Connie's motion. But Mize at last knew that this battle had been lost. He placed his hand on Cox's arm and said, "It's all over, Judge Cox." On September 13, Mize ordered Ole Miss to admit Meredith.

The press, radio, television, and religious leaders began stirring racial emotions more than might have been anticipated even in Mississippi. Governor Ross Barnett, on September 13, went on statewide television and invoked the long-discredited and anarchy-inviting right of "interposition" under the Tenth Amendment, claiming it gave Mississippi the right to defy federal court orders. He issued a proclamation, full of "whereases" and "therefores" and "in witness whereofs," to which he "caused the great Seal of the State of Mississippi to be affixed, on this the 13th day of September in the Year of Our Lord, One Thousand Nine Hundred and Sixty-Two." Musical comedy material, but many of Mississippi's racists took it seriously.

The Justice Department began making preparations for trouble. Alerting federal marshals, corrections officers, and border patrolmen who might function as marshals to stand by, it moved to enter the case as a friend of the court. On September 18, Mize refused to allow the Justice Department to enter the case; Justice then went to the court of appeals, which granted the motion. On the 19th a state court enjoined Meredith, Ole Miss, and federal officials from "performing any act intending to enroll and register the Negro, James Meredith."

On the 20th, violating the federal court order, which prohibited prosecuting Meredith for false registration, Mississippi charged and convicted him of that offense. It also passed a law, Senate Bill (S.B.) 1501, prohibiting any person who has a "criminal charge of moral turpitude pending against him or her" from entering any state institution. The law excepted "any charge or conviction of traffic law violations, violation of the state conservation laws and state game and fish laws, or manslaughter as a result of driving while intoxicated." These exceptions covered thousands of Mississippians.

Back to the court of appeals: It gave us an order enjoining enforcement of S.B. 1501 and prohibiting "any steps to effectuate the conviction and sentence . . . of James Meredith for false registration." One can only imagine the effect this refusal of judges to obey superior courts had on the respect for law among young Mississippians.

Seeking to avoid responsibility, the university's board of trustees, on September 20, "invest(ed) Honorable Ross R. Barnett . . . with the full power . . . to act upon all matters pertaining to or concerned with the registration or non-registration, admission or non-admission and/or attendance or non-attendance of James H. Meredith." The orotund style suggested that they thought the words had a magical quality which would absolve them of responsibility.

In the meantime, from the Justice Department, Bobby Kennedy, Burke Marshall, and John Doar called the governor, attorney general, and lawyer friends in the state in an effort to work out a way to get Meredith into Ole Miss peacefully. Before it was all over, the president would call the governor. But from the outset, Connie and I thought that the only way to get Meredith into Ole Miss was with so overwhelming a show of force that violence would be seen as futile. Mississippi had shown that it would go to unprecedented lengths to keep Meredith out, and the state's propensity for racially motivated violence was well established.

I told Justice Department lawyers—particularly John Doar and Burke Marshall—what we thought, but the administration was driven by political motives both lofty and base. On the one hand, a democracy should govern by persuasion and law, and in the first instance should try to act through moral persuasion, not brute strength. At the same time, President Kennedy, while holding pro-civil rights beliefs, and implementing them to some extent, had an important racist Southern constituency that he preferred not to alienate. He tried to satisfy all considerations at once; in the end he satisfied none.

On September 20, the Justice Department took Meredith from Millington Air Force Base in Memphis, on the Mississippi border, to the university campus in Oxford in a border patrol car. In the auditorium of the university's Continuation Center, the registrar told Meredith that only the governor could register him. The governor then entered the room and denied Meredith's application, handing him the proclamation of September 13, the first of a series of rebuffs at the point of registration.

Meredith then returned to Memphis, and we went back into federal court. Connie and I drove to Meridian to Judge Mize's court and, with the Justice Department at our side, petitioned for an order holding the registrar and other university officials in contempt. But on the following day, September 21, Mize ruled that they were not guilty—the trustees had turned the matter over to Barnett and were powerless to act to admit Meredith.

Nothing succeeds like success, and as the governor seemed to have thumbed his nose at the federal government with impunity, segregationist passions rose. What the states of the old Confederacy had been unable to achieve a hundred years earlier, Mississippi would now attempt on its own. Daily newspapers in the state urged "bitter end defiance."

The Fifth Circuit Court of Appeals was in New Orleans, and we set up LDF headquarters at the Dillard University guest house—a nice two-story cottage, with a half-dozen bedrooms and a kitchen, an ample lawn and lovely trees—courtesy of its president, Albert Dent, father of Tom Dent, then our public information director. Meredith, Connie, other staff lawyers who came and went, secretaries, and I readied ourselves to take the case to the court of appeals. NAACP Mississippi field secretary Medgar Evers stayed with us too, since there was a good chance he would become involved in the aftermath of the case.

After a while the place began to resemble a fraternity house. We kept Meredith's presence secret to avoid the press and possible violence against him, but were deluged with so many phone calls that at times we pressed him into service as telephone operator. No one, however, recognized his voice. One night, Meredith ventured out to a dance on the Dillard campus. He later wrote that when the students learned who he was "they literally swamped me for at least forty-five minutes to an hour. . . . I could not guess how many women must have offered themselves to me or asked me to go home with them."

Many of our meals consisted of takeout food from Levata's, a ramshackle seafood joint near the Dillard campus. Big bags containing boiled crabs, oyster rolls (fried oysters on a roll), lemon meringue pie, and Coca-Cola were brought in daily. This diet gave me a bad case of acne by the time the case ended. Sometimes we ate at Dooky Chase, the best black restaurant in town, later a well-publicized tourist stop. We did our legal work out of A. P. Tureaud's office.

Flush with his success thus far, Barnett raised the stakes. On September 24, he issued another proclamation directing the summary arrest and jailing of any representative of the federal government who arrested or attempted to arrest, or who fined or attempted to fine, any state official in the performance of his official duties.

The same day, Connie and I and the Justice Department lawyers were back at the court of appeals. The issue was no longer just the question of one man's right to go to school at his state university. The authority of the federal judiciary had been called into question, and if its authority weren't established, the ability of one of the three branches of the United States government to fulfill the role given it by our Constitution would be seriously undermined. The court took the extraordinary step of gathering eight judges, not the ordinary panel of three—all the eligible judges, plus the highly respected, retired Joseph C. Hutcheson of Texas, a conservative law-and-order type, who had the right to sit but was not required to. Cameron alone didn't show up. Hutcheson was so old that he ascended the bench with great difficulty, but he was outraged and wanted to be there.

In a hearing that went from 11:30 A.M. to 6:32 P.M. the court heard testimony and received evidence, almost unheard of in appellate courts. Its attitude was exemplified by Hutcheson; in referring to the trustees' order giving the governor control of Ole Miss, he asked the attorney general of Mississippi, "Did you advise them that this monkey business of coming around pretending to take over the school was legal?" Finally, during the hearing, the president of the Board of Trustees of Institutions of Higher Learning announced that the board was ready and willing to obey the court's orders. The registrar caved in too and agreed to be in Jackson not later than 1:00 P.M. on September 25 to register and admit Meredith. The court ordered the board to revoke its action of September 4, which relieved university officials of authority to register Meredith; to revoke appointment of Ross Barnett as the board's agent in matters pertaining to Meredith; and to instruct the registrar to register Meredith between 1:00 P.M. and 4:00 P.M. on September 25.

During all of this, Meredith was curiously emotionless, at least in outward appearance. In court and back on campus, he spoke little and always in a soft voice. Sometimes he tapped a foot lightly a few times and prefaced what he had to say with a soft "mmmmmm." Often, while speaking, he smiled and shook his head a little. But, while he was not outwardly demonstrative, he certainly had great determination.

That should have been the end of it. Conservative judges, all of whom had long sat in the South, had expressed their anger at the disobedience of law and court orders. But reactions based on ignorance, goaded by demagogues, and emboldened by interim successes became difficult to control.

Robert Kennedy and Ross Barnett conferred by phone, but got nowhere. Kennedy told Barnett that the federal courts had ruled, and Barnett replied that the Mississippi courts had ruled to the contrary. Barnett would not agree to permit Meredith to register nor would he guarantee Meredith's safety.

At 8:30 A.M. on the morning of September 25, the court of appeals entered a temporary restraining order prohibiting Barnett, State Attorney General Patterson, and a raft of other officials from interfering with Meredith's registration by arresting, suing, injuring, harassing, or threatening him by force or otherwise. Barnett retaliated with another proclamation, which "denied to you, James H. Meredith, admission to the University of Mississippi."

During some of this time Meredith stayed in Memphis and at other times he stayed with us in New Orleans. He traveled by government plane to Mississippi to attempt to register. We drove from the Dillard guest house to the airport, where two identical aircraft, one carrying Meredith, the other a decoy, took off for the trip, a tactic designed to confuse any Mississippian who might try to end the matter by shooting down Meredith's plane—security people did not dismiss such an outrage as beyond infuriated Mississippians. I thought that if they'd shoot down one plane they'd shoot down two. As it turned out, the greatest peril to materialize appeared when the car taking us to the airport, traveling fast, hit a campus speed bump designed to slow traffic, and we bounced up, banging our heads sharply against the roof of the car.

At the state office building, Meredith, accompanied by John Doar and other Justice Department representatives, once more tried to register. Barnett, reading his latest proclamation, once more denied admission. Meredith turned back, passing through a jeering, threatening crowd, to try again another day.

The court of appeals slapped back an order that evening requiring the governor to appear in court in New Orleans at 10:00 A.M., September 28, "to show cause, if any he has, why he should not be held in civil contempt of the temporary restraining order entered by the Court this day." Justice officials, including Attorney General Kennedy and Burke Marshall, continued their telephone negotiations with the governor, state attorney general, lawyers for the university, and trustees, trying to work out a formula to get Meredith into the university. But Mississippi continued to stonewall.

Although I knew nothing of the details of the negotiations, my own sense of the depth of the racism we were facing was different from that of administration officials. I objected that there was no way the Justice Department would ever persuade Mississippi other than by a show of more than sufficient force, such as Eisenhower had used in Little Rock.

Nevertheless, Justice officers took Meredith from Dillard to Oxford once more on Wednesday, September 26, to try again. This time Lieutenant Governor Paul Johnson turned him away. The *New York Times* reported that the Little Rock confrontation "seemed tonight to be just a shadow of the crisis developing in Mississippi. . . . Officials are in open defiance of Federal Law. Governor Barnett and his aides, evidently supported by state policemen, sheriffs and other law-enforcement officers numbering in the hundreds, are evidently prepared to offer physical resistance to Federal officers."

When mobs become intoxicated on their own rage, there is always someone willing to exploit it, even to raise it to insane levels. A state senator called for resistance "regardless of the cost in human life."

In the meantime Bobby Kennedy and Mississippi representatives were trying to work out a registration charade. They continued to keep Connie and me entirely in the dark, telling us nothing. Later, it was revealed that Mississippi had proposed that federal marshals should draw their guns, at which point Mississippi officials would step aside and, with a show of yielding to federal threats, would permit Meredith to enter the university. Kennedy countered that he preferred that only one marshal draw a gun, but that wasn't enough for Mississippi. Kennedy upped his offer: One marshal would draw a gun; the others would put their hands on their holsters. That still wasn't enough for Barnett, and so Kennedy gave in and agreed that all the marshals would draw their guns.

Kennedy and Mississippi officials having come to an agreement, Meredith's registration was once again attempted. But when a federal convoy carrying Meredith got within fifty miles of Oxford on Thursday the 27th, the mobs had grown so large and threatening that the convoy turned around and headed back. I issued a statement announcing that enough was enough:

> We had advised Mr. Meredith that we do not believe he should return to the University of Mississippi campus unless he is accompanied by sufficient force to assure his enrollment and continued attendance. He agrees with us. We have so informed the Department of Justice.
>
> A trip to the campus, which tentatively had been planned for today, with a force of marshals which may have been insufficient was not made after we asserted this position. Beyond question the United States possesses sufficient power to enforce the orders of its courts and assure the rights of its citizens, and we have no doubt that it will employ that power.

We filed motions, along with the Justice Department, in the court of appeals asking that Barnett be held in civil contempt. At each stage we made sure to file our own motions and be in court ourselves, refusing to allow Justice to conduct alone the case that they had treated with a mix of dither, politics, and principle.

On Friday, September 28, the scene shifted back to the court of appeals in New Orleans. Connie and I represented Meredith; Burke Marshall, John Doar, and St. John Barrett represented the Justice Department; and a team of defense lawyers represented the university, its trustees, and the state of Mississippi. But no one showed up for Governor Barnett. Mississippi's lawyer was John C. Satterfield of Yazoo City, the crown jewel of the Mississippi bar and the 1961–62 president of the American Bar Association, a position, as Satterfield soon showed, that reveals more about bar association politics than about professional skill or responsibility. Satterfield announced that he appeared for the state as a friend of the court and that no one in the courtroom represented Ross Barnett. Barnett was ducking service; Satterfield was claiming he was a friend of the court, not Barnett's counsel, in order to take the position that the court couldn't find Barnett in contempt because he hadn't been served and was not represented.

Looking like a praying mantis, Satterfield tiptoed around the courtroom as he addressed the court in elaborate, deferential tones and filed a motion to dismiss the complaint against Barnett. But the judges immediately caught on. Judge Tuttle replied: "All the Court has given the State of Mississippi the right to do, Mr. Satterfield, is to present the views of the State of Mississippi. The Court has thus far not authorized the State of Mississippi to file any pleadings on behalf of the Defendant . . . Barnett."

Tuttle conferred with the court and announced that Satterfield would not be allowed to proceed until the court determined whether Barnett had been served.

Satterfield asked whether he might make objections to evidence. Tuttle, visibly irritated, answered, "You can assume Counsel for Amicus Curiae has no right to object to any of the evidence." Satterfield replied, "To which we except," using a term that was formerly used to identify a ruling that could be appealed, but that was no longer employed in federal court. Tuttle riposted, "You also have no right to except, I might add." Satterfield, in drippingly deferential tones, responded, "Certainly. That is correct, sir. I am sorry." Tuttle, not letting go, added, "And you needn't do it anyway," pointing out Satterfield's ignorance of the Federal Rules, which had abolished the practice of oral exceptions as repetitive and time consuming.

The government then proved that Barnett had been served, in person, by mail, and by Western Union night letter, with the court order requiring him to admit Meredith. A deputy marshal testified that he went twice to Barnett's office to serve the contempt citation and found it closed, with a piece of paper reading "office closed" affixed to the door. Attempting to serve the citation for a third time that day, the marshal found a group of state police at the door. They refused to state their names, refused to accept service, and warned against leaving the papers on the floor. The marshal left. On a further attempt, the attorney general of Mississippi refused to receive service for the governor. In another effort the marshal was turned away from the governor's home.

Satterfield once more arose to say, "May I respectfully suggest to the Court, it might be of benefit to the Court to have the credentials he exhibited introduced." Tuttle shut him up: "Mr. Satterfield, I do not think you are in a position to make any suggestions." Satterfield, ever obsequious: "Thank you, sir." Judge Rives, exasperated, went after Satterfield, and asked whether he represented the governor. Satterfield said he did not.

Rives then asked, "What communication have you had with the Governor of Mississippi?"

Satterfield evaded, "Within what period of time?"

Rives said, "Since last Tuesday night."

Satterfield once more evaded, "I think it would take several hours to go into that fully."

Rives, now becoming furious, continued the attack:

> RIVES: Have you seen the Governor in person?
> SATTERFIELD: Yes, of course.
> RIVES: . . . Did you discuss this Order with the Governor?
> SATTERFIELD: Do you care to have me sworn as a witness, may it please the Court?
> RIVES: No, I am asking you as attorney.
> SATTERFIELD: I thought I was not privileged to participate in the proceeding until later. I am sorry.
> RIVES: You are an attorney and officer of the Court?
> SATTERFIELD: Correct.
> RIVES: And I ask you as an attorney and officer of the Court.
> SATTERFIELD: May I respectfully object to being questioned by the Court unless I have the status of participating attorney, which I do not have.
> RIVES: Yes, you may object, but I still want an answer.

Rives and Judge Brown then wrung from Satterfield that two days earlier he had discussed with the governor the order to show cause and the time for which it was scheduled to be heard, which Barnett had learned by reading the newspapers, and that Barnett had obtained copies of the recently prepared court papers in the case. At that point Barnett was nailed and Satterfield's petty evasiveness exposed for what it was.

Nevertheless, further into the day Satterfield presented a motion to dismiss the contempt proceedings against Barnett. Tuttle at that point called a brief recess to confer with the court. Satterfield asked for "the privilege of presenting authorities" to the judges. Tuttle, expressing the annoyance of all the judges at Satterfield's temerity in continuing to speak up after he had been silenced, responded: "You don't know what I am talking about to the Court." When the Court finished conferring it lowered the boom on Satterfield. Tuttle announced, "The Court has unanimously voted to revoke its order permitting the State of Mississippi to appear as Amicus Curiae or in any other matter in the case. The Court will hear no further arguments on that. That is a final decision. I want to make it perfectly clear that the Court now revokes its order previously entered orally, permitting the State of Mississippi to appear in the case."

Satterfield tried to come back with another motion "with complete deference and respect." But Tuttle responded curtly, "The motion is denied."

Another Mississippi lawyer tried to pick up where Satterfield left off. Garner W. Green of Jackson challenged the court's jurisdiction and said that "the State of Mississippi is vitally affected by it and bloodshed may result from the continuation."

Tuttle jumped in with, "We have heard about the possibility of bloodshed for the last ten years."

Hutcheson intervened: "You are not threatening the Court with bloodshed, are you?"

Green retreated: "Oh, no, oh, no. I didn't say that at all, Your Honor." And he went on about how he wanted to have the issue resolved by legal proceedings.

Tuttle cut it all off: "Now we will not get into any further Socratic discussion of the case." Satterfield once more tried to participate, but once more was barred. Tuttle announced, "The Court has determined that there was adequate service of the citation."

Later that day the court entered its order holding Barnett in civil contempt, committing him to "the custody of the Attorney General of the United States and . . . [to] pay a fine to the United States of $10,000 per day unless on or before Tuesday, October 2nd, 1962 at 11 A.M.," he ceases resisting the orders of the courts. The order also required the governor to maintain law and order at Ole Miss "to the end that James H. Meredith be permitted to register and remain as a student."

On Saturday, September 29, the President tried his hand at persuading Barnett by phone. The President asked for obedience to the law. Barnett wanted delay. At one point the President made a deal with Barnett by which Meredith would register in Jackson, while Barnett and John Doar would pretend to be in Oxford for the purpose of registering him, thereby diverting mobs from the scene. But then Barnett changed his mind.

In the meantime, the government's inaction left time for passions to rise even more. At the Saturday night Ole Miss football game, fans displayed what must have been the largest Confederate flag in the world. Governor Barnett spoke to the cheering crowd, affirming his allegiance to the customs of Mississippi. Retired General Edwin A. Walker, who had commanded federal troops in Little Rock, and later became a John Bircher, called for volunteers to come to Mississippi to resist federal encroachment.

Finally, on September 30, at long last, President Kennedy issued a proclamation that directed all persons to cease and desist obstruction of justice against court orders that required Meredith's admission. Later that day, Kennedy issued an Executive Order that directed the secretary of defense to take all appropriate steps to enforce orders of the courts in the *Meredith* case. Faced with a threat of violence, that was by now much greater than that at Little Rock, the administration amassed a potential military presence. A few hundred army troops and about five hundred marshals gathered at the Millington Naval Air Station on the Mississippi border—only a fraction of the force mobilized by President Eisenhower—one thousand airborne troops sent right to the scene and 9,936 National Guardsmen federalized and activated.

Late that afternoon, Meredith, with John Doar and the United States marshal in charge, James J. McShane, flew from Millington to Oxford. They drove from the airport to Baxter Hall, a campus dormitory. The Mississippi Highway Patrol, federal marshals, and troops were already on campus. Meredith went to a room that had been selected for him, a second-floor counselor's apartment, and began reading a school assignment. To Meredith it appeared that the campus was deserted—most of the students apparently had gone to Jackson for the football game. In fact, they were beginning to return and, by 7:00 P.M., they formed a mob that was becoming large and nasty, taunting and threatening marshals. One member of the mob sprayed a fire extinguisher in the face of an army truck driver. Soon the rioters began throwing stones. To make things worse, Governor Barnett, or another state official, ordered the highway patrol to leave the campus. Only strenuous efforts by Justice, including phone calls between Bobby Kennedy and the governor, got that decision reversed.

The mob began to turn upon the press, attacking a TV cameraman, reporters, and photographers. They beat a faculty member who attempted to protect a camera that rioters were trying to smash. The crowd threw rocks, bottles, bricks, lead pipes, Coke bottles filled with flaming gasoline, and acid. Finally, the marshals fired tear gas at the mob and, incidentally, at the Mississippi Highway Patrol.

At the same time President Kennedy went on radio and television. He called for adherence to law and urged Mississippians to consider that they had "a new opportunity to show that you are men of patriotism and integrity." Just around that time an unknown person shot and killed an Agence France-Presse photographer. More marshals came to the campus, but rioters continued the fray. More racists began arriving on campus from rural Mississippi. Gunfire against marshals erupted—by 10:00 P.M., four marshals had been hit. Later a bystander was killed and others badly wounded. State police pulled back and allowed events to take their course.

The riot had been going on for three hours and Justice officials still had not called in troops. Finally, the White House decided to permit the National Guard to act. By this time the mob was attacking the marshals and the guard with a bulldozer, a fire engine, and automobiles. They burned cars in the parking lot. As the battle escalated, the President, around midnight, called for troops at Millington to hurry to Oxford. Finally, sometime after 2:00 A.M., they arrived on campus to restore order. By dawn the campus was under control and, before 8:00 A.M., Meredith was driven to the registrar's office in a battered border patrol car, its sides riddled with bullet holes, its windows shot out, and registered.

I had a curious feeling. Along with Meredith we had launched this effort. We had sent him to the University of Mississippi armed with a court order. The courts had acted on our initiative—only after they entered their initial orders did they deal with the Justice Department. We dragged the government reluctantly into doing what it should have done. Indeed, there was an abrasive, sometimes adversarial relationship between us. We weren't sure we trusted them. They wondered what we would do next. But at the moment Meredith entered the university, the government was there, and we were helpless to do anything further to help him.

In 1990, John Doar, agreeing that Justice should have gathered more force sooner, said that it had handled the Meredith case badly: "Would the Justice Department of the United States government ever have done it that way again? No, they wouldn't have. . . . So when we went in with Vivian Malone to the University of Alabama in 1963, we went in in quite a different way. There was lots more military power."

Meredith began attending classes, but his was hardly the conventional life of a student. Other students harassed him and armed guards lived in his suite, but, after all we'd been through, Meredith had what I thought was an oddly relaxed attitude toward his studies. After all the pain and trouble, he didn't seem to take them very seriously. At the end of his first semester he announced that he would withdraw from the university and only just before classes resumed did he decide to return. When Connie and I told him that he hadn't done as well as we thought he could have, he responded that a black man had as much right to fail as a white man. Nevertheless, we arranged tutoring for him in Memphis on weekends. I flew there for the sessions to make sure that he took advantage of them, but he had other ideas and spent his time with a coterie of friends who clustered around him in admiration or at the bowling alley—anywhere but studying. Connie got him up to Yale for Christmas vacation, where she arranged for faculty to work with him on his courses. But Meredith was driven by forces we did not understand. He suddenly left and went to Chicago and then back to Mississippi. It was like trying to get one of your kids to study when he or she didn't want to.

Some years later, Meredith wrote, in a book about the case, "The decisions that I had to make were concerned primarily with the question of my Divine Responsibility. . . . My mission was clear. I had to devote my life to the cause of directing civilization toward a destiny of humaneness." Although we tried to keep him in school, the legal significance of the case dwindled, as did our involvement.

Whatever Meredith lacked in dedication he made up in natural talent. He graduated from Ole Miss and then applied to Columbia Law School. Bill Warren, dean at the time, asked whether I thought the school should admit Meredith. I replied that I didn't know enough about his record to make a judgment. Meredith was admitted and graduated in 1968. Faculty members have told me that he made insightful contributions to classroom discussion. Later he became an assistant to Senator Jesse Helms of North Carolina, and in 1991, announced his candidacy for the office of president of the United States. In 2002, Meredith's son graduated from the Ole Miss Business School with a doctorate and as first in his class.

The Barnett contempt case dribbled away. In 1964, the Supreme Court held that he was not entitled to a jury trial.[10] The Fifth Circuit in 1965, then dismissed the contempt proceedings because, as to civil contempt, the purpose of the decree had been fulfilled: Meredith had been admitted. As to criminal contempt, while all the elements of the crime had been proved except intent, it could not be found fairly by the judges of the Fifth Circuit, because they had predetermined their own positions on the issue. The court also cited *Hamm v. City of Rock Hill,* the case that abated the sit-in prosecutions, to support a let-bygones-be-bygones decision. Judges Tuttle, Wisdom, and Brown dissented.[11] But the case was all over.

---

[10] United States v. Barnett, 376 U.S. 681 (1964).

[11] United States v. Barnett, 346 F.2d 99 (5th Cir. 1965).

George Wallace in the Schoolhouse Door

In May 1963, in the midst of the demonstration turmoil, two bright, attractive black applicants, Vivian Malone and Jimmy Hood, applied to the University of Alabama, were turned down, and came to us for legal help. By then, Alabama was the only state without a black student in its white university system. Rather than starting anew, Connie just added them as plaintiffs to the 1955 *Lucy* case, which still was pending. The registrar tried to squirm out by claiming that the decree bound only his predecessor. Judge Hobart Grooms, no integrationist—he had granted the stay that accompanied the *Lucy* riot—ruled that the new registrar was governed by the decree against his predecessor.

In the meantime, President Kennedy, not wanting a repetition of the *Meredith* case, was cultivating a political climate receptive to admitting the plaintiffs. On May 18, 1963, in a speech at Vanderbilt University in Nashville he said that the efforts of blacks to secure their rights were "in the highest traditions of American freedom." Just in case, he deployed three thousand federal troops to the Birmingham area (five hundred were later withdrawn).

On May 21, 1963, Judge Grooms ordered the university to admit Malone and Hood at the session beginning June 10. Almost immediately, George Wallace announced that he would keep them out and filed a case in the Supreme Court seeking to prohibit the president's deployment of troops. But the Court denied the application because the president's action merely was "preparatory."[12]

Having learned its lesson in Mississippi, the Justice Department moved swiftly for an injunction prohibiting Wallace from interfering. On June 5, 1963, Judge Seybourne Lynne, from whom it was tough to get a desegregation order, granted the motion, but was distressed: "I love the people of Alabama. I know that many of both races are troubled and like Jonah of old are 'angry even unto death' as the result of distortions of affairs within this State, practiced in the name of sensationalism. My prayer is that all of our people, in

---

[12] State of Alabama v. United States, 373 U.S. 545 (1963).

keeping with our fine traditions, will join in the resolution that law and order will be maintained."

That night the National States Rights party held a rally on U.S. Highway 231, on the boundary line between Elmore and Montgomery counties. Edward R. Fields, its leader, made a fiery speech, calling on white people to stand up and fight and not be trampled into the ground any longer. He stated that the NAACP was headed by Jews, that they were "the real enemy," and that Jack Greenberg, a Jew, was the chief counsel for the NAACP, telling the assembled mob, "You are the law of the land." He counseled obeying the court order admitting blacks to the university, "but after Monday, it will be different," recalling the riot that drove Autherine Lucy off the campus after three days.

On June 11, 1963, President Kennedy issued a proclamation commanding the "Governor of Alabama and all other persons . . . to cease and desist" from unlawful obstructions of justice. At the same time he ordered the secretary of defense to take "all appropriate steps to enforce the laws of the United States" within Alabama, and to use such of the armed forces as he deemed necessary. Wallace replied with his own proclamation, which denounced Kennedy's action and said that he forbade "this illegal and unwarranted action by the Central Government."

While this was going on, I was in Birmingham dealing with the demonstrations, along with Connie, who also had her hands full with another case: expulsion of more than a thousand schoolchildren on May 20 from Birmingham's schools for having participated in demonstrations. On May 21, 1963, we filed suit to enjoin the expulsion, and asked for a temporary restraining order. Judge Clarence Allgood denied it, writing that he could "not conceive of a Federal Court saying to the Board of Education . . . made up of dedicated courageous, honorable, men that they should take no action . . . and that the children who deliberately failed to attend school for some several days should not in any way be punished or penalized."

Connie went immediately to Judge Tuttle in Atlanta, who granted a temporary restraining order reinstating the children, holding that they had engaged in constitutionally protected activities. A month later the case came up before a panel of the Fifth Circuit, which reversed Allgood, the court agreeing with Tuttle on the merits. The court also agreed with Connie's argument that allowing the board to go ahead and expel the children, which would have prevented their graduation on time, represented a final, not temporary, denial of relief and that, therefore, the case was appealable.[13] Since then, the case has been more important as a procedural precedent about what is appealable than as a constitutional precedent. After all, the constitutional point should have been obvious from the outset.

The first day of school at the University of Alabama was June 11, 1963, and Jimmy Hood and Vivian Malone went to the campus in Tuscaloosa to register. I met with them before they went up; they were a bit apprehensive, but certainly not jittery. My only advice was simplistic—do your best—but it seemed to reassure them.

Governor Wallace was true to his word. He stood in the schoolhouse door flanked by more than five hundred federalized National Guardsmen. Nicholas Katzenbach, deputy attorney general, walked up to Wallace and, in a planned exchange, asked him to end his defiance. Wallace said he "refuse[d] to willingly submit to illegal usurpation of power by the Central Government." Katzenbach replied, "These students will remain on this campus. They will register today. They will go to school tomorrow." Katzenbach and Malone then walked to her dormitory, and Jimmy Hood and John Doar drove to Hood's dorm. Students greeted them in a friendly manner and later they joined others in the cafeteria without incident.

Wallace's opposition was real, but the incident in the schoolhouse door was strictly for public consumption. Wallace made it into a big media event, which advanced his national political ambitions. No reasonably well-informed person could have had any doubt about the outcome.

As with *Meredith*, I have the feeling that we had sent Vivian Malone and Jimmy Hood out into the struggle alone, with little more than our best wishes that it would all turn out all right. But this time our wishes were fulfilled.

---

[13] Woods v. Wright, 334 F.2d 369 (5th Cir. 1964).

Mississippi's Motley Mystery

Southern segregationists were flummoxed by Connie Motley, who beat them, not only in *Meredith* and *Woods v. Wright*, but almost every time. Once, Attorney General Joe Patterson of Mississippi, possibly feeling that I would confide in him because I was white, asked me whether she really was black. I said I was sure that she was but that I would check with her; I relayed his question to Connie. She replied sardonically, "Tell him I'm an Indian."

In 1989, I visited Ole Miss to take part in a weekend conference celebrating the integration of the university. Connie Motley, John Doar, Burke Marshall, Judges Tuttle, Wisdom, and Brown, and other participants in the Meredith drama participated. Meredith was the only major actor who wasn't there. A bunch of neo-Nazi skinheads gathered outside, displaying racist banners and screaming racial epithets. A much larger integrated group of students gathered across the road and shouted them down. A band of black and white police officers kept order. In 2004, Connie, following a visit to Ole Miss, concluded that it might be the best integrated university in the country. Whether that is true, certainly Ole Miss has come a long way from the way it was in 1962.

CHAPTER 13

EDUCATION FOLLOWING THE DEFEAT OF "ALL DELIBERATE SPEED"

The Civil Rights Acts Begin to Work

The Civil Rights Act of 1964, and the Voting Rights Act of 1965, fulfilled almost all the recommendations of Harry Truman's 1947 Committee on Civil Rights; the Fair Housing Act of 1968, achieved its remaining goals. By prohibiting discrimination in public accommodations, travel, employment, and housing, the acts left the state action issue—which had tormented us in the Restrictive Covenant and sit-in cases—virtually meaningless for the lives of black people. Before these acts we had to prove that the state was somehow meaningfully involved in racial discrimination to establish a denial of equal protection of the laws. Afterward, we had to show only that a law had been broken. The Civil Rights Acts had to be interpreted and enforced, but that was different from the much more uncertain task of interpreting and applying the Constitution. Equally important, the new laws enlisted the federal bureaucracy for enforcement. The 1965 law secured voting rights against tactics that had denied them in the past. Discrimination was now prohibited in most spheres of life.

In the ten years following *Brown II,* from 1955 to 1965, the number of black students attending school with whites throughout the South increased at the rate of about 1 percent per year. The importance of the federal role became manifest in 1965–66; in the first year of Title VI of the 1964 Civil Rights Act, mandating the Department of Health, Education and Welfare (HEW) to cut off federal funds from schools that discriminated, the percentage of black students in previously all-white schools jumped from 10.9 to 15.9 percent; in border states integrated black students rose to 68.9 percent of the black student population. Even in the states of the old Confederacy, we started to see some progress: Fewer than 1 percent of blacks attended school with whites as late as 1962–63, which rose to only 2.25 percent in 1964–65; in 1965–66 the percentage was 6.01. While there was some dispute about how precise these estimates were, and there was no doubt that area-wide statistics masked some local situations of severe racial imbalance, HEW, operating at wholesale, got more blacks into school with whites than our retail lawsuits. Our litigation, however, set standards that kept HEW honest and helped them resist political pressures to do less, especially after 1969, when Richard Nixon, with his Southern strategy, came on the scene.

A Last Chance for Free Choice

Pockets of resistance to the accomplished fact of *Brown* remained among some judges. In June, 1963, Judge Frank M. Scarlett heard a group of witnesses in the Savannah school case, including Professor Emeritus Henry Garrett (who had been Kenneth Clark's professor) of Columbia and Ernest Van den Haag of New York University. At issue was whether *Brown* rested on a conclusion of law—that is, that segregated schools inherently were unequal—or a conclusion of fact—that in the cases before the Supreme Court there was inequality, but other segregated schools might be equal.

Scarlett concluded that desegregation would psychologically harm children of both races in Savannah. Having found that fact, he distinguished his case from *Brown* and decided that segregation was constitutional in Savannah. Connie Motley, immediately appealed to the court of appeals, which entered its own desegregation order.[1]

Typically, however, resistance to segregation took the form of pupil placement laws and so-called "freedom of choice"; litigating forever—appealing, appealing, and appealing; requesting time to formulate plans and then time to comply with these plans, with stays of

---

[1] Stell v. Savanah-Chatham County Board of Education, 220 F. Supp. 667 (S.D. Ga. 1963), *rev'd and remanded*, 333 F.2d 55 (5th Cir. 1964).

execution, while the cases went on. As we fought such tactics in more than one hundred LDF cases through the mid-1960s, the courts began denying stays, requiring that desegregation proceed while the cases were being appealed.

First, courts struck down pupil assignment. When "freedom of choice" replaced it (students might choose any school, but various pressures caused blacks to choose black schools, whites to choose white schools), courts imposed stringent requirements on its exercise, even to the point of prescribing the forms that school boards had to use for transfer applications, times for filing the forms, and other minutiae to prevent onerous procedures from achieving bureaucratically what had been denied the districts legally. John Minor Wisdom of the Fifth Circuit declared, "These cases tax the patience of the Court," and that "the time has come for foot-dragging public school boards to move with celerity toward desegregation."[2]

Wisdom gave free choice a last try in five Fifth Circuit cases from Alabama and Louisiana known as *Jefferson,* in which Jim Nabrit led the argument. Wisdom wrote, "The only school desegregation plan that meets constitutional standards is one that works,"[3] and spelled out every conceivable detail of a free choice plan that would make it work—if it ever could. These were among eleven LDF cases argued in eleven days.[4] We immediately reopened school cases throughout the Fifth Circuit with *Jefferson* motions—twenty cases in Alabama, twenty-seven in Florida, six in Georgia, thirty-three in Louisiana, thirty in Mississippi, and five in Texas.[5]

---

[2] Hudson v. Leake County School Board, 357 F.2d 653, 654 (5th Cir. 1966).

[3] United States v. Jefferson County Board of Education, 372 F.2d 836, 847, 863, 865 (5th Cir. 1966).

[4] A day after the *Jefferson* argument, I argued the Oklahoma City case, Dowell v. Oklahoma City School Board, 375 F.2d 158 (10th Cir. 1967), *cert. denied,* 387 U.S. 931 (1967).

[5] During this period I won Goss v. Knoxville Board of Education, 373 U.S. 683 (1963) (majority to minority transfer). Connie Motley won Watson v. City of Memphis, 373 U.S. 526 (1963) (segregated Memphis park). We also won Bradley v. City of Richmond, 382 U.S. 103 (1965) (teacher segregation), and Rogers v. Paul, 382 U.S. 198 (1965) (transfer to white classes).

The Division of Legal Information and Community Services

The cases couldn't happen by themselves. In 1964, we hired a staff member to help local NAACP branches sign up parents to transfer their children to white schools. Eighty parents in Albany, Georgia, fifty in Jackson, and one hundred in Richmond applied. Then, a remarkable new staff member, Jean Fairfax, created the LDF Division of Legal Information and Community Services, which conducted these kinds of projects, along with others across the range of civil rights. Jean came to LDF from the American Friends Service Committee (AFSC), for which she had been doing similar work in Mississippi. After she escorted Debra Lewis, the first black child to integrate the white elementary school in Leake county, I asked her to join LDF for six months; she stayed for two decades. Jean forged new links between LDF and the black community, organizing community groups to demand desegregated education and fair employment, and published influential pamphlets dealing with the school lunch program, busing, treatment of Native Americans, federal policies affecting elementary and high school education, and exclusion of women from private clubs. She became the most influential single staff member in determining the direction we took on such issues as integration of black colleges and which industries we should target in employment cases.

The Defeat of Free Choice

We struck the final blow against free choice in three Supreme Court cases decided in 1968, that were simple models of why choice didn't work.[6] In rural New Kent County, near Richmond, where one of the cases arose, more than seven hundred blacks and about six hundred whites distributed generally throughout the county at-

---

[6] Green v. New Kent County Board of Education, 391 U.S. 430 (1968) (Virginia); Raney v. Gould County Board of Education, 391 U.S. 443 (1968) (Arkansas); and Monroe v. Board of Comm'r of Jackson, Tennessee, 391 U.S. 450 (1968) (Tennessee).

tended two schools, one black, the other white. In 1964–65 under pupil placement,[7] there was no desegregation. After we won two cases that knocked out Virginia's pupil placement, the state substituted freedom of choice. Thirty-five blacks began going to the formerly white school, but the black school remained all black and unequal; faculties remained segregated. Assigning students by drawing a line down the middle of the county would have integrated both schools.

In opposing our effort to do away with choice, my opponents' brief in one of the cases made much of the fact that I had written in 1959, in *Race Relations and American Law*, that if "there were complete freedom of choice, or geographical zoning, or any other nonracial standard, and all Negroes still ended up in certain schools, there would seem to be no constitutional objection." I had a reply prepared and at an opportune moment during oral argument delivered it: "I did not know then what I know now. And if I had . . ."

Justice Brennan interrupted with a twinkle in his eye: "You might not have written the book . . ."

I responded, "I would have written it differently."

Justice White went after me on whether to take race into account in drawing zone lines: "Even in a city where there are racial problems . . . you could draw school zone lines based on . . . so-called neutral factors."

I replied: "It is inconceivable to me [that] someone facing the situation to redraw the school zones [would] put the consideration of race out of his head. I have heard children play the game, 'Don't think of an elephant.' That is all they think of . . . an elephant."

The cases ended in a smashing victory in *Green v. New Kent County Board of Education*.[8] The Court charged school boards with the "affirmative duty" to "convert to a unitary system in which racial discrimination would be eliminated root and branch." Delay was "no longer tolerable."

---

[7] Marsh v. County School Board of Roanoke, 305 F.2d 94 (4th Cir. 1962); Green v. School Board of City of Roanoke, 304 F.2d 118 (4th Cir. 1962).

[8] Green v. New Kent County Board of Education, 391 U.S. 420, 438 (1968).

We then immediately created a major conflict with the new Nixon administration by filing motions across the South calling for school boards promptly to eliminate segregation "root and branch." HEW also had to revise its guidelines to conform with *Green*. But Nixon didn't want to offend his southern constituency. Leon Panetta, who was in charge of school desegregation at HEW and later became a California congressman and then President Clinton's head of the Office of Management and Budget, pushed to incorporate the latest Supreme Court standards into the HEW guidelines, while the Nixon staff tugged in the opposite direction. The Fifth Circuit then precipitated a crisis by holding that twenty-nine Mississippi districts had to prepare new desegregation plans in consultation with HEW, by August 11, and put them into effect by August 25.

On August 11, 1969, HEW filed plans to integrate thirty Mississippi districts. Senator John Stennis of Mississippi, chair of the Armed Services Committee, retaliated, announcing that constituents were protesting so much that he would have to absent himself from the Senate during consideration of the defense authorization bill. The secretary of HEW, Robert Finch, buckled under White House pressure to delay and wrote to Chief Judge John R. Brown of the Fifth Circuit that he was "gravely concerned that the time allowed for the development of these terminal plans has been much too short." Finch asked that the integration be delayed until December 1, 1969, and sent copies of the letter to the Mississippi district judges.

Nixon's Justice Department asked for the same delay. The Fifth Circuit sent the cases to the district court for hearing on the request. District judges Dan M. Russell, Jr., and Walter L. Nixon, Jr. (no relation to the president), granted the motions and recommended that the court of appeals grant Finch's request. On August 28, the court of appeals put off the requirement to file plans to integrate the Mississippi school districts until December 1, 1969. Pre-Nixon Justice Department lawyers revolted, some resigned, others signed protests.

Deliberate Speed Repudiated

After the five-plus years of Lyndon Johnson's administration, powerful Southern senators and congressmen once again had a sympathetic ear in the White House. To make matters worse, the Fifth Circuit, until then a bastion of civil rights decency, had yielded to President Nixon. With this turn of events our principal allies, the Fifth Circuit and the White House, had disappeared. I concluded that we had no alternative but to appeal to the Supreme Court immediately. I got the staff together to prepare a petition for expedited review, just as we had in Little Rock, quoting with mock bravado Marshal Foch at the second battle of the Marne: "My center is giving way, my right is in retreat . . . I attack."

In addition to our clients in fourteen Mississippi cases, we intervened in sixteen other cases that the Justice Department had initially tried, but that they hadn't appealed. We wanted to have a say in those cases and not allow Justice to give away the rights of black schoolchildren by putting up less than the best case, and then failing to appeal adverse decisions. First, we filed a motion asking Justice Black to vacate the postponement that the Fifth Circuit had entered. On September 5, 1969 he denied the motion, but wrote a stinging opinion rejecting the administration's position, and called for the end of "all deliberate speed." He urged us to appeal right away:

> Deplorable as it is to me, I must uphold the court's order which both sides indicate could have the effect of delaying total desegregation of these schools for as long as a year.
>
> This conclusion does not comport with my ideas of what ought to be done in this case when it comes before the entire Court. I hope these applicants will present the issue to the full Court at the earliest possible opportunity. . . .
>
> In my opinion there is no reason why such a wholesale deprivation of constitutional rights should be tolerated another minute. I feel that this long denial of constitutional rights is due in large part to the phrase "with all deliberate speed." I would do away with that phrase completely.[9]

Then on September 27, 1969, we filed a petition for writ of certiorari and a motion to advance in the Supreme Court. As is custom-

---

[9] Alexander v. Holmes, 396 U.S. 1218, 1222 (1969).

ary, I asked the clerk of the Fifth Circuit to send the records in those cases to the Supreme Court. Part of the record, however, was in Judge Harold Cox's court in Mississippi, and his clerk refused to part with it unless we paid fifty cents per page—for thousands of pages. I asked one of our Mississippi lawyers to see Cox himself, but Cox replied only that the price per page just had gone up. I turned to John F. Davis, clerk of the Supreme Court, who called Cox's clerk and ordered him to send up the record. Cox's clerk complied and sent eight big boxes to Washington.

I asked that the Court consider the petition during the Court's first conference of the term, set for October 6, 1969, and either grant review and reverse summarily or set an expedited schedule. Ordinarily, the case, *Alexander v. Holmes County Board of Education,* would be heard in December, possibly not till the following year. But the Court acted quickly and set argument for October 23, 1969. I asked Louis Oberdorfer, of the Lawyers Committee for Civil Rights Under Law, to take ten minutes of my argument time because I wanted to show that the American legal establishment was on our side.

Instead of facing the friendly Earl Warren, we now had Warren Burger as chief justice. What little was known about him was that he had been chosen because Nixon thought him a fellow conservative. My opponents were Jerris Leonard, Nixon's chief of the Civil Rights Division, and the tiptoeing John Satterfield of Yazoo City, who had been banished from the courtroom in *Meredith.*

The morning of argument I opened my suitcase and discovered that I had forgotten to pack a shirt, rushed out to search for a store, bought one, and dashed off to court.

My only argument was that defendants should integrate immediately. Litigation over schedule, districting, busing, and other details should take place while the schools were integrated in some fashion, and not, as was done in the past, while schools remained segregated. Districts that had swapped "segregation forever" for "litigation forever" then could litigate to their hearts' content, but "I doubt[ed] that there would be the incentive." Leonard argued that it would take time to work out administrative problems, but Justice Black, picking up on my argument, replied, "Why not put [the plan] into effect and make arrangements afterward?" Leonard had no satisfactory answer. Satterfield tried to make something of segregated schools in the North; the Court wasn't interested. He argued that the Court shouldn't decide the case then because it didn't have the record—unaware that I had managed to get it sent up. That was an opening for my observation on Mississippi justice: "This is the story of the litigation in this case. Judge Cox doesn't let you have the record and Mr. Satterfield says you don't belong in this Court if you don't have it."

I reminded the Court that Medgar Evers, a plaintiff in the Jackson, Mississippi, case was assassinated before he could see the schools desegregated, adding, "The question in these cases is whether the children in these school districts, and indeed, the children in any school districts throughout our beloved land, are at last to learn that there is a supreme law of the land, binding upon children and parents; binding upon school boards; binding upon the states; binding upon the United States."

Leon Panetta, who had come to Court hoping to see the HEW guidelines vindicated, observed that as he heard the argument "it was hard to suppress a chill or a tear."

Six days later we won. On October 29, 1969, the Court, in a per curiam opinion, that is, by the Court, not by any identifiable justice, ruled: "The Court of Appeals should have denied all motions for additional time because . . . 'All deliberate speed' is no longer constitutionally permissible."[10]

Then, accepting my argument of integrate first, litigate later, the Court required the court of appeals to order desegregation "forthwith" without "further arguments or submissions." The court of appeals order would remain in effect during district court hearings; only the court of appeals was empowered to make changes, excluding Mississippi district judges from that part of the process. *Alexander* was Warren Burger's first decision, and he went along with the rest of the Court—not an auspicious beginning for the Nixon Court from Nixon's point of view.

---

[10] Alexander v. Holmes County Board of Education, 396 U.S. 19 (1969).

We filed *Alexander* motions across the South demanding immediate desegregation. Still some judges didn't get the message.[11]

Busing Begins

Jim Nabrit and Julius Chambers tried and argued *Swann v. Charlotte-Mecklenburg Board of Education,*[12] which addressed the next
question in the school struggle: What constitutes effective desegregation? In Charlotte, where blacks were concentrated near the center of town, it wasn't possible to desegregate by drawing simple
zone lines. An expert witness, John Finger of the University of Rhode
Island, drew a plan that paired center-city and outlying schools into
single, noncontiguous zones. The inner-city school would teach some
grades and the peripheral school would teach the remaining grades,
so that black and white children would attend each school, many by
bus. The zones were gerrymandered to achieve a black-white ratio
approximating that of the general population, about 71 percent white,
29 percent black. *Swann,* therefore, had to deal with the extent to
which a district court might use such percentages to correct a segregated system; whether every all-black and all-white school must be
eliminated as such and integrated at least to some extent; the limits
on rearranging attendance zones; the limits on busing.

The Supreme Court unanimously approved the Charlotte plan.
The 71 to 29 percent ratio was, in Burger's view, "no more than a
starting point, rather than an inflexible requirement." Gerrymander-
ing, establishing zones that are "neither compact nor contiguous,"
indeed "on opposite ends of a city," though "awkward, inconvenient,
and even bizarre," was permissible. Busing was appropriate. "Eigh-

---

[11] In an opinion covering fifteen cases from six Deep Southern States, Singleton
v. Jackson Municipal Separate School District, 419 F.2d 1211 (5th Cir. 1969), the
Fifth Circuit delayed desegregation until September 1970 (but ordered teachers to
be desegregated by February 1). We asked Justice Black for an order requiring desegregation by February 1, 1970. The entire Court issued the order. Carter v. W.
Feliciana School District, 396 U.S. 290 (1970).

[12] Swann v. Charlotte-Mecklenburg Board of Education, 402 U.S. 1 (1971).
Along with *Swann,* the Court held unconstitutional the North Carolina Anti-Busing
Law. N. Carolina State Board of Education v. Swann, 402 U.S. 43 (1971).

teen million of the Nation's public school children, approximately 39%, were transported to their schools by bus in 1969–1970 in all parts of the country," observed Burger. The "existence of some small number of one-race or virtually one-race schools . . . [was] not in and of itself the mark of a system that still practices segregation by law." As a practical matter, sometimes that would be unavoidable.

With *Swann,* I argued another case, from Mobile, very much like it. To prepare for the argument I drove through the streets of the city at about the speed of a school bus, so that I could tell the Court confidently that busing in Mobile would not be too lengthy or onerous. But Burger had a different question on his mind: Must courts continue to re-zone after population shifts have resegregated integrated districts? I replied, "In a city like Mobile . . . we have a situation in which the Constitution has been violated . . . from 1954 to 1969. . . . It is not as if they have been thoroughly well-integrated for a hundred years and someone is suddenly calling them into court."

We won the Mobile case in a decision much like *Swann.*[13]

Earl Warren later told me that he had learned that Burger originally had voted against us in this group of cases, and others on the Court had supported him. But, little by little, he lost his support, until "he stood there naked," as Earl Warren put it. So he joined the majority and assigned the opinion to himself, making sure that it included his own answer to his question: "Neither school authorities nor district courts are constitutionally required to make year-by-year adjustments of the racial composition of student bodies once the affirmative duty to desegregate has been accomplished and racial discrimination through official action is eliminated from the system."

In those words lie the conflict in the courts over school desegregation. Many formerly desegregated systems have become resegregated as a result of shifting populations, and efforts to undo that regression have run into conflict with Burger's dictum.

We filed *Swann* motions in all our pending cases and, for the first time, thoroughgoing desegregation became widespread.

As busing became a national issue, a recorded telephone message of the National Socialist White People's party denounced it as

---

[13] Davis v. Board of Sch. Comm'r of Mobile County, 402 U.S. 33 (1971).

"a massive attempt to mongrelize the white race with the inferior black race. . . . The man most responsible for busing decisions across the country is Jack Greenberg, a Jew."

Deliberate Speed—Was It Justified?

Was the introduction of the phrase "with all deliberate speed" into *Brown* responsible for the snail's pace of desegregation between 1955 and 1970? Certainly, according to the language in *Brown II*, it couldn't have been. *Brown II* required a "prompt and reasonable start" and permitted delay only for tasks like redrawing zone lines and bus routes, reassigning pupils and teachers, and expressly prohibited delay because of hostility. Criteria of that sort would have been reasonable even if the Court had required desegregation "forthwith." However, the words "deliberate speed" allowed a perception that the Supreme Court had signaled lower courts to tolerate a certain amount of delay. And, if we can believe accounts of conferences among the justices, some indication that delay would be acceptable was the price the majority paid to get a unanimous opinion. Otherwise, there might have been one or more dissents and, some conjectured, opposition to *Brown I* would have been deeper and fiercer.

Furthermore, it's not at all clear that "forthwith" would have produced a quicker pace of desegregation except, perhaps, in a few border areas. The slow pace of desegregation was due almost entirely to factors independent of the language in *Brown II*. The congressional Southern Manifesto, which denounced the Supreme Court for *Brown* and other decisions; a bill in Congress to strip the Supreme Court of its jurisdiction, which failed by a single vote; doctrines of nullification and interposition; state sovereignty commissions; white citizens councils; boycotts and firings of, as well as violence toward, black teachers, civil rights advocates, and parents who tried to transfer their children to white schools—all had the effect of intimidating plaintiffs, white lawyers, and judges.

Other hindrances were that the resources to bring desegregation suits were meager; there were few black lawyers in Southern states; and the Justice Department had no jurisdiction to file school cases. LDF was equipped to assist in only a fraction of the school districts of the South. This environment enabled many districts to do nothing, and in those where something was done, plans like twelve-year grade-a-year "stairstep," minority-majority transfer, pupil assignment, and freedom-of-choice arose, if not simply to maintain the status quo, then at least as sops to those in defiance of the law on this issue. The resources—funds, lawyers, political will—to change that situation were inadequate. Not until the American political agenda changed, as a consequence of the civil rights movement, itself partially a product of *Brown,* were the courts—and the country—ready to move to desegregation "forthwith." By the time of the Johnson administration, the LDF had greater financial resources to draw upon, due to increased giving, more lawyers, and more favorable legal doctrine, and the Justice Department and the Department of Health, Education and Welfare joined the struggle.

At the same time, it may well be true that a dissenting opinion, or maybe more than one, might have undercut the decision's moral imperative, possibly leading to even more intensive opposition. If there had been a dissent, would the congressional effort to diminish the Court's jurisdiction, which failed by a vote, have passed? Would violence have been more widespread? On the other side, would more violent opposition have spurred the civil rights movement into existence earlier and made it stronger? Would a "forthwith" decision have made lower courts act tougher sooner? We should not allow speculation to run amok, for there are no authoritative answers to these questions. I would guess that if I were making the decision in 1955, I would have voted for "forthwith." At least the highest court would not be saying, "Yes, black people have constitutional rights, but we will tolerate deferring them." I have to qualify that stance, however: To guess at what each of us might have done is a far different matter from acting when we know that we will bear the responsibility for the consequences of that decision.

The War on Black Teachers

We had not anticipated how seriously black teachers would be at risk during desegregation. Many whites found it unacceptable to have their children taught by blacks; the firing, or threat of firing, of black teachers created pressures against desegregation, deterring some black teachers from engaging in civil rights activity. Another unhappy development was the demotion of many black principals to second in command, where they would be supervised by white principals. Others were bumped out of administration altogether or simply discharged. Southern states moved quickly after *Brown* to repeal teacher tenure laws, which would give the state a freer hand in dealing with the issue of black teachers and school administrators.

We rapidly developed a docket of teacher cases and incorporated into desegregation suits demands that black teachers be integrated into the school system. I won a Supreme Court decision approving a distribution of black teachers throughout the school system. While not based on a fixed quota, this was the first Supreme Court decision to accept a numerical guideline as a standard for measuring whether equality has been established.[14]

By decade's end we had more than twenty-five teacher dismissal cases across the South. We won a lot, but the problem was more widespread than we could handle, and most cases involved unique circumstances, requiring that they be litigated individually. For example, the Orangeburg, South Carolina, School District fired Gloria Rackley because she had engaged in NAACP activities. By 1966, Matthew Perry and Mike Meltsner got her job back. The Court awarded back pay for one of the three years she had been out of a job, but not for the other two, because she had found a new job after a year.[15] The Court's ruling hardly formed a deterrent to such firings nor was it much of a remedy for the plaintiff herself.

The National Education Association (NEA) found, in a study of the years between 1968 and 1970, that school districts in the Fifth Circuit reduced the number of black teachers by 1,072, while increasing the number of white teachers by 5,575. One out of every five black principal positions was eliminated, while the number of white principals increased.

---

[14] Carr v. Montgomery Board of Education, 395 U.S. 225 (1969).

[15] Rackley v. Sch. Dist. No. 5, Orangeburg County, 258 F. Supp. 676 (D.S.C. 1966).

The *Keyes* Presumption

LDF and the NAACP Special Contribution Fund, led by Bob Carter, tacitly divided up school cases: He mostly filed in the North, we stuck pretty much to the South, where we had our hands full until the *Alexander* decision ordered desegregation "forthwith" without "further arguments or submissions." Carter had a theory of de facto school segregation for Northern school suits—that is, segregation brought about by forces other than an intent to segregate—that I thought wouldn't wash, though the argument was entirely logical: School authorities assign students to neighborhood schools; they know when their actions will create distinctly black and white schools; state action therefore always is involved in creating segregation even when there is no articulated intent to separate by race. The theory continues: what is called *de facto* (literally, according to fact) segregation is really *de jure* (literally, according to the law) and is prohibited by the Fourteenth Amendment in both cases because in both cases state action has denied equal protection. Language in *Brown* supported this approach: "To separate them from others of similar age and qualifications solely because of their race generates a feeling of inferiority that may affect their hearts and minds in a way unlikely ever to be undone."[16]

The theory was cost-effective, too. To prove that school boards had the motive of separating blacks from whites would be difficult, sometimes impossible. Decisions on where to draw lines, build schools, schedule bus routes, and assign teachers were made by many people and were often unexplained, unexpressed, concealed, or simply unfathomable. Making a case for intentional segregation could be as hard as making a case based on bank fraud. Demonstrating racial imbalance would be easier and cheaper. The problem was that it was too easy. If courts were required to correct any racial imbalance, they might have to restructure not only schools, but other institutions that were far from being in racial balance at the time—for example, private housing, higher education, employment. Some would

---

[16] Brown v. Board of Education of Topeka, 347 U.S. 483, 494 (1954).

have been pleased if the courts had undertaken a task of that sort. But without legislation and a bureaucracy to implement it, the courts would have been getting into difficult, uncharted territory, one that I doubted they wanted to enter. I was sure they wouldn't start down that road.

Bob had some early success before state administrative boards and in federal cases in Manhasset, New York, and Springfield, Massachusetts. But the effort soon crashed.[17] Around this time Bob left the NAACP and was replaced by Nathaniel Jones, later to become a judge of the United States Court of Appeals for the Sixth Circuit, with whom there was none of the clash Thurgood and I had with Bob. By then the NAACP theory had run its course and there was no likelihood of conflict, if we were to try an approach of our own. We, therefore, decided to enter a Denver case, in which blacks and Hispanics, on the one hand, and whites, on the other, had been concentrated in separate schools by a complex of factors, including transportation routes, construction, expansion of overcrowded schools with trailer-like portable classrooms to avoid sending students to schools attended by children of another race, optional zones (children might pick their school), and transfer policies. Minority teachers were assigned to minority schools, white teachers to white schools. A school board that had adopted a policy of integration was defeated by candidates pledged to continue segregation.

Colorado, of course, had no law requiring school segregation. We chose not to rely on the mere fact that there were separate minority and white schools, as the earlier NAACP approach would have done, and set out to prove an intent to segregate out of all these circumstances too conveniently contributing to a pattern of quite rigid segregation. I came up with the name "crypto de facto"— meaning a case ostensibly based on government intent which essentially was a de facto case—for this kind of case, but the term never caught

---

[17] Bell v. Sch. City of Gary, 324 F.2d 209 (7th Cir. 1963), *cert. denied*, 377 U.S. 924 (1964); Downs v. Board of Education, 336 F.2d 988 (10th Cir. 1964), *cert. denied*, 380 U.S. 914 (1965); Deal v. Cincinnati Board of Education, 419 F.2d 1387 (6th Cir. 1969), *cert. denied*, 402 U.S. 962 (1971).

on. The new approach left one major gap: Even if intent could be proved as to some area within a school system there was no way of knowing how racial concentrations had come about in other areas within the same system. Would it be impossible to win a comprehensive desegregation order covering the areas about which there wasn't enough information?

Gordon Greiner—a burly, red-bearded, iconoclastic Denver antitrust lawyer in one of Denver's largest firms, a moose and elk hunter in his spare time—along with Vilma Martinez, Conrad Harper, and later Jim Nabrit III, tried and appealed the Denver school case to the Supreme Court in 1973. Jim and Gordon wrote the Supreme Court brief. The decision pointed the way to winning cases across the North. One important part of the decision, which I developed, became known as the *Keyes* presumption: Where a plaintiff establishes that officials segregated in one part of town, the burden shifts to the officials to explain why there are racial concentrations in other parts. Since then, Northern school cases have been winnable because many districts that managed to cover most of their tracks left enough evidence to show some intentional segregation in a local area or two.[18] Such evidence having been uncovered, *they* would have to prove that the rest of the district was segregated by happenstance—something that would be as difficult for them to prove as the contrary would be for us.

Interdistrict Integration

In the late 1960s, and early 1970s, a new issue surfaced: Where there is a district line between city and suburban schools, should city children be sent to suburban schools and vice versa to bring about desegregation? If not, as a city became blacker, the boundary would keep segregation insulated from change. That's what happened in Richmond, as whites left desegregated schools and moved to the suburbs. We then won a court order to desegregate Richmond schools, which treated the city and adjacent districts as a single unit for desegregation purposes. But the court of appeals reversed. Bill Coleman

[18] Keyes v. Sch. Dist. No. 1, Denver, 413 U.S. 189 (1973).

argued the case in the Supreme Court, which upheld the reversal four to four.[19] As is the custom with affirmances by an equally divided Court, it wrote no opinion.

The Court's reasoning emerged in an NAACP case involving Detroit one year later, *Milliken v. Bradley.*[20] Opponents of inter-district integration had argued that where the suburbs had done nothing to segregate they shouldn't compensate for wrongs of the city. They also argued that busing across city boundaries often meant going great distances and that schools work best if parents are in the neighborhood. Moreover, their argument continued, separate tax systems are responsive to their respective constituencies. The decision stated that there would be no inter-district integration unless there had been an inter-district violation, meaning that plaintiffs would have to prove that the suburbs and city were in complicity in segregating.

Nevertheless, there was some city–suburban integration. Charlotte, Jacksonville, Nashville, and their environs, among many other school systems that desegregated under court order, are in single districts that encompass city and suburbs. In Indianapolis, towns near Philadelphia, and elsewhere, courts found that there had been city–suburban complicity and ordered integration.

While it's true that many suburbs became a refuge for whites who didn't want to got to school with blacks, it's also true that many parents who chose suburban over city schools and private over public schools did so because of the terrible state of public education in many cities. These families are disproportionately white; whites more readily afford private and suburban education, and housing discrimination kept many blacks out of the suburbs even when they could afford it.

By 1973, we had 115 school cases where desegregation had been achieved and ninety-nine where we continued to litigate, mostly in rural areas. Thirty-four teacher cases were on the docket.

President Nixon inveighed against busing. The political reaction to busing was hostile; indeed, it became a major national political

[19] Bradley v. State Board of Education, 412 U.S. 92 (1973).
[20] Milliken v. Bradley, 418 U.S. 717 (1974).

issue. Congress and state legislatures passed anti-busing laws, though few of these laws were effective and we struck some down in LDF cases. By October 1972, the Justice Department, now doing the bidding of an anti-busing president, was opposing us in busing cases in Las Vegas, Tulsa, Charlotte, Oklahoma City, and Memphis.

School cases between 1973 and 1984 continued to diminish on the docket as we won greater compliance, and government and other groups also began occasionally litigating educational issues. By 1976, we had ceased filing many new suits and dealt more with issues such as efforts to resegregate, discriminatory discipline, discharge and demotion of black teachers, and a Mississippi board's refusal to use a text book that depicted the role of blacks in state history.[21] We sued to win admission of blacks to state-subsidized private academies and for counsel fees from our opponents.

Forcing HEW to Obey the Law

While HEW had power to enforce *Brown* across the board and was, for all practical purposes, the only source of effective national enforcement, for political reasons it sat on its hands. Motivated by politics of the Nixon administration, HEW adopted a lax stance in gathering complaints and evidence of school segregation and in acting upon them when received. Jean Fairfax's division of Legal Information and Community Services and its deputy director, Phyllis McClure, working with other civil rights groups and a network of black citizens in two hundred districts covering nine Southern states, launched a project to gather facts proving that HEW was not doing its job. Using this information in 1969, with Joe Rauh and his partners, John Silard and Elliot Lichtman, we filed a case (originally called *Adams v. Richardson,* but with name changes over the years, to reflect successive secretaries of HEW) to force HEW to process complaints and withhold federal funds from violators.

At the outset, the case was problematic because administrative agencies, prosecutors, and other law enforcement officials have tra-

---

[21] Loewen v. Turnipseed, 488 F. Supp. 1138 (N.D. Miss. 1980).

ditionally had wide discretion concerning where to target their activities, but Joe and his partners persuaded District Judge John H. Pratt and the court of appeals for the District of Columbia that Congress intended to empower courts to enjoin HEW to enforce Title VI. We won an order setting deadlines to act on complaints. When HEW didn't comply, the court required it to do so. The second prong of the case—requiring HEW to withhold funds from higher education systems that discriminated—at first attracted little attention. When we filed the case, we expected flak from white schools, not black opposition. Yet this is the opposition we found ourselves facing when some blacks feared that West Virginia might be the model for what would happen when black colleges integrated. Dr. John W. Davis, when he was president of West Virginia State College, even before *Sweatt* and *McLaurin* in 1950, had admitted white students— then in violation of state law. In time the college was no longer majority black, although in some ways it preserved its black identity, with a black president, buildings named after prominent blacks, and a substantial number of blacks in the student body. But to some it seemed that such transformations of colleges from majority black to majority white threatened to destroy centers of black power and influence, identity, and jobs.

In response to these fears, in June 1971, Jean Fairfax convened a group chaired by Julius Chambers, Henry Marsh, and John Walker to study how to address the issue of integrating higher education. They concluded that Southern states had no commitment to educating poor black students and wanted instead to admit only a few top black students to their formerly all-white colleges. They called for addressing the problems of job loss among black teachers and of ill treatment of black students.

Another problem requiring attention was black higher education and the all-black schools; the status quo was unacceptable. Most of the best black students and faculty were moving to formerly all-white schools, North and South. Black colleges and universities were becoming backwaters. There was an element of illusion at work too: While many blacks felt that public black colleges belonged to black people, in fact they were under state—that is, majority white—control, particularly with regard to appropriations, and were underfunded.

Jean's group advocated what I would call modulated integration, which combined the integration of higher education with enhancement of formerly black colleges. They advocated that blacks should become trustees, administrators, faculty, students, and non-academic staff in all institutions within the state systems. They advocated numerical guidelines for admissions and appointments. Pointing to the expensive, segregative effect of duplicate programs (identical courses in black and white schools), they called for maintaining, for example, a single racially diverse nursing school and one architecture school or business school, instead of one in a black and another in a white university. But, apart from the political problems involved in closing any program, the proposal suggested other difficulties: What if whites with superior preparation were admitted in disproportionately large numbers to the most attractive programs, shutting out blacks who would have had a program available to them under the old system? Should schools limit white enrollment and use affirmative action in admitting blacks—a solution that would be sure to cause a backlash among whites now shut out? Unraveling segregation in higher education, which Southern states had entrenched even more deeply after *Brown,* was bound to be complicated and controversial.

In 1972, when the government first appealed the order against HEW, the National Association for Equal Opportunity in Higher Education (NAFEO), consisting of heads of black colleges and universities, filed a brief opposing us. The court of appeals, while upholding the judgment, observed that black colleges should be treated with care in the desegregation process. Because the states were making virtually no progress in integrating higher education, in August 1975, we filed a motion asking the court to require HEW to revoke approval of state higher education plans in Florida, Georgia, Maryland, North Carolina, Oklahoma, Pennsylvania, and Virginia, because they had not changed admission requirements to raise black enrollment, re-assigned staff, altered faculty distribution, eliminated duplicative programs, upgraded black institutions, or desegregated institutional governance. That proceeding continued into the 1980s. No longer did higher education cases involve the simple issue of whether G. W. McLaurin might be required to sit in a chair designated for blacks only. Jean worked with coalitions of black educators to shape the role of LDF in regard to these complex issues, but it remained an uneasy relationship.

We continued to try to compel HEW to enforce desegregation of schools wholesale. The district court ordered the Office of Management and Budget to hire hundreds of additional civil rights workers to enforce the decree at all levels. While HEW accepted higher education desegregation plans from Arkansas, Florida, Georgia, Oklahoma, and the North Carolina community college system in 1978 and from Virginia in 1979, North Carolina wouldn't submit an acceptable blueprint to desegregate student bodies and faculties, reduce duplicative programs, and enhance black institutions.

In 1979, therefore, HEW began proceedings before an administrative law judge as the first step toward cutting off federal funds for the North Carolina state system of higher education. Hearings went on for nine months, creating a record of fifteen thousand pages and more than five hundred exhibits. This was what enforcement was coming to.

When Ronald Reagan became president, North Carolina, supported by Senator Jesse Helms, entered into a consent decree with HEW in a North Carolina federal court exonerating the state of its obligations under the original *Adams* decree. We filed a motion in the District of Columbia to enjoin HEW from agreeing to the North Carolina consent decree, but lost six to four in the court of appeals, which held that we should have intervened in the North Carolina federal court. We were running up against political limits to what we could accomplish.[22]

---

[22] Adams v. Bell, 711 F.2d 161 (D.C. Cir. 1983), *cert. denied*, 465 U.S. 1021 (1984). Skelly Wright's dissent in the Court of Appeals case contains the best summary of the case and questions it involved.

CHAPTER 14

SCHOOLS: FINAL THOUGHTS AND REFLECTIONS

Brown Beyond Schools

We couldn't have done what we did in a society and world that wasn't ready.

Neither Thurgood, I, nor anyone else could have won *Plessy v. Ferguson* in 1896. But a half-century later, *Brown v. Board of Education,* which transformed education, race relations and more, would not have happened without us, at least not when it did. *Brown* did more than transform education. It was a catalyst for the Civil Rights Movement that led to the Civil Rights Acts of the mid-sixties, a major factor in breaking up racist domination of national politics. A measure of the difference between now and then is that Strom Thurmond carried four southern states and won 39 electoral votes in the 1948 Presidential election as candidate of the segregationist Dixiecrat party. But in 2002, public protest forced Senator Trent Lott of Mississippi to resign as Republican Senate majority leader when on Thurmond's 100th birthday he said the country would have been better off if Thurmond had been elected. Before the 1965 Voting Rights Act, in counties where blacks were most numerous, black voting was in single digits. Since then Congressional black caucus membership has approached 40 and there have been black mayors in almost every major and smaller cities across the country. Public accommodations, jobs, corporate leadership, the media are all different. It would be silly to claim that *Brown* brought all this about.

It would be equally silly to deny that *Brown* played a larger role than any other event in opening the way to the transformation.

Brown and Schools

While *Brown* contributed to big changes in politics and society, massive resistance (described in detail in Chapter 8) blocked all but slight school integration for fifteen years until 1969 when the Court decided *Alexander v. Holmes County Board of Education.*[1] Even then efforts to integrate never fully overcame the obstacles that massive resistance had raised. Nevertheless by the mid-1980s, when I left LDF, the South was the most desegregated part of the country. Integration was notably successful in Charlotte, Greenville, Jacksonville, Louisville, Nashville, and Tampa. While it was virtually nonexistent in New York, Chicago, Philadelphia, Detroit, Los Angeles, and Atlanta, all big cities with vast populations, great distances, and ghettoes from which whites and middle class blacks had moved, Buffalo, Columbus, Dayton, Denver, Minneapolis, St. Louis, San Diego, and Wilmington, Delaware all had desegregated schools. But from the mid-1980s onward it was mainly downhill for integration.

Segregation increased in elementary and high schools.[2] Dense residential segregation has been central to the increase. Although it declined about 5% over the past 10 years, major urban areas remain as segregated as before. Fair housing laws have not been enforced effectively, but even if they were, the 24% of blacks (and their higher proportion of children) who live in poverty cannot afford better housing. They could not move to integrated neighborhoods (ordinarily suburbs) without subsidies, but the country is not in a mood to subsidize poor people. As a result, over 70% of blacks attend schools in which they are in the majority, so-called majority-minority schools, segregated by race and wealth. Small town and rural southern schools, which had been the most integrated, are also becoming more segre-

---

[1] Alexander v. Holmes County Board of Education, 396 U.S. 19 (1969).

[2] This book concentrates almost entirely on African American Schooling. In recent years the Hispanic population has grown to exceed that of blacks. Many of the issues are the same, but of course not all.

gated. Most of this segregation does not violate any law. It results from where people live, neighborhood school assignment policies, legal doctrine that limits city-to-suburb integration, as well as the rule that dissolves court-ordered integration when systems become "unitary," following which many slip back into segregation.

On Martin Luther King, Jr.'s birthday in January, 2004, this was the situation as described by the Harvard Civil Rights Project:

- In many districts where court-ordered desegregation ended in the past decade, segregation had increased substantially. The courts mistakenly assumed that the forces that produced segregation and inequality no longer were effective.
- Among the four districts included in the original *Brown* decision three of the four cases showed considerable long-term success in realizing desegregated education.
- Rural and small town school districts were, on average, the nation's most integrated for African Americans and Latinos. Central cities of large metropolitan areas are the epicenter of segregation; it is also severe in smaller central cities and in the suburban rings of large metros.
- There has been a substantial slippage toward segregation in most of the states that were highly desegregated in 1991.
- The vast majority of intensely segregated minority schools face conditions of concentrated poverty and related unequal educational opportunity.

Court-ordered integration, and the equality that accompanies it, which once had been widespread, has become virtually impossible to sustain. Judges have been dissolving integration orders on the ground that systems have become "unitary" with no "vestiges" of segregation. With perhaps the rare exception of two judges in Alabama, they accept agreement between lawyers for both sides, who apparently just want the cases to be over. They hardly examine critical school policies, such as tracking, resource allocation, drop-out prevention, graduation rates, and so forth.

While some school integration is possible in an urban district that is not entirely bereft of whites, it has become harder to accomplish as more whites move to the suburbs. Court-ordered integration between those suburbs and nearby cities has become virtually impossible as a result of the doctrine that there will be no interdistrict remedy without proof of an interdistrict violation, that is, collusion between city and suburb to segregate.[2] The integration possibilities, therefore, reduce to: (1) integration within a metropolitan area with the relatively small number of whites who remain; (2) integration within a suburban district, the extent depending on the size and location of black and white populations; (3) integration between districts (suburb and city, suburb and suburb) where population size, location and distances make it feasible.

Why Integration?

Segregated schools, with few exceptions, have always been inferior in terms of tangible, measurable facilities alone. In general, they have been inferior teaching instruments: their students have not done as well academically as students who attend integrated schools, not least because they have not been enabled to overcome handicaps that they brought to school. That was recognized before the Margold Report, which launched the campaign that led to *Brown v. Board of Education:* although plaintiffs originally wanted a better building, Spottswood Robinson and Oliver Hill persuaded them to file a desegregation case. For years they had filed equalization cases, but never accomplished equalization, even when courts ordered it. Repeated return visits to court produced little or nothing. Integrating, however, by definition equalizes by placing all children in the same schools. The ancient dictum, "green follows white," i.e., the funding goes towards white students, holds sway.

Blacks who attend desegregated schools do better in society, getting better jobs after graduation; black young women are less likely to get pregnant while in desegregated schools. Gerald Jaynes and Robin Williams have written, "Children who have attended desegregated schools tend to have more friends who are of another race, to work in higher-status jobs, to attend and graduate from multira-

---

[2] Milliken v. Bradley, 418 U.S. 717 (1974).

cial colleges and universities, and to live in integrated neighborhoods. Blacks from desegregated schools appear to make more money."

As with other social situations, explanations are complex. Better-educated parents (sometimes reflecting the influence of the desegregated schools they attended), more preschool programs, a decline in poverty, black migration from the South to the West and North, and from rural areas to cities and suburbs where schools are better, also have had an effect. Moreover, education in the South improved as the economy became better.

Segregation deprives low-income African American students of social networks that afford personal contact with universities, businesses, law firms, or art museums, for example, and others who can open their eyes to possibilities after high school. Schoolmates and teachers inform about career paths, scholarship programs, internships, help get summer jobs, and opportunities that poor, black segregated children never would have heard of. Integrated schools offer more challenging curricula and teach how to get along in a majority white world. After graduation from integrated schools, black children commonly enjoy higher salaries and better lifestyle than students who attended segregated schools, are less likely to hold negative views about whites, more likely to live in integrated neighborhoods and interact with whites where they live, socially, politically, and economically. Interracial contact dispels stereotypes that whites have of blacks.

Moreover, by commonly accepted measures of academic performance black students who attend integrated schools do better. Consistently, studies show that they achieve higher test scores than blacks who attend segregated schools, and that the performance of whites doesn't suffer. Black IQ has risen to "eras[e] nearly half the gap between blacks' pre-desegregation . . . scores and the national norm." James Liebman's synthesis of studies of the role of school integration reports that black students attending desegregated schools are more likely to have higher IQ scores than their counterparts in segregated schools, less likely to drop out, more likely to complete four-year colleges, and to receive high marks. The largest upward leap in black standardized test scores occurred after 1970 following the Supreme Court decision in *Alexander,* which made possible the greatest increase in desegregation to occur within a brief period of time. The 1966 Coleman Report, which continues to be authoritative, concluded that the most important factors that influence academic performance are family background and the school's social composition. Recent surveys of the effect of integration on academic performance of three separate cohorts of 200,000 Texas school children concluded: "*ceteris paribus* schools with higher concentrations of minority students lead to lower achievement for black students but minimal effects on whites or Hispanics."

Susan Eaton's "The Other Boston Busing Story," relates the superior academic performance and lifetime achievement of Boston black inner city schoolchildren who attended suburban schools through the Boston METCO program. METCO is a voluntary program in which 3,500 Boston black children attend suburban schools. It has a waiting list of 13,000 applicants. Amy Stuart Wells writes of a similar program for black St. Louis school children who attended suburban schools in a city-to-suburb enrollment program:

[N]early twice as many of the transfer students are graduating from their suburban high schools in four years as compared to students who graduate from a City high school. . . .

[F]or every 100 ninth graders in the [almost all black] St. Louis Public Schools, about 74 fail to graduate four years later, and of the 26 students who do graduate, only about 13 go on to post-secondary education. . . . [A]ppproximately eight of these 100 freshmen will find themselves in a four-year university five years after they enter high school.

In contrast, the college-going rate for graduates of the 16 predominantly white suburban districts was about 75 percent on average. . . . [I]n the more affluent of these suburban districts . . . the college-going rates were more than 90 percent. . . . Meanwhile, 68 percent of the African American transfer students who graduate from suburban schools are college bound. Forty-four percent . . . attend four-year colleges . . . nearly three times the national average for black high school graduates. Thus, for every 100 African American transfer students who enroll in suburban schools by the ninth grade, about 60 graduate from the suburbs and 40 of these graduates go on to college.

Following *Alexander,* blacks made great, though uneven progress in education. While in 1972 over 20% of blacks had dropped out of high school by 2000 the percentage was down to 13%, compared to white dropouts of 11%. In 1960 only about 2% of blacks over the age of 25 had a bachelor's degree. By 2002 that had risen to 17% when among whites almost 30% had bachelors' degrees. (Women hold 58% of bachelors' degrees among blacks and, indeed, have a large lead over black men among degree holders at most levels. During the 1990s white enrollment in professional schools, according to the Journal of Blacks in Higher Education, declined slightly, but black enrollment increased about 50%, reflecting widespread adoption of affirmative action policies.

Increased Funding

Litigation to equalize funding between rich and poor, corresponding generally to white and black, schools began in the mid-seventies in response to the obstacles in the way of achieving desegregation. If equal education advocates couldn't achieve their aims by integrating, they hoped to accomplish educational equality by equalizing funds. But, in 1973, in *San Antonio School District v. Rodriguez,*[3] the United States Supreme Court rejected their claims.

I doubt that anyone denies that poor children should attend schools in attractive surroundings and taught by highly competent teachers. But, does equalization or provision for an adequate education upgrade academic performance? It certainly may make available programs, laboratories, library books, and other academic opportunities. Either because money has been misspent, or because it is very difficult to improve by a great deal in a segregated setting, by far, most school districts which have benefited by increased funding have shown no improvement, although a few schools and districts have made gains. In the second phase of the Detroit school case, Milliken II,[4] in lieu of city-to-suburb desegregation, the Supreme Court

---

[3] San Antonio School District v. Rodriguez, 411 U. S. 1 (1973).

[4] Milliken v. Bradley, 433 US 267 (1977).

required remedial programs to compensate for inferior education that had enrolled children while segregating them. Hundreds of millions of dollars later no measurable academic accomplishment was evident. "Milliken II" funding for teachers, librarians, computers, and field trips of $100 million, failed to lift segregated schools in Prince Georges County, Maryland from below the county average academic standing. Kansas City spent about $2 billion dollars awarded to compensate for degradation of its system during years of segregation. The funds were spent in segregated schools on all sorts of things other than superior teaching and administration. There was no change in student performance. Obviously in all such situations more had to be done, certainly reformed teaching and administration, but racial integration—not permitted under prevailing Supreme Court doctrine, almost surely would have made a difference. In any event, Milliken II funding is dwindling and not much more may be expected along that line.

Commencing with cases in California in the early seventies, about twenty state supreme courts have under state constitutional provisions ordered state educational systems to improve (equalize or raise to a level of adequacy) funding of schools in poor districts. Some decisions were based on provisions which require equal protection of the laws; others rely on constitutional language that in general requires states to establish thorough and/or efficient systems of education or furnish a sound basic education. None of the provisions expressly require equal or adequate funding. However, plaintiffs in recent years have most often sued for an "adequate education." Adequacy, even though not a term of great precision is probably easier to compel than "equality" given the diversity of districts, schools, the situation of individual students and other factors. But, cases which involve spending large sums confront the problem that legislatures, not courts, raise taxes and appropriate funds. Even a favorable judicial decision must go through the next step of raising and appropriating money in the legislature, which often faces taxpayer resistance. Race almost inevitably becomes a factor. James E. Ryan has written:

> [M]inority districts do not win school finance cases nearly as often
> as white districts do, and in the few states where minority districts

have successfully challenged school finance schemes, they have encountered legislative recalcitrance that exceeds, in both intensity and duration, the legislative resistance that successful white districts have faced. As this and additional evidence suggests, there are strong reasons to believe that the racial composition of the school district plays an influential role in determining its success or failure in school finance litigation and legislative reform.

The problem is, however, not insurmountable. *Abbot v. Burke*,[5] a New Jersey Supreme Court decision, with ten opinions over thirty years, has been an exception to unpromising results from state equalization litigation. The Court ordered increased funding of students in poor urban districts; needs-based supplemental programs and funding to "wipe out student disadvantages;" comprehensive educational improvement; new and rehabilitated facilities, an end to overcrowding, improved health and safety violations. It required that *"Abbott"* schools introduce "Success for All," an educational reform program that some educators have praised highly, although others have been critical. In 2001–2002, 62 New Jersey elementary schools that used the "Success for All" program gained 9.8 percentage points according to statewide measures of achievement, while the state as a whole gained 1.0 percentage point. Almost all of the Success for All schools are in *Abbott* districts.

Abbott also mandated a preschool program with rigorous quality requirements for three- and four-year-olds. Almost 70% of eligible children have been enrolled, at $10,000 per pupil. The National Institute for Early Education Research placed *Abbott* preschool programs at the top of its rankings in 2004.

The New York Court of Appeals in *Campaign for Fiscal Equity v. State*,[6] that resembles *Abbott*, has ruled that the state is under a duty to provide a sound basic education to all children. According to a March, 2004 estimate the cost of compliance will be $8 billion. There has not yet been a legislative response, but some legislators

---

[5] Abbott v. Burke, 100 NJ 269, 495, A.2d 376 (1985).

[6] Campaign for Fiscal Equity, Inc. v. State, 86 NY.2d 307 (1995).

already are balking at the proposal. Given the reluctance of key members of the legislature to appropriate more money for urban schools, with largely minority populations, the *Campaign for Fiscal Equity* decision is at minimum another weapon in the arsenal of advocates for minority children.

Because effective relief has been so difficult to achieve in funding cases, equal education advocates launched *Sheff v. O'Neill*[7] in Connecticut courts, which has aspired to fund equalization *and* obtain integration as relief. In January 2003, fourteen years after the case was filed, the parties entered into an interim settlement that undertook to expand integrated magnet schools that had been fashioned to reach 30 percent of Hartford's black and Latino students by 2007, although 70% of Hartford students will still be in overwhelmingly segregated schools. The cost will be $245 million over four years. Pursuant to the settlement more than 7,000 Hartford children now are in integrated schools (defined in the settlement as no more than 68 percent black and Latino). The rest are still segregated.

Voluntary Integration

Despite demographics that make it impossible to integrate all African-American children, a great deal more can be done. Various school assignment arrangements, while not primarily integration vehicles, can be used to integrate: charters; vouchers; magnets; No Child Left Behind; voluntary cross-district transfers, exemplified by METCO; assignment by socio-economic class (more or less coinciding with race); assignment from across a range of test scores (coinciding pretty much with race); controlled choice, i.e., limited parental school selection, controlled to prevent racial concentrations. While, none can solve the school segregation problem alone, within a metropolitan or suburban area, a number of the proposals in combination could improve black youngsters' educational opportunities.

Vouchers carry the controversial baggage of church-state issues and a battle over whether they threaten destruction of public educa-

---

[7] Sheff v. O'Neill, 238 Conn. 1, 678 A.2d 1267 (1996).

tion. They, therefore, are not likely to become universal. They have been rejected by recent votes in Maryland, Michigan, Colorado, California, Washington, Michigan and California by margins between 55% and 71%. Because of heavy opposition there may not be enough experience to conclude whether they will affect integration. But, enough is known so that the NAACP Legal Defense Fund, which surely would support them if it believed they would promote integration, is firmly opposed and filed a friend of the court brief against vouchers in the Supreme Court's most recent voucher case. On the other hand many blacks support vouchers, illustrating how controversial they are. Many parochial schools that accept vouchers can afford to educate students cheaply (vouchers typically are about $2,500 per year, but some states offer much more) because they pay their teachers poorly, many of whom work for low pay because of dedication to their religion. But the supply of religiously dedicated teachers is limited. Should voucher programs expand, the supply of cheaply employed teachers may not be sufficient and others will have to be hired at market rates. The cost of voucher subvented education will increase, making the programs difficult to sustain.

Vouchers generally are confined to paying tuition at a school within the voucher holder's district. Where they may be spent outside the district transportation is not available. Vouchers could serve as a city to suburb integration device if they could be redeemed outside the holder's district and transportation were furnished. Suburban schools which take vouchers, however, are likely to cost more than an inner city voucher bearer could afford.

Magnets ordinarily do not draw students across the city-suburb boundary. They are no more likely to be integrated than the general run of schools. But, charter magnets may be used to desegregate as they now are, successfully, in the schools created pursuant to the settlement of *Sheff v. O'Neill.*

A charter school may be organized and taught in various ways, so long as it meets certain requirements. But charters ordinarily have been more segregated than regular public schools and do not necessarily offer a path to integration. If the aim were to promote integration the state might give priority to charters located near district lines, near students from urban and suburban districts. A charter that readily attracts African-Americans might save vacant seats for white children, whose presence would be needed to integrate. On the other hand, they may reject white children to make room for blacks. Both situations can create legal problems that, if its principle reached lower school education, possibly could be mitigated by *Grutter*.[8] Charter schools do not offer an assurance of quality education, although some charters like all black Roxbury Prep in Boston are first-rate. It has a highly dedicated staff that is not often likely to be replicated. New York State closed one of its first three charter schools, partially closed another and placed the third on probation.

Within cities or suburbs, controlled choice has ordinarily been the most effective technique for integrating. In a controlled choice system parents select from a small number of schools that might have the special characteristics of magnet schools. Schools are all of the same quality. Travel distances are convenient. The final assignment is made by lottery, but administrators may make adjustments to maintain some sort of racial balance. I write this not abstractly, but because my granddaughters attend school in a choice district, Montclair, New Jersey, where the schools are excellent and well integrated. I have heard of no dissatisfaction with the program. Ordinarily, most districts don't have enough of a racial mix for controlled choice to serve as a means of promoting integration. There may be objection to magnets in a controlled choice system that set aside some number of seats for minorities if choice does not produce a racially balanced class. Such issues have been litigated occasionally, and usually have been resolved against racial balance, but not always. The Supreme Court has not spoken on the question. *Grutter* may make a difference, but perhaps not, because the Court might view lower schools and higher education differently. Since cross-district school choice is rarely an option, controlled choice cannot

---

[8] Grutter v. Bollinger, 539 U.S. 306 (2003) (upholding University of Michigan Law School's affirmative action program); *see also* Gratz v. Bollinger, 539 U.S. 244 (2003) (striking down University of Michigan's undergraduate affirmative action program).

address the most severe problem of public education, that of the racial divide between city and suburb.

No single technique can work everywhere. In some, perhaps many places, segregated living is so extensive that integration will be difficult or unattainable. Because urban areas are almost all black, the main problem is how to integrate from city to suburb. Unless that is doable, integration will be very limited. James E. Ryan and Michael Heise have persuasively come to a sobering conclusion: the key to integrating schools is the willingness of the suburbs to relinquish their power to keep out racial minorities:

> Our central claim is that unless the politics surrounding school choice are altered, school choice plans will continue to be structured in ways that protect the physical and financial independence of suburban public schools. As a result, school choice plans will be geographically constrained and will generally tend to be intradistrict. Voucher programs, in particular, are likely to be limited to urban areas, where parents feel little attachment to neighborhood public schools and are desperate for relief.

Where schools cannot be integrated the field is wide open for the educational techniques that work. On those I pretend to no exceptional knowledge. Certainly resources matter. But to opt for equalization or adequacy in lieu of integration where it is physically attainable, is to forfeit the best chance for equal education.

A Proposal

The No Child Left Behind Act (NCLB) suggests a conceptual entry to dealing with the problem of interdistrict integration. Where schools, as judged by test scores, are unsatisfactory, NCLB confers the right to transfer to a satisfactory school, but only to one within the same district. Already, transferee schools have been overcrowded and unable to receive new students. Why shouldn't a child be allowed to transfer to a school in another district? I'm not suggesting that the suburban schools be compelled to admit city children. Such a requirement would be counterproductive, because of the resistance it would stir up, to say the least. But suburban districts could be encouraged, voluntarily, or appropriately rewarded, to admit some acceptable number of city children. It would be a patriotic act and suburban districts should, if possible, be persuaded of that. METCO in Boston is a model. Altogether about 3,500 black children bus from Boston to the suburbs. It has been an immense plus for their education and for the health of the general community, at virtually no cost to the suburbs.

The METCO model should be exported from Boston and its suburbs to the rest of the country. METCO's 3500 children, spread out among a large number of suburbs amounts to a small handful of children in each suburban class. If the program were increased several times over the numbers still would be scarcely noticeable. If every suburb across America were to emulate those that surround Boston an immense number of black children would receive a superior education. Their better lives would improve life for everyone.

National leadership, or leadership within states or regions, should establish a national program, or smaller scale programs, to persuade the suburbs that it is in their interest and the national interest to upgrade the education of as many metropolitan area minority children as they feel they can absorb. That program should celebrate also the benefits white, middle-class kids would gain by attending racially diverse schools. Montclair, once more, is an example. Not only are the schools well integrated, but the educational experience, which includes attending school with a mix of classmates, is first-rate. The upscale Montclair housing market is booming, testimony to how families view the opportunity for their children to attend school there.

A first step would be to establish national, statewide or regional bodies to ascertain how many children could conveniently be accommodated if, across the country, a city-to-suburb program were introduced into NCLB; how many would probably transfer, costs, logistical factors and so forth. The leadership should promote public understanding that it is in the national interest to furnish the best possible education to the most disadvantaged children. Without city-to-suburb integration how can a substantial number of urban black kids be integrated? Without city to suburb integration the debilitated state of black education and quality of life will continue.

Powerful arguments and interests will be marshaled against such a proposal: travel expense; burden of the bus ride; inequality of black children busing to distant schools while white children go to school nearby; costs incurred by the transferee district; social problems for children on both sides of the divide; skimming the best students from city schools; obstacles to parental involvement in after school activities at children's distant schools; a disconnect between tax rates set by the vote of parents in one district to pay for the education of children who come from another. Some of these barriers are unavoidable. Yet, many children bus to school in all-black or all-white systems, some parents are distant from their children's schools, many of the best students seize distant opportunities. As to expense, a necessary part of the program would be that the state or federal governments would pay the extra costs that benefit the entire community. Transfer should be accompanied by a social support program, for which Roma-Bulgarian integration, described at the beginning of this volume, offers a lesson: social workers, teacher preparation, tutoring, social and cultural programs for children and families, and so forth. Just as the President of that Eastern European country praised its Roma integration program, political leaders here should do the same.

Persuading suburbs will not be the only problem. Some blacks see integration as renouncing their own racial identification, losing power over school funds and the power to hire. The black mayor of St. Louis opposed interdistrict busing, advocating, instead, spending the money on all-black city schools over which he would have influence. The black leadership in Atlanta settled the Atlanta school desegregation case, in which I was their lawyer, against my advice. They gained administrative control and such power and patronage as it commanded. In exchange they agreed not to seek integration with the suburbs. Julian Bond has called this "the second Atlanta Compromise." "The community settled for black control of the school system in exchange for an integrated school system. . . . At the time it had a lot of attractiveness to it, but in hindsight it was an awful mistake." (The first Atlanta Compromise was Booker T. Washington's 1895 speech in Atlanta to the Cotton States and International Exposition in which he said, "The wisest among my race understand that the agitation of questions of social equality is the extremest folly. . . .")

I have no illusions that this proposal be adopted with alacrity. But as the need to do something about segregated schools sinks in, as they become commonly recognized as a breeding ground for no end of social dislocation, the attraction of integration should become manifest. I think of Adam Clayton Powell's Powell Amendment. In 1950 he proposed the incontestable proposition that recipients of federal funds should not be permitted to discriminate on grounds of race. It was regularly defeated until 1964 when it finally was enacted into law in the Civil Rights Act of that year. I hope that the country will not wait for fourteen years to do something meaningful about school segregation. But sooner or later, the need for action will produce action. The sooner the start, the sooner the result. Does that possibly distant goal mean that I despair of improving black education until it is achieved? Obviously, steps can be taken to ameliorate present conditions. But until schools are desegregated, until black and white children go to school in racially unified systems, I don't see how black children can attain their full potential. Until then, white children will be going to school in an environment much different from the one in which they will later work.

School desegregation alone will not end the enduring subordination of large parts of the black population. To integrate is necessary, but not sufficient. Other remedies have been employed and must continue. Affirmative action in higher education has increased the number of black professional and business people. Enforcing fair employment and fair housing laws have made a difference. Other aspects of living will have to change as well. Then, at least a generation will have to pass through the new system. But, still, without integration, the path to equality will be much longer than it could be.

Critics of what might be called this traditional civil rights agenda prefer to focus on self-help. Among them have been Abigail and Stephan Thernstrom, most recently authors of "No Excuses" and John McWhorter, author of "Losing the Race." They advocate hard work, study and personal responsibility, giving up a mindset of anti-intellectualism and victimology. Surely, anyone, black or white, would benefit from those prescriptions. But, integration, not exhortation, would more likely promote the attitudes they prescribe. Black students in integrated schools are more likely than those who are isolated in the ghetto to assimilate such standards from classmates (although, to be sure, not all classmates).

Do I think this will happen soon? I doubt it, absent leadership that we do not now have. *Brown,* the Civil Rights Movement and the Civil Rights Acts of the mid-sixties effected a great transformation. Nevertheless, black income persists at about 60% of white, black unemployment double that of white. One third—*one third*—of all black males will spend time in prison. Twenty-four percent of African Americans, 30% of black children, live in poverty. A black man in Harlem has less chance of living to age 65 than a man in Bangladesh. The discrepancy is not as visible as black and white drinking fountains or the back of the bus. But periodic race riots bring it to the forefront. Perhaps the next one or two will be a spur to amending NCLB to permit cross district transfers or otherwise commencing a program of desegregating black education. Or perhaps unanticipated leadership will emerge. There may be other ways of accomplishing the same result that I don't know or don't appreciate.

Charles Sumner, in years preceding the Civil War, energized public opinion against slavery. John Brown, became a national icon around whom anti-slavery opinion formed, despite the fact that he was a murderer. Martin Luther King, Jr., provided non-violent inspiration in the sixties in the last great struggle against racial segregation. Perhaps change must crystallize around a leader; rational contemplation is not enough. That asks: Who can become a Sumner, Brown or King of today's world?

But to integrate schools should not require charisma. Rational contemplation of what is at stake should be enough. As a nation there is plenty of capacity for that when it is unencumbered by centuries of meaning attached to race. What if the issue were approached with the resolve and the billions of dollars that might be invested in putting an astronaut on Mars?

APPENDICES

[edited]

PLESSY v. FERGUSON

1896

163 U.S. 537 (1986)

MR. JUSTICE BROWN delivered the opinion of the court.

The first section of the statute enacts "that all railway companies carrying passengers in their coaches in this State, shall provide equal but separate accommodations for the white, and colored races, by providing two or more passenger coaches for each passenger train, or by dividing the passenger coaches by a partition so as to secure separate accommodations: Provided, That this section shall not be construed to apply to street railroads. No person or persons, shall be admitted to occupy seats in coaches, other than, the ones, assigned, to them on account of the race they belong to."

By the second section it was enacted "that the officers of such passenger trains shall have power and are hereby required to assign each passenger to the coach or compartment used for the race to which such passenger belongs; any passenger insisting on going into a coach or compartment to which by race he does not belong, shall be liable to a fine of twenty-five dollars, or in lieu thereof to imprisonment for a period of not more than twenty days in the parish prison, and any officer of any railroad insisting on assigning a passenger to a coach or compartment other than the one set aside for the race to which said passenger belongs, shall be liable to a fine of twenty-five dollars, or in lieu thereof to imprisonment for a period of not more than twenty days in the parish prison; and should any passenger refuse to occupy the coach or compartment to which he or she is assigned by the officer of such railway, said officer shall have power to refuse to carry such passenger on his train, and for such refusal neither he nor the railway company which he represents shall be liable for damages in any of the courts of this State."

The third section provides penalties for the refusal or neglect of the officers, directors, conductors and employes of railway companies to comply with the act, with a proviso that "nothing in this act shall be construed as applying to nurses attending children of the other race." The fourth section is immaterial.

The petition for the writ of prohibition averred that petitioner was seven eighths Caucasian and one eighth African blood; that the mixture of colored blood was not discernible in him, and that he was entitled to every right, privilege and immunity secured to citizens of the United States of the white race; and that, upon such theory, he took possession of a vacant seat in a coach where passengers of the white race were accommodated, and was ordered by the conductor to vacate said coach and take a seat in another assigned to persons of the colored race, and having refused to comply with such demand he was forcibly ejected with the aid of a police officer, and imprisoned in the parish jail to answer a charge of having violated the above act.

1. That it does not conflict with the Thirteenth Amendment, which abolished slavery and involuntary servitude, except as a punishment for crime, is too clear for argument. Slavery implies involuntary servitude—a state of bondage; the ownership of mankind as a chattel, or at least the control of the labor and services of one man for the benefit of another, and the absence of a legal right to the disposal of his own person, property and services. This amendment was said in the Slaughter-house cases, 16 Wall. 36, to have been intended primarily to abolish slavery, as it had been previously known in this country, and that it equally forbade Mexican peonage or the Chinese coolie trade, when they amounted to slavery or involuntary servitude, and that the use of the word "servitude" was intended to prohibit the use of all forms of involuntary slavery, of whatever class or name. It was intimated, however, in that case that this amendment was regarded by the statesmen of that day as insufficient to protect the colored race from certain laws which had been enacted in the Southern States, imposing upon the colored race onerous disabilities and burdens, and curtailing their rights in the pursuit of life, liberty and property to such an extent that their freedom was of little value; and that the Fourteenth Amendment was devised to meet this exigency.

So, too, in the Civil Rights cases, 109 U.S. 3, 24, it was said that the act of a mere individual, the owner of an inn, a public conveyance or place of amusement, refusing accommodations to colored people, cannot be justly regarded as imposing any badge of slavery or servitude upon the applicant, but only as involving an ordinary civil injury, properly cognizable by the laws of the State, and presumably subject to redress by those laws until the contrary appears. "It would be running the slavery argument into the ground," said Mr. Justice Bradley, "to make it apply to every act of discrimination which a person may see fit to make as to the guests he will entertain, or as to the people he will take into his coach or cab or car, or admit to his concert or theatre, or deal with in other matters of intercourse or business."

A statute which implies merely a legal distinction between the white and colored races—a distinction which is founded in the color of the two races, and which must always exist so long as white men are distinguished from the other race by color—has no tendency to destroy the legal equality of the two races, or reestablish a state of involuntary servitude. Indeed, we do not understand that the Thirteenth Amendment is strenuously relied upon by the plaintiff in error in this connection.

2. By the Fourteenth Amendment, all persons born or naturalized in the United States, and subject to the jurisdiction thereof, are made citizens of the United States and of the State wherein they reside; and the States are forbidden from making or enforcing any law which shall abridge the privileges or immunities of citizens of the United States, or shall deprive any person of life, liberty or property without due process of law, or deny to any person within their jurisdiction the equal protection of the laws.

The proper construction of this amendment was first called to the attention of this court in the Slaughter-house cases, 16 Wall. 36, which involved, however, not a question of race, but one of exclusive privileges. The case did not call for any expression of opinion as to the exact rights it was intended to secure to the colored race, but it was said generally that its main purpose was to establish the citizenship of the negro; to give definitions of citizenship of the United States and of the States, and to protect from the hostile legislation of the States the privileges and immunities of citizens of the United States, as distinguished from those of citizens of the States.

The object of the amendment was undoubtedly to enforce the absolute equality of the two races before the law, but in the nature of things it could not have been intended to abolish distinctions based upon color, or to enforce social, as distinguished from political equality, or a commingling of the two races upon terms unsatisfactory to either. Laws permitting, and even requiring, their separation in places where they are liable to be brought into contact do not necessarily imply the inferiority of either race to the other, and have been generally, if not universally, recognized as within the competency of the state legislatures in the exercise of their police power. The most common instance of this is connected with the establishment of separate schools for white and colored children, which has been held to be a valid exercise of the legislative power even by courts of States where the political rights of the colored race have been longest and most earnestly enforced.

One of the earliest of these cases is that of Roberts v. City of Boston, 5 Cush. 198, in which the Supreme Judicial Court of Massachusetts held that the general school committee of Boston had power to make provision for the instruction of colored children in separate schools established exclusively for them, and to prohibit their attendance upon the other schools. "The great principle," said Chief Justice Shaw, p. 206, "advanced by the learned and eloquent advocate for the plaintiff," (Mr. Charles Sumner,) "is, that by the constitution and laws of Massachusetts, all persons without distinction of age or sex, birth or color, origin or condition, are equal before the law. . . . But, when this great principle comes to be applied to the actual and various conditions of persons in society, it will not warrant the assertion, that men and women are legally clothed with the same civil and political powers, and that children and adults are legally to have the same functions and be subject to the same treatment; but only that the rights of all, as they are settled and regulated by law, are equally entitled to the paternal consideration and protection of the law for their maintenance and security." It was held that the powers of the committee extended to the establishment of separate schools for children of different ages, sexes and colors, and that they might also establish special schools for poor and neglected children, who have become too old to attend the primary school, and yet have not acquired the rudiments of learning, to enable them to enter the ordinary schools. Similar laws have been enacted by Congress under its general power of legislation over the District of Columbia, §§ 281, 282, 283, 310, 319, as well as by the legislatures of many of the States, and have been generally, if not uniformly, sustained by the courts.

Laws forbidding the intermarriage of the two races may be said in a technical sense to interfere with the freedom of contract, and yet have been universally recognized as within the police power of the State.

The distinction between laws interfering with the political equality of the negro and those requiring the separation of the two races in schools, theatres and railway carriages has been frequently drawn by this court. Thus in Strauder v. West Virginia, 100 U.S. 303, it was held that a law of West Virginia limiting to white male persons, 21 years of age and citizens of the State, the right to sit upon juries, was a discrimination which implied a legal inferiority in civil society, which lessened the security of the right of the colored race, and was a step toward reducing them to a condition of servility. Indeed, the right of a colored man that, in the selection of jurors to pass upon his life, liberty and property, there shall be no exclusion of his race, and no discrimination against them because of color, has been asserted in a number of cases. So, where the laws of a particular locality or the charter of a particular railway corporation has provided that no person shall be excluded from the cars on account of color, we have held that this meant that persons of color should travel in the same car as white ones, and that the enactment was not satisfied by the company's providing cars assigned exclusively to people of color, though they were as good as those which they assigned exclusively to white persons. Railroad Company v. Brown, 17 Wall. 445.

Upon the other hand, where a statute of Louisiana required those engaged in the transportation of passengers among the States to give to all persons travelling within that State, upon vessels employed in that business, equal rights and privileges in all parts of the vessel, without distinction on account of race or color, and subjected to an action for damages the owner of such a vessel, who excluded colored passengers on account of their color from the cabin set aside by him for the use of whites, it was held to be so far as it applied to interstate commerce, unconstitutional and void. Hall v. De Cuir, 95 U.S. 485. The court in this case, however, expressly disclaimed that it had anything whatever to do with the statute as a regulation of internal commerce, or affecting anything else than commerce among the States.

While we think the enforced separation of the races, as applied to the internal commerce of the State, neither abridges the privileges or immunities of the colored man, deprives him of his property without due process of law, nor denies him the equal protection of the laws, within the meaning of the Fourteenth Amendment, we are not prepared to say that the conductor, in assigning passengers to the coaches according to their race, does not act at his peril, or that the provision of the second section of the act, that denies to the passenger compensation in damages for a refusal to receive him into the coach in which he properly belongs, is a valid exercise of the legislative power.

It is claimed by the plaintiff in error that, in any mixed community, the reputation of belonging to the dominant race, in this instance the white race, is property, in the same sense that a right of action, or of inheritance, is property. Conceding this to be so, for the purposes of this case, we are unable to see how this statute deprives him of, or in any way affects his right to, such property. If he be a white man and assigned to a colored coach, he may have his action for damages against the company for being deprived of his so called property. Upon the other hand, if he be a colored man and be so assigned, he has been deprived of no property, since he is not lawfully entitled to the reputation of being a white man.

In this connection, it is also suggested by the learned counsel for the plaintiff in error that the same argument that will justify the state legislature in requiring railways to provide separate accommodations for the two races will also authorize them to require separate cars to be provided for people whose hair is of a certain color, or who are aliens, or who belong to certain nationalities, or to enact laws requiring colored people to walk upon one side of the street, and white people upon the other, or requiring white men's houses to be painted white, and colored men's black, or their vehicles or business signs to be of different colors, upon the theory that one side of the street is as good as the other, or that a house or vehicle of one color is as good as one of another color. The reply to all this is that every exercise of the police power must be reasonable, and extend only to such laws as are enacted in good faith for the promotion for the public good, and not for the annoyance or oppression of a particular class. Thus in Yick Wo v. Hopkins, 118 U.S. 356, it was held by this court that a municipal ordinance of the city of San Francisco, to regulate the carrying on the public laundries within the limits of the municipality, violated the provisions of the Constitution of the United States, if it conferred upon the municipal authorities arbitrary power, at their own will, and without regard to discretion, in the legal sense, of the term, to give or withhold consent as to persons or places, without regard to the competency of the persons applying, or the propriety of the places selected for the carrying on the business. It was held to be a covert attempt on the part of the municipality to make an arbitrary and unjust discrimination against the Chinese race. While this was the case of a municipal ordinance, a like principle has been held to apply to acts of a state legislature passed in the exercise of the police power.

So far, then, as a conflict with the Fourteenth Amendment is concerned, the case reduces itself to the question whether the statute of Louisiana is a reasonable regulation, and with respect to this there must necessarily be a large discretion on the part of the legislature. In determining the question of reasonableness it is at liberty to act with reference to the established usages, customs and traditions of the people, and with a view to the promotion of their comfort, and the preservation of the public peace and good order. Gauged by this standard, we cannot say that a law which authorizes or even requires the separation of the two races in public conveyances is unreasonable, or more obnoxious to the Fourteenth Amendment than the acts of Congress requiring separate schools for colored children in the District of Columbia, the constitutionality of which does not seem to have been questioned, or the corresponding acts of state legislatures.

We consider the underlying fallacy of the plaintiff's argument to consist in the assumption that the enforced separation of the two races stamps the colored race with a badge of inferiority. If this be so, it is not by reason of anything found in the act, but solely because the colored race chooses to put that construction upon it. The argument necessarily assumes that if, as has been more than once the case, and is not unlikely to be so again, the colored race should become the dominant power in the state legislature, and should enact a law in precisely similar terms, it would thereby relegate the white race to an inferior position. We imagine that the white race, at least, would not acquiesce in this assumption. The argument also assumes that social prejudices may be overcome by legislation, and that equal rights cannot be secured to the negro except by an enforced commingling of the two races. We cannot accept this proposition. If the two races are to meet upon terms of social equality, it must be the result of natural affinities, a mutual appreciation of each other's merits and a voluntary consent of individuals. As was said by the Court of Appeals of New York in People v. Gallagher, 93 N.Y. 438, 448, "this end can neither be accomplished nor promoted by laws which conflict with the general sentiment of the community upon whom they are designed to operate. When the government, therefore, has secured to each of its citizens equal rights before the law and equal opportunities for improvement and progress, it has accomplished the end for which it was organized and performed all of the functions respecting social advantages with which it is endowed." Legislation is powerless to eradicate racial instincts or to abolish distinctions based upon physical differences, and the attempt to do so can only result in accentuating the difficulties of the present situation. If the civil and political rights of both races be equal one cannot be inferior to the other civilly or politically. If one race be inferior to the other socially, the Constitution of the United States cannot put them upon the same plane.

The judgment of the court below is, therefore,

Affirmed.

DISSENT: MR. JUSTICE HARLAN dissenting.

* * *

Only "nurses attending children of the other race" are excepted from the operation of the statute. No exception is made of colored attendants travelling with adults. A white man is not permitted to have his colored servant with him in the same coach, even if his condition of health requires the constant, personal assistance of such servant. If a colored maid insists upon riding in the same coach with a white woman whom she has been employed to serve, and who may need her personal attention while travelling, she is subject to be fined or imprisoned for such an exhibition of zeal in the discharge of duty.

While there may be in Louisiana persons of different races who are not citizens of the United States, the words in the act, "white and colored races," necessarily include all citizens of the United States of both races residing in that State. So that we have before us a state enactment that compels, under penalties, the separation of the two races in railroad passenger coaches, and makes it a crime for a citizen of either race to enter a coach that has been assigned to citizens of the other race.

Thus the State regulates the use of a public highway by citizens of the United States solely upon the basis of race.

However apparent the injustice of such legislation may be, we have only to consider whether it is consistent with the Constitution of the United States.

That a railroad is a public highway, and that the corporation which owns or operates it is in the exercise of public functions, is not, at this day, to be disputed.

In respect of civil rights, common to all citizens, the Constitution of the United States does not, I think, permit any public authority to know the race of those entitled to be protected in the enjoyment of such rights. Every true man has pride of race, and under appropriate circumstances when the rights of others, his equals before the law, are not to be affected, it is his privilege to express such pride and to take such action based upon it as to him seems proper. But I deny that any legislative body or judicial tribunal may have regard to the race of citizens when the civil rights of those citizens are involved. Indeed, such legislation, as that here in question, is inconsistent not only with that equality of rights which pertains to citizenship, National and State, but with the personal liberty enjoyed by every one within the United States.

The Thirteenth Amendment does not permit the withholding or the deprivation of any right necessarily inhering in freedom. It not only struck down the institution of slavery as previously existing in the United States, but it prevents the imposition of any burdens or disabilities that constitute badges of slavery or servitude. It decreed universal civil freedom in this country. This court has so adjudged. But that amendment having been found inadequate to the protection of the rights of those who had been in slavery, it was followed by the Fourteenth Amendment, which added greatly to the dignity and glory of American citizenship, and to the security of personal liberty, by declaring that "all persons born or naturalized in the United States, and subject to the jurisdiction thereof, are citizens of the United States and of the State wherein they reside," and that "no State shall make or enforce any law which shall abridge the privileges or immunities of citizens of the United States; nor shall any State deprive any person of life, liberty or property without due process of law, nor deny to any person within its jurisdiction the equal protection of the laws." These two amendments, if enforced according to their true intent and meaning, will protect all the civil rights that pertain to freedom and citizenship. Finally, and to the end that no citizen should be denied, on account of his race, the privilege of participating in the political control of his country, it was declared by the Fifteenth Amendment that "the right of citizens of the United States to vote shall not be denied or abridged by the United States or by any State on account of race, color or previous condition of servitude."

These notable additions to the fundamental law were welcomed by the friends of liberty throughout the world. They removed the race line from our governmental systems. They had, as this court has said, a common purpose, namely, to secure "to a race recently emancipated, a race that through many generations have been held in slavery, all the civil rights that the superior race enjoy." They declared, in legal effect, this court has further said, "that the law in the States shall be the same for the black as for the white; that all persons, whether colored or white, shall stand equal before the laws of the States, and, in regard to the colored race, for whose protection the amendment was primarily designed, that no discrimination shall be made against them by law because of their color." We also said: "The words of the amendment, it is true, are prohibitory, but they contain a necessary implication of a positive immunity, or right, most valuable to the colored race—the right to exemption from unfriendly legislation against them distinctively as colored—exemption from legal discriminations, implying inferiority in civil society, lessening the security of their enjoyment of the rights which others enjoy, and discriminations which are steps towards reducing them to the condition of a subject race." It was, consequently, adjudged that a state law that excluded citizens of the colored race from juries, because of their race and however well qualified in other respects to discharge the duties of jurymen, was repugnant to the <u>Fourteenth Amendment</u>. At the present term, referring to the previous adjudications, this court declared that "underlying all of those decisions is the principle that the Constitution of the United States, in its present form, forbids, so far as civil and political rights are concerned, discrimination by the General Government or the States against any citizen because of his race. All citizens are equal before the law."

The decisions referred to show the scope of the recent amendments of the Constitution. They also show that it is not within the power of a State to prohibit colored citizens, because of their race, from participating as jurors in the administration of justice.

It was said in argument that the statute of Louisiana does not discriminate against either race, but prescribes a rule applicable alike to white and colored citizens. But this argument does not meet the difficulty. Every one knows that the statute in question had its origin in the purpose, not so much to exclude white persons from railroad cars occupied by blacks, as to exclude colored people from coaches occupied by or assigned to white persons. Railroad corporations of Louisiana did not make discrimination among whites in the matter of accommodation for travellers. The thing to accomplish was, under the guise of giving equal accommodation for whites and blacks, to compel the latter to keep to themselves while travelling in railroad passenger coaches. No one would be so wanting in candor as to assert the contrary. The fundamental objection, therefore, to the statute is that it interferes with the personal freedom of citizens. "Personal liberty," it has been well said, "consists in the power of locomotion, of changing situation, or removing one's person to whatsoever places one's own inclination may direct, without imprisonment or restraint, unless by due course of law." 1 Bl. Com. *134. If a white man and a black man choose to occupy the same public conveyance on a public highway, it is their right to do so, and no government, proceeding alone on grounds of race, can prevent it without infringing the personal liberty of each.

It is one thing for railroad carriers to furnish, or to be required by law to furnish, equal accommodations for all whom they are under a legal duty to carry. It is quite another thing for government to forbid citizens of the white and black races from travelling in the same public conveyance, and to punish officers of railroad companies for permitting persons of the two races to occupy the same passenger coach. If a State can prescribe, as a rule of civil conduct, that whites and blacks shall not travel as passengers in the same railroad coach, why may it not so regulate the use of the streets of its cities and towns as to compel white citizens to keep on one side of a street and black citizens to keep on the other? Why may it not, upon like grounds, punish whites and blacks who ride together in street cars or in open vehicles on a public road of street? Why may it not require sheriffs to assign whites to one side of a court-room and blacks to the other? And why may it not also prohibit the commingling of the two races in the galleries of legislative halls or in public assemblages convened for the considerations of the political questions of the day? Further, if this statute of Louisiana is consistent with the personal liberty of citizens, why may not the State require the separation in railroad coaches of native and naturalized citizens of the United States, or of Protestants and Roman Catholics?

The answer given at the argument to these questions was that regulations of the kind they suggest would be unreasonable, and could not, therefore, stand before the law. Is it meant that the determination of questions of legislative power depends upon the inquiry whether the statute whose validity is questioned is, in the judgment of the courts, a reasonable one, taking all the circumstances into consideration? A statute may be unreasonable merely because a sound public policy forbade its enactment. But I do not understand that the courts have anything to do with the policy or expediency of legislation. A statute may be valid, and yet, upon grounds of public policy, may well be characterized as unreasonable.

The white race deems itself to be the dominant race in this country. And so it is, in prestige, in achievements, in education, in wealth and in power. So, I doubt not, it will continue to be for all time, if it remains true to its great heritage and holds fast to the principles of constitutional liberty. But in view of the Constitution, in the eye of the law, there is in this country no superior, dominant, ruling class of citizens. There is no caste here. Our Constitution is color-blind, and neither knows nor tolerates classes among citizens. In respect of civil rights, all citizens are equal before the law. The humblest is the peer of the most powerful. The law regards man as man, and takes no account of his surroundings or of his color when his civil rights as guaranteed by the supreme law of the land are involved. It is, therefore, to be regretted that this high tribunal, the final expositor of the fundamental law of the land, has reached the conclusion that it is competent for a State to regulate the enjoyment by citizens of their civil rights solely upon the basis of race.

In my opinion, the judgment this day rendered will, in time, prove to be quite as pernicious as the decision made by this tribunal in the Dred Scott case. It was adjudged in that case that the descendants of Africans who were imported into this country and sold as slaves were not included nor intended to be included under the word "citizens" in the Constitution, and could not claim any of the rights and privileges which that instrument provided for and secured to citizens of the United States; that at the time of the adoption of the Constitution they were "considered as a subordinate and inferior class of beings, who had been subjugated by the dominant race, and, whether emancipated or not, yet remained subject to their authority, and had no rights or privileges but such as those who held the power and the government might choose to grant them." 19 How. 393, 404. The recent amendments of the Constitution, it was supposed, had eradicated these principles from our institutions. But it seems that we have yet, in some of the States, a dominant race—a superior class of citizens, which assumes to regulate the enjoyment of civil rights, common to all citizens, upon the basis of race. The present decision, it may well be apprehended, will not only stimulate aggressions, more or less brutal and irritating, upon the admitted rights of colored citizens, but will encourage the belief that it is possible, by means of state enactments, to defeat the beneficent purposes which the people of the United

States had in view when they adopted the recent amendments of the Constitution, by one of which the blacks of this country were made citizens of the United States and of the States in which they respectively reside, and whose privileges and immunities, as citizens, the States are forbidden to abridge. Sixty millions of whites are in no danger from the presence here of eight millions of blacks. The destinies of the two races, in this country, are indissolubly linked together, and the interests of both require that the common government of all shall not permit the seeds of race hate to be planted under the sanction of law. What can more certainly arouse race hate, what more certainly create and perpetuate a feeling of distrust between these races, than state enactments, which, in fact, proceed on the ground that colored citizens are so inferior and degraded that they cannot be allowed to sit in public coaches occupied by white citizens? That, as all will admit, is the real meaning of such legislation as was enacted in Louisiana.

The sure guarantee of the peace and security of each race is the clear, distinct, unconditional recognition by our governments, National and State, of every right that inheres in civil freedom, and of the equality before the law of all citizens of the United States without regard to race. State enactments, regulating the enjoyment of civil rights, upon the basis of race, and cunningly devised to defeat legitimate results of the [*561] war, under the pretence of recognizing equality of rights, can have no other result than to render permanent peace impossible, and to keep alive a conflict of races, the continuance of which must do harm to all concerned. This question is not met by the suggestion that social equality cannot exist between the white and black races in this country. That argument, if it can be properly regarded as one, is scarcely worthy of consideration; for social equality no more exists between two races when travelling in a passenger coach or a public highway than when members of the same races sit by each other in a street car or in the jury box, or stand or sit with each other in a political assembly, or when they use in common the streets of a city or town, or when they are in the same room for the purpose of having their names placed on the registry of voters, or when they approach the ballot-box in order to exercise the high privilege of voting.

There is a race so different from our own that we do not permit those belonging to it to become citizens of the United States. Persons belonging to it are, with few exceptions, absolutely excluded from our country. I allude to the Chinese race. But by the statute in question, a Chinaman can ride in the same passenger coach with white citizens of the United States, while citizens of the black race in Louisiana, many of whom, perhaps, risked their lives for the preservation of the Union, who are entitled, by law, to participate in the political control of the State and nation, who are not excluded, by law or by reason of their race, from public stations of any kind, and who have all the legal rights that belong to white citizens, are yet declared to be criminals, liable to imprisonment, if they ride in a public coach occupied by citizens of the white race. It is scarcely just to say that a colored citizen should not object to occupying a public coach assigned to his own race. He does not object, nor, perhaps, would he object to separate coaches for his race, if his rights under the law were recognized. But he objects, and ought never to cease objecting to the proposition, that citizens of the white and black races can be adjudged criminals because they sit, or claim the right to sit, in the same public coach on a public highway.

The arbitrary separation of citizens, on the basis of race, while they are on a public highway, is a badge of servitude wholly inconsistent with the civil freedom and the equality before the law established by the Constitution. It cannot be justified upon any legal grounds.

If evils will result from the commingling of the two races upon public highways established for the benefit of all, they will be infinitely less than those that will surely come from state legislation regulating the enjoyment of civil rights upon the basis of race. We boast of the freedom enjoyed by our people above all other peoples. But it is difficult to reconcile that boast with a state of the law which, practically, puts the brand of servitude and degradation upon a large class of our fellow-citizens, our equals before the law. The thin disguise of "equal" accommodations for passengers in railroad coaches will not mislead any one, nor atone for the wrong this day done.

The result of the whole matter is, that while this court has frequently adjudged, and at the present term has recognized the doctrine, that a State cannot, consistently with the Constitution of the United States, prevent white and black citizens, having the required qualifications for jury service, from sitting in the same jury box, it is now solemnly held that a State may prohibit white and black citizens from sitting in the same passenger coach on a public highway, or may require that they be separated by a "partition," when in the same passenger coach. May it not now be reasonably expected that astute men of the dominant race, who affect to be disturbed at the possibility that the integrity of the white race may be corrupted, or that its supremacy will be imperilled, by contact on public highways with black people, will endeavor to procure statutes requiring white and black jurors to be separated in the jury box by a "partition," and that, upon retiring from the court room to consult as to their verdict, such partition, if it be a moveable one, shall be taken to their consultation room, and set up in such way as to prevent black jurors from coming too close to their brother jurors of the white race. If the "partition" used in the court room happens to be stationary, provision could be made for screens with openings through which jurors of the two races could confer as to their verdict without coming into personal contact with each other. I cannot see but that, according to the principles this day announced, such state legislation, although conceived in hostility to, and enacted for the purpose of humiliating citizens of the United States of a particular race, would be held to be consistent with the Constitution.

I do not deem it necessary to review the decisions of state courts to which reference was made in argument. Some, and the most important, of them are wholly inapplicable, because rendered prior to the adoption of the last amendments of the Constitution, when colored people had very few rights which the dominant race felt obliged to respect. Others were made at a time when public opinion, in many localities, was dominated by the institution of slavery; when it would not have been safe to do justice to the black man; and when, so far as the rights of blacks were concerned, race prejudice was, practically, the supreme law of the land. Those decisions cannot be guides in the era introduced by the recent amendments of the supreme law, which established universal civil freedom, gave citizenship to all born or naturalized in the United States and residing her, obliterated the race line from our systems of governments, National and State, and placed our free institutions upon the broad and sure foundation of the equality of all men before the law.

I am of opinion that the statute of Louisiana is inconsistent with the personal liberty of citizens, white and black, in that State, and hostile to both the spirit and letter of the Constitution of the United States. If laws of like character should be enacted in the several States of the Union, the effect would be in the highest degree mischievous. Slavery, as an institution tolerated by law would, it is true, have disappeared from our country, but there would remain a power in the States, by sinister legislation, to interfere with the full enjoyment of the blessings of freedom; to regulate civil rights, common to all citizens, upon the basis of race; and to place in a condition of legal inferiority a large body of American citizens, now constituting a part of the political community called the People of the United States, for whom, and by whom through representatives, our government is administered. Such a system is inconsistent with the guarantee given by the Constitution to each State of a republican form of government, and may be stricken down by Congressional action, or by the courts in the discharge of their solemn duty to maintain the supreme law of the land, anything in the constitution or laws of any State to the contrary notwithstanding.

[edited]

BROWN ET AL. v. BOARD OF EDUCATION OF TOPEKA ET AL.

347 U.S. 483

1954

MR. CHIEF JUSTICE WARREN delivered the opinion of the Court.

These cases come to us from the States of Kansas, South Carolina, Virginia, and Delaware. They are premised on different facts and different local conditions, but a common legal question justifies their consideration together in this consolidated opinion.

In each of the cases other than the Delaware case, a three-judge federal district court denied relief to the plaintiffs on the so-called "separate but equal" doctrine announced by this Court in *Plessy v. Ferguson, 163 U.S. 537.* Under that doctrine, equality of treatment is accorded when the races are provided substantially equal facilities, even though these facilities be separate. In the Delaware case, the Supreme Court of Delaware adhered to that doctrine, but ordered that the plaintiffs be admitted to the white schools because of their superiority to the Negro schools.

The plaintiffs contend that segregated public schools are not "equal" and cannot be made "equal," and that hence they are deprived of the equal protection of the laws. Because of the obvious importance of the question presented, the Court took jurisdiction.

Reargument was largely devoted to the circumstances surrounding the adoption of the Fourteenth Amendment in 1868. It covered exhaustively consideration of the Amendment in Congress, ratification by the states, then existing practices in racial segregation, and the views of proponents and opponents of the Amendment. This discussion and our own investigation convince us that, although these sources cast some light, it is not enough to resolve the problem with which we are faced. At best, they are inconclusive. The most avid proponents of the post-War Amendments undoubtedly intended them to remove all legal distinctions among "all persons born or naturalized in the United States." Their opponents, just as certainly, were antagonistic to both the letter and the spirit of the Amendments and wished them to have the most limited effect. What others in Congress and the state legislatures had in mind cannot be determined with any degree of certainty.

An additional reason for the inconclusive nature of the Amendment's history, with respect to segregated schools, is the status of public education at that time.[4] In the South, the movement toward free common schools, supported by general taxation, had not yet taken hold. Education of white children was largely in the hands of private groups. Education of Negroes was almost nonexistent, and practically all of the race were illiterate. In fact, any education of Negroes was forbidden by law in some states. Today, in contrast, many Negroes have achieved outstanding success in the arts and sciences as well as in the business and professional world. It is true that public school education at the time of the Amendment had advanced further in the North, but the effect of the Amendment on Northern States was generally ignored in the congressional debates. Even in the North, the conditions of public education did not approximate those existing today. The curriculum was usually rudimentary; ungraded schools were common in rural areas; the school term was but three months a year in many states; and compulsory school attendance was virtually unknown. As a consequence, it is not surprising that there should be so little in the history of the Fourteenth Amendment relating to its intended effect on public education.

---

[4] For a general study of the development of public education prior to the Amendment, see Butts and Cremin, A History of Education in American Culture (1953), Pts. I, II; Cubberley, Public Education in the United States (1934 ed.), cc. II–XII. School practices current at the time of the adoption of the Fourteenth Amendment are described in Butts and Cremin, *supra*, at 269–275; Cubberley, *supra*, at 288–339, 408–431; Knight, Public Education in the South (1922), cc. VIII, IX. See also H. Ex. Doc. No. 315, 41st Cong., 2d Sess. (1871). Although the demand for free public schools followed substantially the same pattern in both the North and the South, the development in the South did not begin to gain momentum until about 1850, some twenty years after that in the North. The reasons for the somewhat slower development in the South (*e.g.*, the rural character of the South and the different regional attitudes toward state assistance) are well explained in Cubberley, *supra*, at 408–423. In the country as a whole, but particularly in the South, the War virtually stopped all progress in public education. *Id.*, at 427–428. The low status of Negro education in all sections of the country, both before and immediately after the War, is described in Beale, A History of Freedom of Teaching in American Schools (1941), 112–132, 175–195. Compulsory school attendance laws were not generally adopted until after the ratification of the Fourteenth Amendment, and it was not until 1918 that such laws were in force in all the states. Cubberley, *supra*, at 563–565.

In the first cases in this Court construing the Fourteenth Amendment, decided shortly after its adoption, the Court interpreted it as proscribing all
state-imposed discriminations against the Negro race.[5] The doctrine of "separate but equal" did not make its appearance in this Court until 1896 in the
case of _Plessy v. Ferguson, supra,_ involving not education but transportation.[6] American courts have since labored with the doctrine for over half a
century. In this Court, there have been six cases involving the "separate but
equal" doctrine in the field of public education. In _Cumming v. County
Board of Education, 175 U.S. 528,_ and _Gong Lum v. Rice, 275 U.S. 78,_ the
validity of the doctrine itself was not challenged. In more recent cases, all
on the graduate school level, inequality was found in that specific benefits
enjoyed by white students were denied to Negro students of the same educational qualifications. _Missouri ex rel. Gaines v. Canada, 305 U.S. 337;
Sipuel v. Oklahoma, 332 U.S. 631; Sweatt v. Painter, 339 U.S. 629; McLaurin
v. Oklahoma State Regents, 339 U.S. 637._ In none of these cases was it
necessary to re-examine the doctrine to grant relief to the Negro plaintiff.
And in _Sweatt v. Painter, supra,_ the Court expressly reserved decision on the
question whether _Plessy_ v. _Ferguson_ should be held inapplicable to public
education.

---

[5] _Slaughter-House Cases, 16 Wall. 36, 67–72 (1873); Strauder v. West Virginia,
100 U.S. 303, 307–308 (1880):_

"It ordains that no State shall deprive any person of life, liberty, or property,
without due process of law, or deny to any person within its jurisdiction the equal
protection of the laws. What is this but declaring that the law in the States shall be
the same for the black as for the white; that all persons, whether colored or white,
shall stand equal before the laws of the States, and, in regard to the colored race, for
whose protection the amendment was primarily designed, that no discrimination
shall be made against them by law because of their color? The words of the amendment, it is true, are prohibitory, but they contain a necessary implication of a positive immunity, or right, most valuable to the colored race,—the right to exemption
from unfriendly legislation against them distinctively as colored,—exemption from
legal discriminations, implying inferiority in civil society, lessening the security of
their enjoyment of the rights which others enjoy, and discriminations which are
steps towards reducing them to the condition of a subject race."

[6] The doctrine apparently originated in _Roberts v. City of Boston, 59 Mass.
198, 206 (1850),_ upholding school segregation against attack as being violative of
a state constitutional guarantee of equality. Segregation in Boston public schools
was eliminated in 1855. Mass. Acts 1855, c. 256. But elsewhere in the North segregation in public education has persisted in some communities until recent years. It
is apparent that such segregation has long been a nationwide problem, not merely
one of sectional concern.

In the instant cases, that question is directly presented. Here, unlike *Sweatt* v. *Painter,* there are findings below that the Negro and white schools involved have been equalized, or are being equalized, with respect to buildings, curricula, qualifications and salaries of teachers, and other "tangible" factors.[9] Our decision, therefore, cannot turn on merely a comparison of these tangible factors in the Negro and white schools involved in each of the cases. We must look instead to the effect of segregation itself on public education.

In approaching this problem, we cannot turn the clock back to 1868 when the Amendment was adopted, or even to 1896 when *Plessy* v. *Ferguson* was written. We must consider public education in the light of its full development and its present place in American life throughout the Nation. Only in this way can it be determined if segregation in public schools deprives these plaintiffs of the equal protection of the laws.

Today, education is perhaps the most important function of state and local governments. Compulsory school attendance laws and the great expenditures for education both demonstrate our recognition of the importance of education to our democratic society. It is required in the performance of our most basic public responsibilities, even service in the armed forces. It is the very foundation of good citizenship. Today it is a principal instrument in awakening the child to cultural values, in preparing him for later professional training, and in helping him to adjust normally to his environment. In these days, it is doubtful that any child may reasonably be expected to succeed in life if he is denied the opportunity of an education. Such an opportunity, where the state has undertaken to provide it, is a right which must be made available to all on equal terms.

We come then to the question presented: Does segregation of children in public schools solely on the basis of race, even though the physical facilities and other "tangible" factors may be equal, deprive the children of the minority group of equal educational opportunities? We believe that it does.

---

[9] In the Kansas case, the court below found substantial equality as to all such factors. 98 F.Supp. 797, 798. In the South Carolina case, the court below found that the defendants were proceeding "promptly and in good faith to comply with the court's decree." 103 F.Supp. 920, 921. In the Virginia case, the court below noted that the equalization program was already "afoot and progressing" (103 F.Supp. 337, 341); since then, we have been advised, in the Virginia Attorney General's brief on reargument, that the program has now been completed. In the Delaware case, the court below similarly noted that the state's equalization program was well under way.

In *Sweatt v. Painter, supra,* in finding that a segregated law school for Negroes could not provide them equal educational opportunities, this Court
relied in large part on "those qualities which are incapable of objective measurement but which make for greatness in a law school." In *McLaurin v.
Oklahoma State Regents, supra,* the Court, in requiring that a Negro admitted to a white graduate school be treated like all other students, again re-
sorted to intangible considerations: ". . . his ability to study, to engage in
discussions and exchange views with other students, and, in general, to learn
his profession." Such considerations apply with added force to children in
grade and high schools. To separate them from others of similar age and
qualifications solely because of their race generates a feeling of inferiority as
to their status in the community that may affect their hearts and minds in a
way unlikely ever to be undone. The effect of this separation on their educational opportunities was well stated by a finding in the Kansas case by a
court which nevertheless felt compelled to rule against the Negro plaintiffs:

"Segregation of white and colored children in public schools has a detrimental effect upon the colored children. The impact is greater when it has
the sanction of the law; for the policy of separating the races is usually
interpreted as denoting the inferiority of the negro group. A sense of inferiority affects the motivation of a child to learn. Segregation with the sanction of law, therefore, has a tendency to [retard] the educational and mental
development of negro children and to deprive them of some of the benefits
they would receive in a racial[ly] integrated school system."[10]

Whatever may have been the extent of psychological knowledge at the time
of *Plessy* v. *Ferguson*, this finding is amply supported by modern authority.[11] Any language in *Plessy* v. *Ferguson* contrary to this finding is rejected.

---

[10] A similar finding was made in the Delaware case: "I conclude from the testimony that in our Delaware society, State-imposed segregation in education itself
results in the Negro children, as a class, receiving educational opportunities which
are substantially inferior to those available to white children otherwise similarly
situated." 87 A. 2d 862, 865.

[11] K. B. Clark, Effect of Prejudice and Discrimination on Personality Development (Midcentury White House Conference on Children and Youth, 1950); Witmer
and Kotinsky, Personality in the Making (1952), c. VI; Deutscher and Chein, The
Psychological Effects of Enforced Segregation: A Survey of Social Science Opinion,
26 J. Psychol. 259 (1948); Chein, What are the Psychological Effects of Segregation
Under Conditions of Equal Facilities?, 3 Int. J. Opinion and Attitude Res. 229 (1949);
Brameld, Educational Costs, in Discrimination and National Welfare (MacIver, ed.,
1949), 44–48; Frazier, The Negro in the United States (1949), 674–681. And see
generally Myrdal, An American Dilemma (1944).

We conclude that in the field of public education the doctrine of "separate but equal" has no place. Separate educational facilities are inherently unequal. Therefore, we hold that the plaintiffs and others similarly situated for whom the actions have been brought are, by reason of the segregation complained of, deprived of the equal protection of the laws guaranteed by the Fourteenth Amendment. This disposition makes unnecessary any discussion whether such segregation also violates the Due Process Clause of the Fourteenth Amendment.[12]

Because these are class actions, because of the wide applicability of this decision, and because of the great variety of local conditions, the formulation of decrees in these cases presents problems of considerable complexity. On reargument, the consideration of appropriate relief was necessarily subordinated to the primary question—the constitutionality of segregation in public education. We have now announced that such segregation is a denial of the equal protection of the laws. In order that we may have the full assistance of the parties in formulating decrees, the cases will be restored to the docket, and the parties are requested to present further argument on Questions 4 and 5 previously propounded by the Court for the reargument this Term.[13] The Attorney General of the United States is again invited to

---

[12] See *Bolling* v. *Sharpe, post,* p. 497, concerning the Due Process Clause of the Fifth Amendment.

[13] "4. Assuming it is decided that segregation in public schools violates the Fourteenth Amendment

"(a) would a decree necessarily follow providing that, within the limits set by normal geographic school districting, Negro children should forthwith be admitted to schools of their choice, or

"(b) may this Court, in the exercise of its equity powers, permit an effective gradual adjustment to be brought about from existing segregated systems to a system not based on color distinctions?

"5. On the assumption on which questions 4 (a) and (b) are based, and assuming further that this Court will exercise its equity powers to the end described in question 4 (b),

"(a) should this Court formulate detailed decrees in these cases;

"(b) if so, what specific issues should the decrees reach;

"(c) should this Court appoint a special master to hear evidence with a view to recommending specific terms for such decrees;

"(d) should this Court remand to the courts of first instance with directions to frame decrees in these cases, and if so what general directions should the decrees of this Court include and what procedures should the courts of first instance follow in arriving at the specific terms of more detailed decrees?"

participate. The Attorneys General of the states requiring or permitting segregation in public education will also be permitted to appear as *amici curiae* upon request to do so by September 15, 1954, and submission of briefs by October 1, 1954.

It is so ordered.

BOLLING ET AL. v. SHARPE ET AL.

SUPREME COURT OF THE UNITED STATES

347 U.S. 497

May 17, 1954

MR. CHIEF JUSTICE WARREN delivered the opinion of the Court.

This case challenges the validity of segregation in the public schools of the District of Columbia. The petitioners, minor of the Negro race, allege that such segregation deprives them of due process of the law under the Fifth Amendment. They were refused admission to a public school attended by white children solely because of their race. They sought the aid of the District Court for the District of Columbia in obtaining admission. That court dismissed their complaint. The Court granted a writ of certiorari before judgment in the Court of Appeals because of the importance of the constitutional question presented.

We have this day held that the Equal Protection Clause of the Fourteenth Amendment prohibits the states from maintaining racially segregated public schools.[1] The legal problem in the District of Columbia is somewhat different, however. The Fifth Amendment which is applicable in the District of Columbia, does not contain an equal protection clause as the Fourteenth Amendment which applies to the states. But the concepts of equal protection and due process, both stemming from our American ideal of fairness, are note mutually exclusive. The "equal protection of the laws" is a more explicit safeguard of prohibited unfairness than "due process of law," and, therefore, we do not imply that the two are always interchangeable phrases. But as this Court has recognized, discrimination may be so unjustifiable as to violative of due process.[2]

Classification based solely upon race must be scrutinized with particular care, since they are contrary to our traditions and hence constitutionally

---

[1] Brown v. Board of Education.

[2] Detroit Bank v. United States, 317 U.S. 329.

suspect.[3] As long ago as 1896, this Court declared the principle "that the Constitution of the United States, in its present form, forbids, so far as civil and political rights are concerned, discrimination by the General Government, or by the sates, against any citizen because of his race.[4] And in Buchanan v. Warley, 245 U.S. 60, the Court held that a statute which limited the right of a property owner to convey his property to a person of another race, was as an unreasonable discrimination, a denial of due process of law.

Although the Court has not assumed to define "liberty" with any great precision, that term is not confined to mere freedom from bodily restraint. Liberty under law extends to the full range of conduct which the individual is free to pursue, and it cannot be restricted except for a proper governmental objective. Segregation in a public school is not reasonably related to any proper governmental objective, and thus it imposes on Negro children of the District of Columbia a burden that constitutes an arbitrary deprivation of their liberty in violation of the Due Process Clause.

In view of our decision that the Constitution prohibits the states from maintaining racially segregated public schools, it would be unthinkable that the same Constitution would impose a lesser duty on the Federal Government.[5] We hold that racial segregation in the public schools of the District of Columbia is a denial of the due process of law guaranteed by the Fifth Amendment to the Constitution.

For reasons set out in Brown v. Board of Education, this case will be restored to the docket for reargument on Questions 4 and 5 previously propounded by the Court. 345 U.S. 972

It is so ordered.

---

[3] Korematsu v. United States, 323 U.S. 214.

[4] Gibson v. Mississippi, 162 U.S. 565.

[5] Hurd v. Hodge, 334 U.S. 24.

BROWN v. BOARD OF EDUCATION

349 U.S. 294

MR. CHIEF JUSTICE WARREN delivered the opinion of the Court.

These cases were decided on May 17, 1954. The opinions of that date, declaring the fundamental principle that racial discrimination in public education is unconstitutional, are incorporated herein by reference. All provisions of federal, state, or local law requiring or permitting such discrimination must yield to this principle. There remains for consideration the manner in which relief is to be accorded.

Because these cases arose under different local conditions and their disposition will involve a variety of local problems, we requested further argument on the question of relief. In view of the nationwide importance of the decision, we invited the Attorney General of the United States and the Attorneys General of all states requiring or permitting racial discrimination in public education to present their views on that question. The parties, the United States, and the States of Florida, North Carolina, Arkansas, Oklahoma, Maryland, and Texas filed briefs and participated in the oral argument. These presentations were informative and helpful to the Court in its consideration of the complexities arising from the transition to a system of public education freed of racial discrimination. The presentations also demonstrated that substantial steps to eliminate racial discrimination in public schools have already been taken, not only in some of the communities in which these cases arose, but in some of the states appearing as amici curiae, and in other states as well. Substantial progress has been made in the District of Columbia and in the communities in Kansas and Delaware involved in this litigation. The defendants in the cases coming to us from South Carolina and Virginia are awaiting the decision of this Court concerning relief.

Full implementation of these constitutional principles may require solution of varied local school problems. School authorities have the primary responsibility for elucidating, assessing, and solving these problems; courts will have to consider whether the action of school authorities constitutes good faith implementation of the governing constitutional principles. Because of their proximity to local conditions and the possible need for further hearings, the courts which originally heard these cases can best perform this judicial appraisal. Accordingly, we believe it appropriate to remand the cases to those courts.

In fashioning and effectuating the decrees, the courts will be guided by equitable principles. Traditionally, equity has been characterized by a practical flexibility in shaping its remedies and by a facility for adjusting and reconciling public and private needs. These cases call for the exercise of these traditional attributes of equity power. At stake is the personal interest of the plaintiffs in admission to public schools as soon as practicable on a nondiscriminatory basis. To effectuate this interest may call for elimination of a variety of obstacles in making the transition to school systems operated in accordance with the constitutional principles set forth in our May 17, 1954, decision. Courts of equity may properly take into account the public interest in the elimination of such obstacles in a systematic and effective manner. But it should go without saying that the vitality of these constitutional principles cannot be allowed to yield simply because of disagreement with them. While giving weight to these public and private considerations, the courts will require that the defendants make a prompt and reasonable start toward full compliance with our May 17, 1954, ruling. Once such a start has been made, the courts may find that additional time is necessary to carry out the ruling in an effective manner. The burden rests upon the defendants to establish that such time is necessary in the public interest and is consistent with good faith compliance at the earliest practicable date. To that end, the courts may consider problems related to administration, arising from the physical condition of the school plant, the school transportation system, personnel, revision of school districts and attendance areas into compact units to achieve a system of determining admission to the public schools on a nonracial basis, and revision of local laws and regulations which may be necessary in solving the foregoing problems. They will also consider the adequacy of any plans the defendants may propose to meet these problems and to effectuate a transition to a racially nondiscriminatory school system. During this period of transition, the courts will retain jurisdiction of these cases.

The judgments below, except that in the Delaware case, are accordingly reversed and the cases are remanded to the District Courts to take such proceedings and enter such orders and decrees consistent with this opinion as are necessary and proper to admit to public schools on a racially nondiscriminatory basis with all deliberate speed the parties to these cases. The judgment in the Delaware case—ordering the immediate admission of the plaintiffs to schools previously attended only by white children—is affirmed on the basis of the principles stated in our May 17, 1954, opinion, but the case is remanded to the Supreme Court of Delaware for such further proceedings as that Court may deem necessary in light of this opinion.

It is so ordered.

A Note on Sources

*B*rown v. Board of Education: *Witness to a Landmark Decision,* extracts and edits the history of the *School Segregation Cases,* as *Brown* also is known, from *Crusaders in the Courts: Legal Battles of the Civil Rights Movement ("Crusaders").* My purpose in this separate volume devoted only to Brown has been to makes its history readily accessible to those who want to focus only on the school cases. This separate volume, therefore, does not treat all of the history of the NAACP Legal Defense and Educational Fund, Inc. as does *Crusaders.* It omits describing the many criminal cases, representations of the Civil Rights Movement and Martin Luther King, Jr., fair employment and housing litigation, the campaign against the death penalty, organizational rivalries, and other matters. It omits also the Bibliographical Notes in *Crusaders,* much of which has some connection with *Brown,* but also covers ground beyond it and would occupy about 20% of the length of this volume. *Crusaders* also has a complete table of cases more than a dozen pages in length, which I am omitting here. For anyone interested in more fully tracing or consulting sources related to the material in this volume, *Crusaders* and its Bibliographical Notes would provide a useful start. Colleagues and students were immensely helpful in writing these pages: Dana Neacsu, law school Reference Librarian, was of immeasurable assistance in obtaining information of all sorts, for this project and others. Columbia Law students Philip Evan Cummins, James Kan, Anna Wagner and Moez Kaba provided superb and efficient research assistance.

The sources that I have consulted, which are cited fully in *Crusaders,* include LDF dockets, board minutes, financial reports, press releases, annual and periodic reports, briefs, memoranda, correspondence, interview notes, and other materials. All of these are in LDF files, which will be available at the Library of Congress. I also consulted books, journals, and other secondary materials.

I will list here, in a general way, some of the principal sources upon which I drew.

I have cited reported cases in footnotes on the pages where they appear in the text.

General Sources

Race Relations Law Reporter and *Southern School News* chronicle legal decisions, legislation, and other legal materials that bear on race relations and events related to school segregation beginning with the days following *Brown*. Indispensable.

The *Journal of Blacks in Higher Education* is another indispensable resource. It reports perhaps anything one might want to know about blacks in higher education, and much more about black America's situation.

Richard Kluger, *Simple Justice: The History of* Brown v. Board of Education *and Black America Struggle for Equality* (New York: Knopf, 1976), has become the classic recounting of the story of *Brown v. Board of Education.*

The *Journal of Negro Education,* Summer 1935 issue, contains early debates about what to do concerning black education. The Summer 1952 issue contains articles by lawyers who litigated *Brown* and their associates on issues that the cases presented.

The Harvard Civil Rights Project, www.civilrightsproject.harvard.edu/ , regularly reports on civil rights developments particularly with regard to education.

The Schomburg Center for Research in Black Culture, 515 Lenox Ave., New York, N.Y. 10037, is a library decided to African American history.

United States Government Statistics

Readily available on the web, I will list several examples that I consulted. Government sources are countless and are consistently being updated:

"Digest of Education Statistics Tables and Figures," National Center for Education Statistics (1996), *at* http://www.nces.ed.gov/programs/digest/ /d96/D96T008.asp.

"Historical Income Tables—Families," U.S. Census Bureau, *at* http:// www.census.gov/hhes/income/histinc/f05.html; 1991 to 2002, *at* http:// www.census.gov/hhes/www/income02.html.

"Income in the United States: 2002," P60-221, U.S. Census Bureau (Sept. 2003), *at* http://www.census.gov/hhes/www/income02.html.

"Moving to America—Moving to Homeownership: 1994 to 2002," U.S. Census Bureau, *at* http://www.census.gov/hhes/www//housing/movingto america2002/tab7.html (last revised Oct. 7, 2003).

Labor Force Statistics from the Current Population Survey, Unemployment Rate 1991–2003, U.S. Department of Labor, Bureau of Labor Statistics, *at* http://data.bls.gov/cgi-bin/surveymost?bls.

Life Expectancy at Birth by Race and Sex, National Vital Statistics Report 52.3, Centers for Disease Control and Prevention (Sept. 18, 2003).

Crime Statistics

"U.S. Prison Population Passes 2 Million Mark," Drug Policy Alliance, Feb. 15, 2000, *at* http://www.lindesmith.org/news/2million_inmates2.cfm. *Lindesmith is an excellent source of crime statistics.*

"Lifetime Likelihood of Going to State or Federal Prison," Criminal Offenders Statistics, Bureau of Justice Statistics, U.S. Department of Justice, *at* http://www.ojp.usdoj.gov/bjs/crimoff.htm#lifetime (last revised Aug. 7, 2003).

Commission of Crime: James Alan Fox & Marianne W. Zawitz, "Homicide Trends in the United States," Bureau of Justice Statistics, U.S. Department of Justice 9, *at* http://www.ojp.usdoj.gov/bjs/pub/pdf/htius.pdf (last revised Nov. 12, 2002).

Black Economic Status

Robert Lieberman, *Shifting the Color Line* (Cambridge: Harvard University Press, 1998).

Melvin L. Oliver and Thomas M. Shapiro, *Black Wealth, White Wealth* (New York: Routledge, 1995).

Poverty Status of People by Race: 1991–2001, "Poverty in the United States: 2002," P60-222, U.S. Census Bureau, *at* http://www.census.gov/hhes/www/poverty02.html.

Affirmative Action

William G. Bowen, & Derek Curtis Bok, *The Shape of the River: Long-Term Consequences of Considering Race in College and University Admissions* (Princeton University Press, 1998).

Joel Dreyfuss and Charles Lawrence, *The Bakke Case: The Politics of Inequality* (New York: Harcourt Brace, 1979).

Jack Greenberg, "Diversity, the University and the World Outside," 103 *Columbia Law Review* 1610 (2003) and "Affirmative Action In Higher Education: Confronting the Condition and Theory," 43 *Boston College Law Review* 521 (2002). *Among other things, catalogs and evaluates all arguments pro and con affirmative action.*

Charles Lawrence & Mari J. Matsuda, *We Won't Go Back: Making the Case for Affirmative Action* (Houghton Mifflin, 1997).

Roma

Roma in Eastern Europe, Open Society Institute, EU Accession Monitoring Program, Monitoring the EU Accession Process, Minority Protection, vol. I (2002).

Civil Rights Organizations and Leadership

Harry S. Ashmore, *The Negro and the Schools* (Chapel Hill: University of North Carolina Press, 1954).

H. Ball, *A Defiant Life: Thurgood Marshall and the Persistence of Racism in American* (Crown, 1999).

Taylor Branch, *Parting the Waters: America in the King Years, 1954–63* (New York: Simon & Schuster, 1988).

Clayborne Carson, *In Struggle: SNCC and the Black Awakening of the 1960s* (Cambridge: Harvard University Press, 1981).

William Elwood, *Civil Rights Lawyers Project*, University of Virginia, Charlottesville, 1990.

James Forman, *The Making of Black Revolutionaries* (New York: Macmillan, 1972).

David Garrow, *Bearing the Cross: Martin Luther King, Jr. and the Southern Christian Leadership Conference* (New York: Morrow, 1986). *By a knowledgeable and long time involved observer.*

Henry Hampton and Steve Fayer, eds., *Voices of Freedom: An Oral History of the Civil Rights Movement from the 1950s Through the 1980s* (New York: Bantam, 1990).

Charles Flint Kellogg, *NAACP: A History of the National Association for the Advancement of Colored People* (Baltimore: John Hopkins University Press, 1967).

Walter Lord, *The Past That Would Not Die* (New York: Harper and Row, 1965).

Genna Rae McNeil, *Groundwork: Charles Hamilton Houston and the Struggle for Civil Rights* (Philadelphia: University of Pennsylvania Press, 1983).

August Meier and Elliot Rudwick, *CORE: A Study in the Civil Rights Movement* (Urbana: University of Illinois Press, 1973).

James Meredith, *Three Years in Mississippi* (Bloomington: Indiana University Press 1966). *A strange memoir revealing a mystical side to Meredith, who went on to Columbia Law School, then working for Jesse Dukes and Jesse Helms, later becoming candidate for President of the United States.*

Mark Tushnet, *Making Civil Rights Law: Thurgood Marshall and the Supreme Court, 1936–1961* (New York: Oxford University Press, 1994).

Mark Tushnet, *Making Constitutional Law: Thurgood Marshall and the Supreme Court, 1961–1991* (Oxford University Press, 1997).

Walter White, *A Man Called White: The Autobiography of Walter White* (New York: Viking, 1948). *A forgotten highly influential, character, executive secretary of the NAACP, who had immense influence before, during, and after World War II.*

Roy Wilkins and Tom Mathews, *Standing Fast: The Autobiography of Roy Wilkins* (New York: Viking, 1982).

Juan Williams, *Thurgood Marshall: American Revolutionary* (Times Books, 1998).

Brown v. Board of Education, Supreme Court Decision Making

Mary L Dudziak, "Desegregation as a Cold War Imperative," 41 *Stanford Law Review* 61 (1988). *A seminal article that has raised to prominence the role of foreign policy in coming to the decision in Brown.*

Philip Elman interviewed by Norman Silber, "Essays Commemorating the One Hundredth Anniversary of *The Harvard Law Review*: The Solicitor General's Office, Justice Frankfurter and Civil Rights Litigation, 1946–1960: An Oral History," 100 *Harvard Law Review* 817 (1987). *A highly controversial article, in which the author describes his relationship with Justice Felix Frankfurter during the Court's deliberations in Brown. His dismissive remarks about some of the counsel attracted a lot of attention.*

Leon Friedman, ed., *Argument: The Oral Argument in* Brown v. Board of Education of Topeka, *1952–1955* (New York: Chelsea House, 1969).

Mark Tushnet, "What Really Happened in *Brown v. Board of Education*," 91 *Columbia Law Review* 1867 (1991).

Paul E. Wilson, *A Time to Lose: Representing Kansas in* Brown v. Board of Education (Lawrence, Kan.: University Press of Kansas, 1995).

Desegregation Methods

Davison M. Douglas, *School Busing: Constitutional and Political Developments* (Garland Press, 1994).

Jack Greenberg, *Race Relations and American Law* (New York: Columbia University Press, 1959).

Richard D. Kahlenberg, *Public School Choice vs. Private School Vouchers* (New York: Century Foundation Press, 2003).

James S. Liebman, "Desegregating Politics," 90 *Columbia Law Review* 1463 (1990).

Gary Orfield, *Must We Bus?: Segregated Schools and National Policy* (Washington, D.C.: The Brookings Institution, 1978).

Leon E. Panetta and Peter Gall, *Bring Us Together: The Nixon Team and the Civil Rights Retreat* (Philadelphia: J. B. Lippincott, 1971), 249.

James Ryan, "The Political Economy of School Choice," 111 *Yale Law Journal* 2043 (2002). *An immensely illuminating article on desegregation and the relationship between city and suburb.*

President's Committee on Civil Rights

To Secure These Rights: The Report of the President's Committee on Civil Rights (New York: Simon & Schuster, 1947). *One of the most influential documents in civil rights history. Within about twenty years of its publication, all of its key recommendations became law.*

Reconstruction

Eric Foner, *Reconstruction: America's Unfinished Revolution 1863–1877* (New York: Harper and Row, 1988). *Key to understanding development of the Reconstruction amendments by the leading historian of that period.*

C. Vann Woodward, *Reunion and Reaction: The Compromise of 1877 and the End of Reconstruction* (Boston: Little, Brown, 1951). *Essential to understanding the regression to Plessy v. Ferguson, by an outstanding historian whose work informed lawyers in Brown v. Board.*

C. Vann Woodward, *The Strange Career of Jim Crow*, 3d ed. (New York: Oxford University Press, 1974).

Legislative History of the 14th Amendment

Howard Jay Graham, "Proposed Amendment to Appellants' Briefs," LDF archives. *Graham, an important constitutional scholar, consulted with plaintiffs' counsel.*

Dr. Alfred H. Kelly, "When the Supreme Court Ordered Desegregation," *U.S. News & World Report*, February 5, 1962, 86–88. *Kelly was an important consultant with counsel for plaintiffs, but outraged them when he asserted that he had shaped his conclusions about history to suit their argument. Later he characterized his experience differently. Discussed in the text.*

Michael McConnell, "Originalism and the Desegregation Decisions," 81 *Virginia Law Review* 947 (1995).

C. Vann Woodward, "The Background of the Abandonment of Reconstruction," LDF archives. *Van Woodward was among the most influential historians of the Civil War period. He consulted with counsel for plaintiffs.*

Little Rock Desegregation

Daisy Bates, *The Long Shadow of Little Rock* (New York: David McKay, 1962).

I. Wilmer Counts, Will D. Campbell, Ernest Dumas, et. al., *A Life Is More than a Moment: The Desegregation of Little Rock's Central High* (Bloomington, IN: Indiana University Press, 1999).

Robert Somerlott, *The Little Rock School Desegregation Crisis in American History* (Berkeley Heights, NJ: Enslow Publishers, 2001).

Meredith and Ole Miss

Henry Hampton and Steve Fayer, eds., *Voices of Freedom: An Oral History of the Civil Rights Movement from the 1950s Through the 1980s* (New York; Bantam, 1990), 119–20.

Walter Lord, *The Past That Would Not Die* (New York: Harper and Row, 1965), 169.

James Meredith, *James Meredith vs. Ole Miss.* (Jackson, MS: Meredith Publishers, 1995).

James Meredith, *Three Years in Mississippi* (Bloomington: Indiana University Press 1966).

Fred Powledge, *Free at Last! The Civil Rights Movement and the People Who Made It* (Boston: Little, Brown, 1991), 437–42.

University of Alabama Desegregation

Arthur Carter, "Ike Calls Mob Action 'Deplorable,'" and "'I'm Ready to Go Back to School,'" *Afro American*, February 18, 1956.

Wayne Phillips, "Tuscaloosa: A Tense Drama Unfolds," *New York Times Magazine*, February 26, 1956, 17.

"First Alabama Negro Enrollment Brings 3-Day Demonstration," *Southern School News* 2, no. 9 (March 1956), 6.

E. Culpepper Clark, *The Schoolhouse door: Segregation's Last Stand at the University of Alabama* (Bridgewater N.J.: Replica Books, 1995).

Freedom Rides

Taylor Branch, *Parting the Waters: America in the King Years, 1954–63* (New York: Simon & Schuster, 1988), 427.

James Farmer, *Lay Bare the Heart* (New York: Arbor House, 1985), chap. 17.

James Haskins, *The Freedom Rides: Journey for Justice* (New York: Hyperion Books for Children, 1995).

August Meier and Elliot Rudwick, *CORE: A Study in the Civil Rights Movement* (Urbana: University of Illinois Press, 1973), 139.

Victor Navasky, *Kennedy Justice* (New York: Atheneum, 1971), 204–5.

Sit-ins

Taylor Branch, *Parting the Waters: America in the King Years 1954–63* (New York: Simon & Schuster, 1988), see chap. 7.

David McCullough, *Truman* (New York: Simon & Schuster, 1992), 971.

Fred Powledge, *Free At Last! The Civil Rights Movement and the People Who Made It* (Boston: Little, Brown, 1991), see chap. 12.

Robert Weisbrot, *Freedom Bound: A History of America's Civil Rights Movement* (New York: Norton, 1990), see chap. 2.

Robert Weisbrot, *Marching toward Freedom, 1957–1965: From the Founding of the Southern Christian Leadership Conference to the Assassination of Malcolm X* (Chelsea House, 1994).

Paul A.Winters, *The Civil Rights Movement* (Greenhaven Press, 2000).

Margold Report

A fabulous, prescient work that was the roadmap to Brown, often departed from, but nonetheless setting the direction.

Jack Greenberg, *Judicial Process and Social Change: Constitutional Litigation* (Minneapolis, Minn.: West, 1977) [partially reprinted].

New York Public Library, complete copy on file.

Mark Tushnet, *The NAACP Legal Strategy Against Segregated Education, 1925–1950* (Chapel Hill: University of North Carolina Press, 1987).

Black Summit at Howard University (1952) and NAACP Strategizing

Harry S. Ashmore, "Some Major Problems Involved in Achieving Racial Integration, with Especial Reference to Education in the South," *Journal of Negro Education* 21, no. 3 (Summer 1952).

Robert L. Carter, "Review of Mark Tushnet's *The NAACP's Legal Strategy Against Segregated Education 1925–1950*," 86 *Michigan Law Review* 1089 (1988).

John P. Frank, "Can the Courts Erase the Color Line?" "Discussion of Papers—Third Session," *Journal of Negro Education* 21, no. 3 (Summer 1952).

James M. Nabrit, Jr., "An Appraisal of Court Action as a Means of Achieving Racial Integration in Education," *Journal of Negro Education* 21, no. 3 (Summer 1952).

"Discussion of Papers—Third Session," *Journal of Negro Education* 21, no. 3 (Summer 1952).

"General Discussion—Third Session," *Journal of Negro Education* 21, no. 3 (Summer 1952).

"Discussion of Papers—Seventh Session," *Journal of Negro Education* 21, no. 3 (Summer 1952).

NAACP, *New Blueprint for Legal Action Against Racial Segregation and Discrimination* (New York: NAACP, 1953).

NAACP, *Civil Rights Handbook*, (New York: NAACP, 1953).

Social Science Studies

Kenneth B. Clark, *Effect of Prejudice and Discrimination on Personality Development*, Fact Finding Report, Mid-Century White House Conference on Children and Youth, Children's Bureau, Federal Security Agency, 1950, Columbia University, Social Work Library, New York, N.Y. *Clark's studies, made with Mamie Clark, were used by plaintiffs in Brown in the form of Clark's testimony and reference to his writings.*

"Effects of Segregation and the Consequences of Desegregation: A Social Science Statement" 37 *Minnesota Law Review* 427 (1953).

Kenneth B. Clark, *Prejudice and Your Child* (Middletown, Conn.: Wesleyan University Press, 1988).

Inter-district Busing

Davison M. Douglas, *School Busing: Constitutional and Political Developments* (Garland Press, 1994).

Gary Orfield, *Must We Bus?: Segregated Schools and National Policy* (Washington, D.C.: The Brookings Institution, 1978), 99–101.

INDEX

A

Alexander v. Holmes County
    Board of Education, xiii

B

Baker, Russel, 176
Black Teachers Targeted, 239
Black, Charles, 93–94
Bolling v. Sharpe, 137
Briggs v. Elliot, 67–74, 89
Busing, 236–238
Brown v. Board of Education of
    Topeka, 13
    Brown II, 238
    Initial Trial, 62–66, 74–88
    Legal Academy Reaction, 152,
        156
    Little Rock, 162–182
    Reflections, 249
    Second Reargument, 145
    States Reaction, 140–142,
        161–195
    Supreme Court Brief and Oral
        Argument, 95–109, 111–133
    Victory, 137–140
    "With All Deliberate Speed,"
        147, 232, 238

C

Civil Rights Movement, 199, 227
Carter, Robert L., 8
Clark, Kenneth B., 70, 84

Coleman, William T., 93
Corngold, Stanley, xv

D

Davis v. County School Board of
    Prince Edward County,
    Virginia, 82
Delaware Cases (Wilson v. Beebe
    and Johnson v. Beebe), 49
Du Bois, W. E. B., 15, 51

E

Eisenhower, Dwight, 150

F

Freedom House, 7

G

Greenberg, Jack
    Director Counsel, 206
    First days at LDF, 9, 56

H

Hand, Learned, 152
Handler, Milton, 56
Hastie, William H, 3
Health, Education and Welfare
    Department (HEW), 227, 245
Houston, Charles Hamilton, 3–5
Howard University, 4, 61

J

Journal of Negro Education, 59

K

King Jr., Martin Luther, 149

L

Little Rock Nine, 162–182
Lucy v. Board of Trustees, 159

M

Marhshall, Cecelia S., ix
Marshall Thurgood
  Briggs trial, 90–92
  Description, 8
  Summit, 60
  Supreme Court Preparation,
    Team, 92, 93
  United States Court of Appeals,
    206
McLaurin v. Oklahoma, 25, 29–39
Meltsner, Michael, 240
Meredith, James, 204–222
Montgomery Bus Boycott
Motley, Constance Baker, 7,
  201–226

N

Nabrit, Jr., Jim, 61
Nabrit, Jim, III, 63
NAACP, 43, 143
NAACP Legal Defense and Educa-
  tional Fund
  Internal Revenue Challenge to
  Tax Exemption, 157

Southern States Efforts to
  Destroy LDF, 155
No Child Left Behind (NCLB),
  261–265

P

Parks, Rosa, 149
Pearson v. Murray, 20
Plessy v. Ferguson, 12, 14, 138
Pollak, Louis H., 93

R

Redding, Louis, 50
Robinson, Spotts, 60

S

Segregation's end, 47
Sipuel v. Board of Regents of the
  University of Oklahoma,
  21–26
Sweatt v. Painter, 29–38

T

Thurmond, Strom, 151

W

Wallace, George, 223
Wechsler, Herbert, 152
Weinstein, Jack, 93, 95
Williams, Franklin H., 7
Wisdom, John Minor, 186, 229